Chelsea School Research Centre Edition
Volume 2

Graham McFee/ Alan Tomlinson (eds.)

Education, Sport and Leisure

Connections and Controversies

Meyer & Meyer Verlag

First published in 1993 by
CSRC
Chelsea School Research Centre
Chelsea School of Physical Education,
Sports Science, Dance and Leisure
University of Brighton
CSRC Topic Report 3
Education, Sport and Leisure: Connections and Controversies

Die Deutsche Bibliothek – CIP-Einheitsaufnahme

Education, sport and leisure :
connections and controversies / Graham McFee/Alan Tomlinson (eds.).
– Aachen : Meyer und Meyer, 1997
(Chelsea school research centre edition ; Vol. 2)
ISBN 3-89124-442-8
NE: McFee, Graham [Hrsg.]; GT

© 1997 by Meyer & Meyer Verlag, Aachen
Cover design: Walter J. Neumann, N & N Design-Studio, Aachen
Cover exposure: frw, Reiner Wahlen, Aachen
Typesetting: Myrene L. McFee
Printed by Druckerei Hahnengress, Aachen
Printed in Germany
ISBN 3-89124-442-8

PREFACE

This is the third publication in the Chelsea School Research Centre (CSRC) Topic Report series, first published by the University of Brighton. These reports represent the range of work which has been generated by the scholarly and research activities of academics and researchers in the Chelsea School of Physical Education, Sport Science, Dance and Leisure (Faculty of Education, Sport and Leisure), University of Brighton.

Chelsea has long been at the forefront of multi-disciplinary and specialist scholarship in physical education, human movement studies and the sport sciences. More recently, the research activity of members of the School has been organised into specialist research groupings within the Chelsea School Research Centre.

This volume has blended central interests of those groups, and represents the established strengths and the continued aspirations of the Chelsea School in contributing to high level scholarship in this and other important areas.

We are particularly pleased to have brought together in this volume expertise from prominent figures in other institutions. This has been aided by funding from the former Polytechnics and Colleges Funding Council.

Professor Alan Tomlinson
Chelsea School Research Centre (CSRC)
September 1993

I am pleased to be able to write an extension to the above, four years on from the publication of this volume. The collection has been consistently in demand, and its re-issue is the first publication in the CSRC Editions launched by Meyer & Meyer in partnership with the Chelsea School Research Centre, The University of Brighton.

Professor Alan Tomlinson
CSRC
January 1997

Contents

Glossary of abbreviated terms

AT	Attainment Target
BANC	British Association of National Coaches
BCPE	British Council of Physical Education
BOA	British Olympic Association
BSAD	British Sports Association for the Disabled
CATE	Council for the Accreditation of Teacher Education
CCPR	Central Council for Physical Recreation
CCT	Compulsory Competitive Tendering
CDO	Curriculum Development Officer
CNAA	Council for National Academic Awards
DES	Department of Education and Science
DFE	Department For Education
DoE	Department of the Environment
EEC	European Economic Community (now EC)
EOC	Equal Opportunities Commission
ERA	Education Reform Act [1988]
GMS	Grant-Maintained Status
GCSE	General Certificate of Secondary Education
HEFC	Higher Education Funding Council
HMI	Her Majesty's Inspectorate
HRE	Health related exercise
INSET	In-Service Education and Training
ITT	Initial Teacher Training
KS	Key Stage. Four of these are specified: KS 1: ages 5–7 KS 2: ages 8–11 KS 3: ages 12–14 KS 4: ages 15–16
LEA	Local Education Authority
LMS	Local Management of Schools
NC	National Curriculum
NCC	National Curriculum Council

NCPE	National Curriculum Physical Education
NGB	National Governing Body
PE	Physical Education
PEA	Physical Education Association
PSD	Personal and Social Development
QTS	Qualified Teacher Status
SARD	Sport and Recreation Division
SDO	Sports Development Officer
SEAC	Schools Examination and Assessment Council
UFC	Universities Funding Council

I.

INTRODUCTION

CURRICULUM, CHANGE AND CRITIQUE: THEMES IN THE STUDY OF EDUCATION, SPORT AND LEISURE

Graham McFee and Alan Tomlinson
Chelsea School Research Centre
University of Brighton

I.   Introduction

This report grew from a workshop held at the Chelsea School Research Centre (CSRC), the University of Brighton (then Brighton Polytechnic), in conjunction with the Joint Study Group on Leisure and Recreation of the Leisure Studies Association (LSA) and the British Sociological Association (BSA). The workshop functioned as an element in the Chelsea School's part-time MA(PE) programme, and presenters there included graduates of the course. As had been the case at previous LSA/BSA workshops, the collaboration of the 'host' organisation was seen as a crucial element in what turned out to be a stimulating (and therefore successful) event. The event was also supported by the CSRC's Research Initiative from PCFC (The Polytechnics and Colleges Funding Council) and by the BSA Study-Group budget.

The Workshop struck its organisers as timely for a number of reasons: first, the National Curriculum proposals for England and Wales had been in the public domain long enough to elicit informed (and research-based) commentary, yet were fresh enough to be a major topic in the minds of educationalists — and we were fortunate to have with us two members from the Working Party that composed the proposals; second, the Chelsea School had recently been part of a reorganisation in the University which, by creating the Faculty of Education, Sport and Leisure, had made explicit some of the appropriate constituencies for cross-disciplinary investigation; and third, the relation of the educational sphere to others — in particular, to the sphere of local leisure provision — was a 'hot' topic, in the light of funding changes in both these spheres (LMS for schooling, CCT for leisure provision) as well as such reorganisations as the 'change' from Department of Education and Science (DES) to Department for Education (DFE).

3

Given this history, and the buoyancy of the exchanges and dialogues, it seemed appropriate to preserve in many cases the 'spirit' of the event in this report by retaining references to "in this room", "yesterday", and the like.

II.　The National Curriculum in the United Kingdom — an introduction

To many, the National Curriculum has been such an obsession that it is taken-for-granted. Here we rehearse some of the main themes and professional concerns raised by it. The National Curriculum in the United Kingdom poses, in a concrete form, a set of major questions for the curriculum in general and the role of physical education in particular. As Kenneth Baker (then Secretary of State for Education) said in a speech in January 1987, by the expression 'National Curriculum' was meant "...a school curriculum governed by national criteria which are promulgated by the Secretary of State..." (quoted Maw, 1988: p. 49). In fact, this idea was enshrined in the 1988 Education Reform Act (for England and Wales); and in the comparable Acts applying to Scotland and Northern Ireland. In the Education Reform Act (1988), this amounted to a specification of (1) subjects to be taught; (2) organisation of subjects into core and foundation categories; (3) percentages of the curriculum dedicated to particular subjects; and (4) an elaborate pattern of regular testing.

As summarised by the former Department of Education and Science (DES, 1989: § 3.3), the National Curriculum comprises:

- *foundation* subjects — including three *core* subjects and seven *other* foundation subjects which must be included in the curricula of all pupils;
- *attainment targets* — to be specified up to ten levels of attainment, covering the ages 5–16, setting objectives for learning;
- *programmes of study* — specifying essential teaching within each subject area;
- *assessment arrangements* — related to the ten levels of attainment.

The core subjects were English, Mathematics and Science; the other foundation subjects were Technology (including design), History, Geography, Music, Art, Physical Education, and (from 11–16) a modern foreign language. Moreover, it is acknowledged that "the foundation subjects are certainly *not* a complete curriculum...", the *whole* curriculum for *all* pupils will certainly need to include at appropriate (and in some cases all) stages (DES, 1989: § 3.8):

- careers education and guidance;
- health education;
- other aspects of personal and social education; and
- coverage across the curriculum of gender and multi-cultural issues.

The National Curriculum involves testing "at the ages of 7, 11, 14 and 16 for most pupils" (DES, 1989: § 6.4) — these ages representing the end-points of the so-called Key Stages 1 to 4.

It is not the intention here to debate the educational credentials of the 'proposals' in this Act: by now, they represent the legal obligations of Local Authorities in England and Wales. One might think of the whole idea as "...a folly of unprecedented proportions" (Simons, 1988: p. 89), or agree with White's tart comment (White, 1988: p. 113):

> You pick ten foundation subjects to fill 80-90% of the school time table, highlight three as of particular importance and arrange tests at different ages. I could have worked out the National Curriculum years ago. Anyone could.

But it is never as simple as that — choices about what constitutes 'particular importance' and 'tests' will greatly vary. Such trenchantly expressed views have, though, been a feature of professional debates ranging across all of the subjects of the National Curriculum; and this form of professionally-motivated tendentiousness was a prominent feature of the Workshop on which this collection is based. In this Introduction, we contextualise such debates by:

(a) offering a succinct survey of the main thrusts of the National Curriculum for Physical Education (Section III);

(b) looking at other, related yet different, formulations of a national physical education curriculum — in particular, that in Northern Ireland (Section IV);

(c) signalling the themes raised in the presentations at the Workshop (Section V);

(d) pointing towards key professional and research implications in this area (Section VI).

III. The National Curriculum for Physical Education in England and Wales

In its final form, the Physical Education National Curriculum document puts forward (as the Secretary of State had requested) a single Attainment Target (AT) — it was:

> ...the sum total of all the end of key stage statements. (DES, 1992: p. 2)

But it is revealing of the structure of the final curriculum to remind oneself of the three ATs originally proposed in the Working Party's Interim Report — these were to take account, respectively, of the following "facets" of progressive learning in physical education:

> Planning and composing Participating and performing
> Appreciating and evaluating. (DES, 1991a: p. 23)

Although this structure is not formally in place, its emphasis is visible in the detail of what is proposed — indeed, explicitly so, since the Working Party's proposals, which formed the basis of the statutory guidance, includes mention of the earlier proposals (DES, 1991b: p. 17). So that the explication of each 'end of Key Stage' statement tends to be employing just such notions as the "facets" above.

The Programmes of study for Physical Education are based on an initial 'definition' of six areas of activity: games, dance, athletic activities, gymnastic activities, swimming, and outdoor and adventurous activities. In Key Stages 1 and 2, all of these areas of activity should be experienced by all pupils, but the emphasis should be on games, dance and gymnastic activities. In addition, by the end of Key Stage 2, all pupils should be able to swim at least 25 metres and to demonstrate an understanding of water-safety. (With this in place, swimming is incorporated within other areas of activity for the purposes of later Key Stages.)

In Key Stage 3 pupils should follow the Programmes of study for a minimum of 4 of the areas of activity, with games compulsory in each year; while in Key Stage 4, two activities should be experienced — although these may be from the same or different areas of activity as 'defined' above.

Further, there are general requirements, designed to "apply to all key stages and to be taught through all areas of activity" (DES, 1992: p. 3). The first is worth quoting in full here:

In physical education lessons pupils should be taught to:

- be physically active;

- demonstrate knowledge and understanding mainly through physical actions rather than verbal explanations;

- be aware at the same time of the terminology relevant to activities undertaken; and

- engage in activities that involve the whole body, maintain flexibility and develop strength and endurance. (DES, 1992: p. 3)

The other general requirements enjoin pupils to become independent learners, to develop positive attitudes and be concerned that practice be safe — and each is expanded in terms of what this might amount to and how it might be brought about through physical education.

The Working Party's Report includes a section entitled "A Rationale for Physical Education", a section which has been criticised (see Alderson in this volume, and Talbot's response, reflecting aspects of the Workshop exchanges) for its direction: its account of physical education emphasises education "in and through the use of the body and its movement" (DES, 1991b: p. 5). That is, there was no explicit mention of specific activities — for example, sport — although there was an acknowledgement of the wide range of activities that might be embraced within physical education. In this way, the 'principle of selection' operative in the classification of areas of activity remained implicit. This rationale also makes explicit reference to pupils' need for a broad, balanced and differentiated curriculum and, in doing so in that language, reaffirmed its commitment to earlier educational documents (see Tomlinson, this volume, pp. 85–92).

IV.   A contrasting view?

It is revealing here to briefly compare the National Curriculum proposals for physical education for England and Wales with those for Northern Ireland, since there seem marked differences (within an allegedly *national* curriculum). Within broadly the same framework of Key Stages and Attainment Targets and the rest, two differences are immediate: the nature of the 'rationale' and the selection of the activities. To take them in that order, in the Northern Ireland document there is no rationale section as such; rather the document begins by describing the nature and scope of physical education, but soon makes plain its commitment to "a health focus" (DENI, 1990: p. 10), as an important central aspect of physical education. So that the health focus is not, as in the proposals for England and Wales, consigned to the cross-curricular. In this way, the proposal for Northern Ireland is more polemical, taking a stance on what are recognised to be contentious issues. And it recognises the contentiousness not least in how the proposals are contextualised — for instance: scholarly references in support of its position are included.

It is also noticeable that the document for Northern Ireland is written — or at least appears to be — with the teacher in mind. So that it is briefer, blunter, and more directly in the language of teachers of physical education — for example, in writing of "gymnastics", rather than "gymnastic activities". (One might speculate on whether or not this reflects the make-up of the panel — which might be thought to contain a heavier weighting towards practitioners in physical education and related areas than was the case for the England and Wales proposals, although this is not easy to quantify, given difficulties in precisely defining the backgrounds of some of those involved: see Appendix 1 and Appendix 2.)

If the Northern Ireland document is more polemical than its Anglo-Welsh counterpart, it is also explicit in employing its focus in justifying its conclusions. So that it identifies health-related physical education as a specific topic area — almost as a separate area of activity, although in fact the health-related physical education is taught through athletics, dance, games, gymnastics and swimming in Key Stages 1, 2 and 3: only in Key Stage 4 is health-related physical education a discrete element in the programme of study (DENI, 1991 p. 3). Nonetheless, it is seen as one of the organising principles, one which "pervades physical education" (DENI, 1991: p. 10). In this way, it can be used in explanation of the selection of areas of activity.

Of course, the conclusions reached in the Northern Ireland case may not be appealing ones: in particular, one might dispute the centrality, within physical education proper, of health-related concerns (we would want to raise such questions) — but at least there is fairly clear demarcation of the battleground. And that is the heart of our conclusion from this comparison: that the Anglo-Welsh version is evocative, rather than explicit. Perhaps that is a Good Thing, leaving suitable freedom of interpretation. Certainly, the Workshop concerned itself with a number of related issues, turning on the possible sites of curriculum innovation; and recurrent concerns with the question of implementation as well as issues of critical analysis. But if a clear demarcation *is* available, perhaps an ease of implementation will follow. (On this, see Walter Bleakley, 'Assessment of Practical Performance — Guidelines', included here as Appendix 3.)

V.   The Physical Education Curriculum: political and policy issues and the curriculum context

The content of this collection is arranged according to clusters of themes, and also includes three contributions not made at the Workshop. In this section we recall some of the main emphases in the presentations of the Workshop; and outline the further contributions in the volume.

John Alderson got the Workshop off to a lively start with his talk on physical education, sport development and leisure management. He argued that the physical education profession "has never really differentiated fully between its role in offering/facilitating extracurricular opportunities for recreation... and the education for recreation/leisure that should occur in curriculum time". Developing this distinction, he moved towards five concluding points. First, a question — should education for leisure have a more formal place in the school curriculum? Second, there is a strong case to be made for 'Sport Education' within a widened view of leisure education. Third, current practice in physical education in schools (and the practice proposed in the PE national curriculum document) does not really meet the needs of 'Sport Education'. Fourth, a developed model of 'Sport Development' would identify roles for sports leaders/ coaches and recreation resource managers as well as sports teachers. Finally, such a model is premised on a "complementarity in the training" of these 'leisure professionals'.

Margaret Talbot's talk took the cloak of secrecy away from the process of the production of the Physical Education National Curriculum, revealing a policy-maker's world of ignorance and prejudice, and riveting the Workshop with insider accounts of the process. The Education Minister Angela Rumbold might have chosen John Fashanu to sit on the Working Party as (her words) "black street-cred": but how many of us knew that Ms. Rumbold was also a season-ticket holder at Wimbledon Football Club? Such are the networks of power and culture. Margaret Talbot's talk covered too the intra-professional politics of the physical education world and the politics of professional belief in government and its servicing bureaucracies. She also reminded the Workshop that physical education remains "the most deeply gendered subject" in the curriculum; and that many PE teachers are still professionally under-prepared, seeing the National Curriculum as a side issue — "it won't catch on", many teachers are seeming to say, a little like many of the early responses to decimal currency. The talk concluded with a list of 16 points, presented as a context which physical education teachers needed to be knowledgeable about or understand.

John Evans provided a theoretical framework for understanding the making of policy, addressing issues of power and agency in a framework which located the 'policy text' in the context of its formative discourses and its professional ramifications. "In the recursive flow of policy, creative activity may occur but the text and the conditions/contexts in which people work may constrain and narrow the possibilities for action". These theoretical issues provided a highly appropriate framework for further discussion of the involvement of professionals in the policy-making process, and for the recognition of the political and ideological contexts in which policy is made, adapted and potentially remade.

In two sessions on the first day the focus was upon teachers' aims, and pupils' conceptions of femininity. **Lesley Lawrence** reported on her survey of 165 teachers (from 61 schools), and looked at the leisure aims of those teachers. She argued that "on the whole, the teachers' leisure aim and practice fails to account for: the significance of leisure in life; the meaning of leisure; and in particular, consideration of subjective conceptualisations of leisure". **Bev Miller** presented an outline of her study of the conceptions of femininity held by secondary school girls who were particularly committed to sports and dance.

Leo Hendry led off the second day of the Workshop in genuine workshop style. All of us were asked to list some 'keywords' which described the main elements of our lifestyle. Some of these were clearly influenced by the informal proceedings between the Saturday and Sunday sessions! We were also given some sheets of data on young people's lifestyles, and set about interpreting them. Within the context of the transitions characteristic of young people's lives (psychosocial, institutional, and leisure-based), and drawing upon the vast database of the Aberdeen-based studies, this presentation brought the realities of young people's lives into the centre of the Workshop's concerns. These data made it clear that there are a lot of stereotypes of young people's lifestyles and cultures which operate as mis-information; and that despite a contemporary rhetoric of classlessness, class is still a major determinant of lifestyle.

Scott Fleming raised questions about the PE curriculum, ethnicity and racism, drawing upon his own ethnographic fieldwork in a London secondary school. He argued persuasively for the need to develop anti-racist PE practices in the context of a commitment to equal opportunities. **Gill Lines** presented data from her study of young people's media/sport interests, based on a survey of fourth-year pupils in schools in London, Essex and Sussex, and drew out the implications of these data for the practitioner in the school.

The final session of the Workshop was a presentation by **Elizabeth Murdoch** in which different initiatives and responses of the physical education profession were graded/marked. The profession was awarded 5 stars, for instance, for its intentions regarding the unification of the profession; but a mere half a star for achievement or implementation. The session provided a comprehensive over-view of developing partnerships, and a realistic appraisal of problems and achievements in the professional worlds of education, sport and leisure.

Three further contributions are included in this report. **Joy Standeven** reaffirms the appositeness of the 'leisure education' theme for the physical educationist. **Graham McFee** argues the case for the distinctiveness of dance studies in any higher educational consideration of the physical education curriculum. **Alan Tomlinson** selects one piece of policy text and subjects it to critical scrutiny, to a form of textual interrogation. This piece is further evidence of the importance of the critical analysis of policy that is argued for in several papers in this collections, particularly in that by John Evans *et al*. None of those three pieces were included in the Workshop programme, but they are right at the heart of the volume's concerns.

The Workshop brought together academics, researchers, policy-makers, and schoolteachers. There was usually time in the sessions for fully-developed discussion, and the applied professional issues were as prominent as the more theoretical/academic questions. In this sense the Workshop was a striking success, and moved towards a consensus on some very central questions such as the need for the physical education profession, nationally, to achieve integration and to speak with one voice; and the urgent need for a coherent programme of in-service education for teachers in schools, alongside a recognition that the role of the physical education teacher now embraces a lot of challenging inter-agency demands.

The presentations made at the Workshop, and the three further contributions, have been reassembled in this collection, and situated in two main sections, addressing aspects of 'The Curriculum — political and policy issues', and 'The Curriculum Context — deliverers and users'. For the collection itself, some contributors have produced amended, revised or fully reworked versions of what was presented at the Workshop. There is a mixture of types here too, including individual studies, embryonic blueprints, and experiential retrospective accounts.

VI.   Policy and research questions — emergent and recurrent workshop themes

Several recurrent and challenging points emerged during the course of the Workshop, and characterise the themes and debates as presented in this volume. These points can be seen as both professional concerns and indications of important research areas — for the concerns need to be monitored and systematically researched and reviewed, and with changes in Initial Teacher Training (ITT), there is the opportunity for the development of new, perhaps research-based, professional relations between University and School-based physical education professionals. The Economic and Social Research Council (ESRC, 1992) has identified four main areas for educational research, at least in terms of its own funding priorities. These are 'Learning in Educational Settings'; 'Management and Organisation in Educational Institutions'; 'Enhancing Professional Training and Development'; and 'Informing Policy Development'. In the light of those four areas, physical education specialists would do well to think through the connections between education, sport and leisure, in terms of the six points with which we conclude this piece.

First, the necessity for critical professional reflection upon the policy process was widely recognised — at all levels. Policy making should not be taken-for-granted, but its processes should be constantly re-evaluated. One way of doing this is to recognise the importance of lobbies and constituencies in the power networks of policy making. Teachers themselves — as the 'core-subject English' lobby so conspicuously showed in its opposition to end of key stage testing in early 1993 — must see their own professional activities as a form of engagement, related to a key site of policy making and evaluation.

Second, the changing role of the physical education teacher remains an important area of enquiry. What kind of "provider" should the professionally prepared physical educator be? What are the new constituencies or markets to which his/her expertise should be directed? How do school-based physical educators work with the new breed of sports developers elsewhere in the public sector? Or with coaching specialists in clubs and the private sector? While none of these questions is definitively answered in this volume, their urgency surely is now unquestionable. Other providers are also facing severe pressures to change traditional roles. Compulsory competitive tendering, for instance, is leading to a rethinking of the rationale for public sector provision in leisure and sport. The physical education professional in the school and the community cannot afford to ignore this.

The third point follows from the second point, in that new partnerships must be forged around the complementarity of interests among professionals in cognate fields. This is not news to some professional peers in other societies, such as Sweden and Cuba. For a long time, in Sweden, physical education professionals have worked side by side with further and adult education specialists, in the same facilities. In Cuba's experiment in integrating social service delivery across the leisure, health and physical activity spheres, professionals are given a general training followed by a specialist emphasis, and work in a variety of settings alongside fellow professionals with complementary skills. Here, in Britain, such complementarity of interests should also be recognised, in the areas of both policy making and professional implementation.

Fourth, several of the presentations/papers remind us that the social and cultural determinants of the "clients'" experiences must be seriously considered. The classic determinants of social division — class, gender and ethnicity — must be truly grasped and countered at the level of practice. Any understanding of this should never be merely tokenistic, but should be genuinely incorporated into an expanding physical education discourse, more sensitive to the physical education teachers' actual and real, rather than idealised, constituencies.

The fifth point raises the question of whose concerns, and consequently definitions, determine the curriculum. To what extent does any specific collection of proposals — as manifest, for instance, in the National Curriculum document for physical education — foreclose interesting and important debates, for teachers as well as theorists and other practitioners? The 1933 syllabus was widely taken as a definitive blueprint for physical education teaching in perpetuity. It is important to understand the problems that such an uncritical acceptance can lead to. As the debate at the Workshop and in the papers illustrates, there is clearly room for further argument on what constitutes appropriate practice in the development and delivery of a physical education curriculum.

Finally, the profession is faced with a big challenge. Should it leave definitions of physical education practice and development to state mandarins and their appointees? Or should it seek to marshal its resources and integrate professional interests in a programme of professional and in-service development, so maximizing its potential input into policy and practice alike? It seems remarkable that a policy initiative on the scale and with the profile of the National Curriculum has lacked the core funding for in-depth and sustained professional preparation which has characterised, for example, the Probation Service's in-service training pack developed for the implementation of the Criminal Justice Act of 1992. Perhaps what physical education has chiefly lacked is a single voice speaking for the profession.

The relationship between change and critique is an unpredictable, volatile one — never measurable by any voguish conception of cost-benefit analysis or performance indicators. But recognising that there is and can be such a relationship is a source of substantial professional commitment, and an antidote to apathy. The Workshop initiative which was the source of this volume was living testimony to this.

This collection documents that testimony, and encourages professionals — practitioners and researchers alike — to continue or begin to explore the central challenges in the area. These challenges and the themes within and around them are not peripheral or transitory, and they will be at the heart of professional and policy debates for the foreseeable future. The 1995 (Easter) Annual Conference of the Leisure Studies Association (hosted by the Chelsea School, University of Brighton, Eastbourne), on 'Leisure, Sport and Education — the interfaces' offers a further forum for reflection upon these questions.

This collection is offered as a hitch-up — alongside other important interventions (Armstrong, 1990; 1992; Evans, 1992) to a horse that will run and run.

References

Armstrong, N. (ed) (1990) *New Directions in Physical Education Vol. I*. Rawdon: Human Kinetics Publishers.

―――― (1992) *New Directions in Physical Education Vol. II*. Rawdon: Human Kinetics Publishers.

Armstrong, N. and A. Sparkes (1991) *Issues in Physical Education*. London: Cassell Educational.

DENI (1990) *Proposals for Physical Education in the Northern Ireland Curriculum*. Belfast: HMSO.

DES (1989) *The National Curriculum: From Policy to Practice*. London: DES Publications.

―――― (1991a) *National Curriculum Physical Education Working Group. Interim Report*. DES/Welsh Office.

―――― (1991b) *Physical Education for ages 5–16. Proposals of the Secretary of State for Education and Science and the Secretary of State for Wales*. DES/ Welsh Office.

―――― (1992) *Starting Out with the National Curriculum*. York: National Curriculum Council.

ESRC (1992) *Frameworks and Priorities for Research in Education: Towards a Strategy for Future Research in Education*. Report of the Working Party on the Future of Research in Education, to the Education and Social Research Council, Revised Draft Version, April.

Evans, J. (ed) (1986) *Physical Education, Sport and Schooling: Studies in the Sociology of Physical Education*. Lewes, Falmer Press.

―――― *(1988) Teachers, Teaching and Control in Physical Education*. Lewes, Falmer Press.

Maw, J. (1988) 'National Curriculum policy: coherence and progression?', in D. Lawton and C. Chitty (eds) *The National Curriculum (The Bedford Way Series)*. London: Kogan Page, pp. 49–64.

Simons, H. (1988) 'Teacher professionalism and the new curriculum', in D. Lawton and C. Chitty (eds) *The National Curriculum (The Bedford Way Series)*, London: Kogan Page, pp. 78–90.

White, J. (1988) 'An unconstitutional National Curriculum', in D. Lawton and C. Chitty (eds) *The National Curriculum (The Bedford Way Series*. London: Kogan Page, pp. 113–122.

II.

THE PE CURRICULUM:
POLITICAL AND POLICY ISSUES

PLAYING BY MARKET RULES: PHYSICAL EDUCATION IN ENGLAND AND WALES AFTER ERA

John Evans, Dawn Penney and Amanda Bryant
Department of Physical Education
University of Southampton

I. Introduction

Given the level of emotion expended by politicians and educationalists on Physical Education and Sport in state schools in the years prior to the arrival of The Education Reform Act (ERA) 1988 and the noise of proper debate that has surrounded the 'making' of the National Curriculum Physical Education (NCPE), the relative hush accompanying the 1992 delivery of the 'final orders' (the statutory requirements for PE) into the education system can seem somewhat surprising. The 'final order' arrived with all the cacophony of a falling feather and we might ask whether it will also have a similar impact. Of course this quiescence could be illusory, merely an artefact of our distance in academia from the NCPE's important point of impact: teachers and pupils in schools. The effects of the NCPE and other ERA legislation will take years not days, weeks or months to materialise. What we hear now may be only the calm of reflective activity as teachers deliberate on the demands of a National Curriculum Physical Education (NCPE). It remains to be seen whether this foreruns a noisy storm of celebration or despair as the impact and implications of ERA really begin to dawn.

The National Curriculum (NC) has been implemented by law for all pupils (age 5–16) registered in state schools in England and Wales on and after 1989. The NCPE has been amongst the last of the subjects to 'come on line', arriving for pupils at key stage 1, 2 and 3 in September 1992. As it will be AD 2000 before the NC in its entirety is fully operative in schools, we have to acknowledge and stress that anything we say here is necessarily speculative, though it is not guesswork. Although our analysis is based on research[1] which is still largely at the stage of data gathering, our comments are informed by data which indicate that difficult issues are already being raised and worrying trends may be developing. For example, we can make more than an informed guess that there are a good many teachers in the Primary sector, under-trained in PE, low in time and energy, already submerged by silver ring leaf folder NC demands reaching EEC food mountain proportions, who will receive the NCPE documentation with all the enthusiasm of a vegetarian at a burger bar. They will not receive a curriculum — packaged with all the imagination of a Halfords car manual without the pictures — which prescribes what to do in some detail while saying little about how and next to nothing about why, with open and out-stretched arms. It is no over-statement to say that PE in the Primary and the Secondary sectors of education is at a crossroads. Whether teachers go forward, make progress, retreat or stay still will depend not only on the professional resources (motivations, knowledge and skills) that they bring to the subject but also on many other aspects of the socio-cultural and economic conditions and contexts in which they work. At the heart of our argument is the claim that teachers are not operating on a level playing surface. They are not equally well-equipped to meet the requirements of ERA and NCPE or to play by 'free market rules'. The difficulties they are likely to experience over the next few years cannot be dismissed simply as 'teething troubles' which accompany all education reforms. The problems facing teachers in schools post-ERA will not go away because they derive from the ideological intent, principles, inconsistencies and contradictions which are inherent in the ERA legislation (Evans *et al.*, 1993).

II. Market rules

The ideological orthodoxy, popularly termed the 'New Right', which has driven the construction of the 1988 ERA has been outlined on many occasions elsewhere (Davies, 1988; Evans & Davies, 1993; CCCS, 1991; Troyna, 1992; Evans *et al.*, 1990) and we have no need or wish to cover this ground again in detail here. But given the importance of ERA — it has sponsored the re-constitution of the state education system and radically altered the distribution of power between interested parties within it — and our assumption that what emerges as NCPE in schools over the next few years will depend much on what went into the construction of ERA in the first place (in the form of ideological intent and principles), we do need to remind ourselves of the nature of the New Right discourse which fuelled the making of the 'great' education Act.

This was neither homogeneous nor without contradiction (Troyna, 1992; Ball, 1990). As Troyna points out, on the one hand the neo-conservative voices of the New Right celebrated strong interventionist central state control in educational matters. This found expression in appeals for a National Curriculum, formal assessment, targets of attainment and strong directives for the content and orientation of teacher education courses. On the other, the voices of neo-liberals, fuelled by the work of Hayek and the monetarist theories of Friedman, championed decentralisation and deregulation and inspired the move towards Grant-Maintained Status (GMS), Local Management of Schools (LMS) and Opting Out of local education authority control. In the making of ERA, compromises were inevitable and they account for the contradictions we find in its legislation and the difficulties which are now beginning to emerge for LEAs and teachers in schools. However, the principal ideological thrust of the ERA is that market principles can be applied as well to education as to any other sector of the economy. In the eyes of the Right, 'the market' is the natural guarantor both of our children's wellbeing and our educational, economic and moral welfare. The cry is 'give power to parents, head teachers and governors', only decentralisation will raise standards and change the form and the content of education in accordance with that which the market demands. The main means of achieving all this—more competition, accountability and improved standards in schools—are putatively present in ERA legislation, particularly LMS, Open Enrolment and the terms of the NC with an accompanying system of testing (Evans *et al.*, 1993).

Not everyone shares this view of how education can best function. Other counter-positional viewpoints, ours amongst them, state that, far from raising standards in school as the rhetoric of ERA and the NC would have us believe, both ERA and the NC may produce and exacerbate educational and social inequalities in the state education system, erode the egalitarian values and commitments that were embodied in the 1944 Education Act and seriously damage the quest of providing a quality PE for *all*.

Given these claims and counter-claims, set against a backdrop of the apparent awesome potency of the central state, how are we to think about and study the impact of ERA on the state school system and PE within it? Are we to think that the work of policy making in education has now been completed and that the NCPE now 'made' has only to be 'implemented' in schools? How are we to conceptualise this phenomenon called policy? How are teachers implicated in the 'making' or 'implementation' of a PE curriculum in schools?

III. Conceptualising policy

In the last decade the study of education policy has, once again, become fashionable. Troyna is not far off the mark when he claims that the "theoretical and empirical furrows channelled by sociologists and educationalists" (such as Ahier & Flude, 1983; Troyna & Williams, 1986; Ozga, 1987; Dale, 1989; Ball, 1990) is some "testimony to the steps taken in 'policy sociology' by British educational researchers" (Troyna, 1992: p. 3). This body of work is contributing not only to our understanding of the policy process but also to those more enduring sociological and epistemological issues in the social sciences concerning the relationships between agency and structure. Needless to say, the 1988 ERA has given the study of education policy added impetus. Hardly a stone of ERA's legislative measures has now been left unturned. This is very good news. ERA represents the most significant piece of legislation to have entered the education system in post-war Britain. As government has sometimes treated the process of educational reform with all the skill, care and sensitivity of a bull in a glass factory and as its actions may be equally dangerous and undemocratic, there has never been a time more in need of researchers 'whacking in the evidence' to monitor the claims of untried and untested policies. There have also been many times in recent years when many good educationalists, receiving the latest policy 'initiative' from the central state, have wondered whether they any longer had the professional authority and responsibility to determine or influence the work that they do. The central state has seemed all powerful and the 'agency' of professional educators sadly missing from the arena of decision making.

However, the development of the National Curriculum subjects, and most recently the NCPE, has not only highlighted that the 'making' of state education policy is a complex phenomenon involving social and political processes in which vested interests and values are always and inevitably at play, but has also revealed both the range and the limits of the central state's power to determine the thinking of educationists and control the constitution of the curriculum of schools (Ball, 1990; Bowe *et al.*, 1992). Furthermore, research in other subject areas is revealing that the creation of a NC by subject working groups is not the only 'point' at which the 'making' of a curriculum occurs. This may also be so in PE. The sort of conflicts and contestation over the form and content of PE which have accompanied the actions of the working group on the NCPE are unlikely to cease with the publication of the final order for the NCPE. Rather, struggles in these terms will continue throughout its 'implementation' in schools as the NCPE is recursively made and remade in very different circumstances of resourcing and educational work. The claim made by the DES (1987) — that offering clear NC statements of objectives, programmes of study, attainment levels and regular assessment of the levels of attainment, *will* entitle pupils in all schools to the same opportunities and a curriculum that is "... balanced and broadly based ..." (DES, 1989) — is therefore no guarantee that this is either what schools can or will deliver or what children will receive.

If we accept this view, that policy is potentially something which is made and remade at all sites of educational practice, we immediately have to exercise caution with concepts — such as 'making' and 'implementation' — used to describe the policy process. Indeed we have come to share the view of Hill and others that policy is a complex social process, in which 'making' and 'implementation' are difficult divide. As Hill (1980) states:

> It is hard to identify a dividing line at which making can be said to be completed and implementation to start. There is also a considerable amount of feedback from implementation which influences further policy making and many policies are so skeletal that their real impact depends upon the way they are interpreted at the implementation stage. (p. 44)

In this view, policy is not an event or an action undertaken at a single point in time only by powerful 'others' who operate 'somewhere', either outside schools or in the upper echelons of an institution's hierarchy, who hand on policy for others — their subordinates — to implement. Policies are always and inevitably interpreted and in the process they may be adapted, adopted, contested and resisted at various 'sites' of educational practice as they are 'put into practice' (Hill, 1980; Ball, 1990). Richard Bowe and his colleagues (1992), for example, have illustrated how policies are 'made' at all sites in the education system and are not just 'legislative moments'. Policy making is a continual process of engagement, interpretation and struggle.

However, although we endorse this view, we also have some reservations about the emphasis placed upon human agency within the policy *process*. Policies are not always made in conditions of the agent's own making. The relationship between a policy text and the context of its location is essentially problematic. The policy process like all other forms of human endeavour has to be viewed as a "relational activity" (Evans & Penney, 1992): a process in which the actions of individuals not only act upon and help shape, create and/or recreate the social and organisational contexts in which they are located, but are also shaped by those contexts and the political, social and cultural influences or constraints which are found within them. In such an analysis the issue of what power is and how power operates within the policy process is forced to the foreground of concern.

There are very good reasons for wanting either to dissolve altogether, obfuscate or underplay the boundaries of policy making and *implementation*. Richard Bowe and his colleagues are quite right to point out that what they call the "state control model of policy" distorts the policy process with its conception of distinct policy makers and policy implementors and that this model does serve the ideological purposes of reinforcing a linear conception of policy in which theory and practice are separate and the former is privileged (Bowe *et al.*, 1992). As already mentioned, we too have made much of the limits of such a linear model and its tendencies to represent policy as something made only by powerful others (in government) which is then handed on to those (less powerful) for implementation in practice in schools. Such a model (Bowe, *et al.*, 1992)

> ... is not the best place to start for research into the effects of ERA, or if we want to know who is involved in the policy process, or how and why they are so involved. (p. 10)

Viewing policy as a lengthy, indeed a constantly ongoing 'complex and often recursive' set of interactions of a political kind, between groups in government and other groups (Buachalla, 1988; Penney & Evans, forthcoming) has considerable merits. It presses us to problematise conventional wisdom on policy 'making', consider policy as complex social and political process, acknowledge human agency, and focus on the ways in which this is expressed in action which may contest, resist, or in some other way mediate what sometimes seem to be the awesome and 'determining' powers of capital and the state. Our empirical work provides much evidence to support this less deterministic view. But an overemphasis on process and human agency may inadvertently occlude the analysis of the way in which power operates, resides and moves within the social system, and underplay the constraints within which people work. If our analysis does do this it may help sustain that very ideology — individualism — which so often in the same literature we and so many authors contest and deride.

In Western democracies power is widely distributed among different interest or pressure groups and these play an important part in the policy making process. Such groups, with interests in particular issues, aggregate to form "issues communities". In many cases policy is then formed within these communities and thus the policy process may become "segmented" (Buachalla, 1988). This 'pluralist' view of policy is helpful and it has informed our analysis of policy and power. At a glance it seems to offer the basis for a pretty accurate description of the way in which ERA and particularly the NC has been constructed in recent years. However, whilst pluralist theory may have much to offer our understanding of how policy is made, it does not really prompt us to consider the issue of what power is and how the capacities of actors to influence policy are differently distributed within and between individuals and interest groups in the social system. While a Foucauldian analysis offers further insight into this matter, this too has its limitations.

For Foucault, power cannot be located in either agency or structures; instead it is everywhere expressed discursively through:

> ... a multiple and mobile field of force relations where far reaching but never complete stable effects of dominations are produced. (Foucault, 1980: p. 102; quoted in Best & Kellner, 1991: p. 51)

Modern power is:

> ... relational power that is exercised from innumerable points, is highly indeterminate in character, and is never something acquired, seized or shared. There is no source of power or centre of power to contest, nor are there any subjects holding it; power is a purely structural activity for which subjects are anonymous conduits or by products. (Best & Kellner, 1991: p. 52)

As Best and Kellner point out, this is a "pluralised analysis of power and rationality as they are inscribed in various discourses and institutional sites" (p. 52). Power literally is everywhere and as such it is purportedly indissoluble either from 'structures' or 'agency', from contestation and struggle:

> I am saying: as soon as there is a power relation, there is a possibility of resistances. We can never be ensnared by power: we always modify its grip in determinate conditions and according to precise strategy. (Foucault, in Best & Kellner, 1991: p. 123)

Foucault does sensitise us to how power is woven through discourses into all aspects of social and personal life, including the policy process. Our own and others' research on policy (*cf.* Ball, 1990) draws heavily on this and other structuralist views (Bernstein, 1990). But a Foucauldian view also brackets "the question of who controls and uses power for which interests in order to focus on the means by which power operates" (Bernstein, 1990: p. 70). Like pluralist theory it therefore occludes the extent to which power is still controlled and administered by specific and identifiable agents in positions of economic and political power and underplays the analysis of what Best and Kellner call "macro-powers" such as that of the state and capital. While pluralist and structuralist theories force us to both complexify our view of power and consider it not just as a state of affairs but as a 'property', a potential which resides in all human endeavour, the other dimension of power, "the capability of actors to secure outcomes where the realisation of these outcomes depends upon the agency of others" (Giddens, 1979: p. 3) is perhaps underplayed. Both views are necessary in policy analysis, although the latter in particular challenges us to look not only at "the media [the resources] through which power is *exercised* but also how structures of domination are *reproduced* " (Giddens, 1979: p. 91, our emphasis).

IV.   'Making' the PE Curriculum

Policy is, of course, not only a process: it is also a *text* constituted by discourses which emerge from and continually interact with a variety of inter-related *contexts*. The concept of discourse now much used in the language of social science theory is of immense utility in policy analysis. Discourses define what can be said and thought, who can speak, when, where, and with what authority (Ball, 1990); they contain claims about how the world, education and individuals should and might be. Viewing policy as a text presses us to ask, for example, how ERA and the NCPE are constituted, what gives them their distinctive features, which discourses within them are given privileged status and which were marginalised or omitted (Penney & Evans, forthcoming). For example, we might ask why the discourse on Games teaching is so privileged in the NCPE. Why is a progressive discourse on 'Equal Opportunities' excluded from the text of the Final Order? While further analysis of the textual content of the NCPE is vital to our understanding of the policy process, it is not our purpose here: alone it will not be sufficient to inform us of what PE in schools will become in future years. Although particular texts and the discourses within them may have great potency and even be accompanied by the order of the law, their power is never complete. As we have discussed above, the policy process is such that as a text is relayed from Government (or quasi-Government bodies) to agencies of sub-government and thence on to arenas of practice in schools, there is inevitably a re-contextualisation of policy. In this respect, ERA and the NC legislation have to be considered as but one aspect of a continual process in which "the loci of power are constantly shifting as various resources implicit and explicit in a text are contextualised and employed in the struggle to maintain or change views of schooling" (Bowe, *et al,* 1992: p. 13). For Bowe *et al.,* the efforts of the NC Subject Working Parties nicely illustrate and underline this view; that policy as knowledge and practices, as a discourse, is always and inevitably 'made'. Our evidence, however, suggests that these efforts also illustrate the unevenness and asymmetry of the power relations in this process, the differences in the capabilities of actors to influence the content of a policy text and both the explicit and the subtle way in which power is exercised in the policy making process.

For example, the planning of the NCPE, like all other National Curriculum subjects, has been conducted in three phases. Firstly an overall structure (of programmes of study, attainment targets) is established by Government and its aids. Secondly professionals from education and industry are brought in to construct a curriculum and express its form and content. Thirdly the 'findings' (interim and final reports) of the Working Party are referred back to Government for its 'approval' via the National Curriculum Council (and mediated by it). Throughout this process, struggle over the meaning given to the teaching of PE has been in evidence. But neither the distribution nor the exercise of power has been equitable within this contest. Physical Educationists had no control over the structure of the NC or the selection of the Working Party members, and throughout the process of constructing the NCPE certain parameters were firmly set by the Secretaries of State. For example, an initial request to the Secretaries of State to stipulate (in the statutory requirements) how much timetable should be given to PE in the NC was simply rejected out of hand. The Working Group was also consistently reminded of the "resource implications" of its recommendations. In his response to its Interim Report (DES, 1991a) the Secretary of State for Education assiduously underlined the need for the group to consider again the economic "feasibility" of the proposals and implored the Group to ensure that the recommendations in their final report were "…realistically related to the general level of school funding which can reasonably be expected to be available" (DES, 1991a). Effectively the group was being 'asked' to construct a curriculum with respect to its economic viability, rather than its educational desirability, or so it seemed. Thus although we can find evidence of resistance and opposition in the actions of the Working Group, it would be folly to ignore the way in which its actions were framed by the policy statements of more powerful others. The Group had neither the authority nor the resources to contest the power of the central state. There were elements of the policy text which could not be 'made'.

In this respect the development of the NCPE vividly illustrates not only the tension between stated 'ideal' ERA intentions (that the curriculum should be 'broad and balanced' and 'available to all children') and harsh economic realities (the limits of economic resources), but also that policy 'making' is a political process in which not all parties have similar capabilities to determine or privilege elements of a text. It also shows that the power of the central state can be expressed simultaneously in very obvious and very subtle forms of control.

In a period of recession central Government is faced with an acute dilemma. Having created in the public mind the view that education is both a cause of and a solution to the nation's economic problems, it is confronted with the dilemma of how to provide, or at least appear to provide, more and better quality education (in this instance Physical Education) for less economic investment. In this context, a key concept — 'flexibility' — has emerged in Government texts and discourse on curriculum provision as the principal means of resolving the problem. The importance of this concept as a rhetorical device cannot be overstated. It has been used systematically not only to reduce the level of prescription in the NCPE throughout its various stages of development, but also to obscure the limited commitments of the state to PE and shift the onus of responsibility for the provision of this curriculum from central government to schools. For example, the NC recommendations for the PE curriculum at key stages 3 and 4 have undergone significant changes in the course of its development within each of the phases mentioned above. The Working Group interim report recommended that in order to experience a broad and balanced curriculum at key stage 3, pupils should experience physical activities from six areas of physical activity and at key stage 4 at least three activities including games and either gymnastics or dance and one other activity (DES, 1991a). The final report, however, either expressing or anticipating pressure from central government, reduced the number of areas of activity at key stages 3 and 4 to five, and recommended that in key stage 3 pupils should experience all areas, but in any one year at least four including games and either gymnastics or dance, and in key stage 4 two activities from the same or different areas (DES, 1991b).

Subsequently the recommendations for key stage 4 were endorsed by the NCC (1992) and the Secretaries of State. However, those for key stage 3 were deemed to be "...too prescriptive", and in the interest of "greater flexibility" the NCC recommended that pupils should experience a minimum of four of the five activities by the end of key stage 3, with games being the only compulsory activity in each year (NCC, 1991: p. 14).

On the surface, a policy text ascribing 'flexibility' to a subject area does sound like good news (and no doubt it is intended to). It seems to offer scope for the level of human agency in 'policy making' which we and others stress in our conceptualisations of policy and which has been observed in other subject areas in schools (Bowe *et al.*, 1992). In this sense the flexibility embedded in the PE curriculum for pupils at key stages 3 and 4 seems to make the NCPE a 'writerly text'. It "invites the reader to 'join in', to co-operate and co-author" (see Bowe *et al.*, 1992: p. 11), the 'making' of the NCPE. However, in a highly differentiated state school system and in an organisational context of competition for limited resources, this 'ascription' can not be equated either with freedom from constraint or unlimited possibilities for teachers to engage in either policy making or curriculum development. Although in a liberal discourse 'flexibility' does signify possibility, in reality a school's or teacher's capacity to act upon such 'freedom' will be dependent upon existing levels of available (physical and human) resources, and these may vary considerably across the subject areas of the curriculum within them.

Thus schools and teachers are being issued opportunity without statutory support for their curriculum initiatives: a version of a classic para-professional dilemma, responsibility without power. It is as well to remember that in the eyes of the political Right the lower the status of a curriculum subject the greater the 'flexibility' it is afforded. Needless to say, the status imputed to a subject will have an important bearing on whether it is privileged or disadvantaged in the acquisition of resources. The low status historically imputed to PE in the school curriculum, and endorsed and hardened by the political culture and educational outlook of the conservative New Right in recent years (see Evans, 1990; Evans, 1993; Kirk, 1992), therefore potentially has very serious implications for the future of PE.

As indicated earlier, the struggles and conflicts evident throughout the development of the NCPE are likely to be equally apparent in its implementation in schools. Within LEAs and schools, issues of resourcing and how the curriculum is to be paid for will continue to dominate discussions of the future provision of PE for the foreseeable future. In a context of scarce resources, 'entitlement' and 'flexibility' may be fundamentally incompatible. Armed with 'flexibility' as a 'rhetorical device', schools, headteachers and governing bodies may free themselves from the task of having to deliver a 'broad and balanced' PE curriculum for all pupils.

It may be evident in what we have said above that whether a text is perceived or received as a resource, an opportunity, a barrier or a constraint will depend not only on the narrative of the text or the discourses within it, but also on many other aspects of the contexts with which it inter-relates. For us the concept of *context* addresses the environment in which policy 'making' and implementation occurs. It includes the influences of past policies and practices, the parallel implementation of other policies, competing ideologies and the policies, practices and ideologies of other sites. ERA of course is not a single piece of legislation: it is a package of measures which together are intended to bring about quite radical changes in the organisation and structure of the education system. An understanding of the 'impact' of the NCPE is not going to be achieved unless we study it in relation to other ERA policy measures.

Particularly pertinent in this respect are the possible implications of LMS for the future provision of PE. LMS aims to make schools in England and Wales more accountable for their operations and encourage more efficient use of resources. It makes fundamental changes in the financial and management structures of education, placing limitations on the function of LEAs and giving greater autonomy to schools and governing bodies. The two key features of this policy are *formula funding* and *delegation management*. Formula funding introduces the allocation of schools budgets on the basis of the number and age of pupils, with certain mandatory exceptions. Delegation of management makes governing bodies responsible for the management of school budgets, thereby significantly reducing the power of LEA with respect to school finances, resources and personnel, and giving far greater 'opportunities' and autonomy to governing bodies in these respects. Although the effects of these budgetary and management changes will take time to materialise, it has already been noted that LMS not only exacerbates levels of competition *between* schools, but also creates competition *within* them.

Physical educationists now work in contexts in which subjects are forced to vie with each other for resources in terms of staffing levels and financial support.

Whilst all subjects will feel the effects of these policy changes to some degree, their impact across the curriculum will be far from even. In the case of PE, where the resources available are a key determinant of provision, the effects may be particularly serious. Tighter or reduced budgets will jeopardise the upkeep of facilities, prohibit the purchase of new equipment or replacement of old, or mean that travel to off-site facilities is no longer a viable option. As one secondary school teacher in our study remarked, "We now have to hire fields and transport. Thus [our] administration has increased dramatically. We also have to be aware how frequently we go off-site. This may need to be cut in the future" (Head of PE, Secondary). Clearly the financial implications of LMS in these terms may have a direct impact on the PE experiences and opportunities a school can provide.

It is naive to assume that all subjects are equal in the competition for resources within schools. As indicated earlier, subjects differ in their historical, social and political 'status' and this will undoubtedly be influential when schools are forced to prioritise curriculum areas for budget allocations. Furthermore they have entered the competition at different points in time. The phased implementation of the NC has created a situation in which the subjects 'settled' first are at an advantage in competing for timetable time, staffing and physical resources. Conversely, those arriving late in the NC implementation process, and pariculary those with low status subject matter, are disadvantaged. As a subject, PE may therefore be particularly disadvantaged with consequences that are potentially very severe. As one head teacher remarked, it's a case of "first come first served. PE comes later". Another stressed that the main effect of the NC has been "to squeeze curriculum time for PE as other subjects have come on stream".

'Open Enrolment' also challenges both the quality and level of provision of PE in schools. Open enrolment promises parents greater freedom to choose the school to which they will send their children. With the introduction of formula funding this has created a situation in which schools are competing for pupils. Schools are forced to market their services and records — a key aspect of which may be their available facilities, including those for PE and sport. Clearly schools vary in their capacity to compete in these terms and such inequalities may exacerbate extant differences in the provision of PE and sport. Schools having the facilities and staffing levels to provide a wide range of activities may find financial support for PE, and thus for curriculum development, far more forthcoming than in schools lacking such 'luxuries'. Thus schools will not enter the marketplace on anything like 'equal terms'. As one Head of a Secondary school remarked, "other neighbouring schools with more on-site facilities including fields are attractive to 12 year olds", and presumably to their parents too. The difficulties may be even more pronounced in the Primary sector. Historically under-funded in comparison to the secondary sector, Primary schools have often had to 'make do' with the limited facilities for PE to which they have access. A wide variety of schools — including First (5–8), Middle (8–12), Infant (5–7) and Junior (7–11) — characterise this sector, each differing in pupil roll, class size, physical size and equipment available. Small and rural schools face the greatest problems as formula funding will ensure that their income is very low in comparison to other primary and secondary schools. Such schools may be unable by virtue of their geographical location to attract further pupils and so concomitantly to swell their funds.

Whether or not these fears are justified will only be apparent in time. Our point is simply that the effects of ERA, and the NCPE in particular, will not be experienced evenly or uniformly in the system. As the text of the NCPE actively co-mingles with other aspects of ERA legislation there inevitably will be winners and losers in an 'educational game' played by market principles and rules. Bowe *et al.* (1992) point out that:

> LEA control of the size of the General School Budget and Government controls over LEA spending via the central spending estimates and poll capping are major sources of constraint and inequality. What is more, most writers seem to conveniently ignore the fact that student recruitment is inelastic, the student population is fixed. Increases in the roll of one school can only be achieved by decreases elsewhere. Greater budgetary flexibility in one school will mean additional constraints and a reduction in services in another. This is already happening as historic budgets are adjusted in relation to current levels of recruitment. Many schools are starting out by losing cash. (p. 29)

The upshot of all this is likely to be an increase in the number of more highly segregated schools as parents weigh issues such as quality of education, levels of resource, racial mix, religion or culture in their choices. The sort of school differences, both in terms of the quality of educational experience they can provide and social and ability mix which bedevilled the development of 'comprehensive schools' in the UK, may accumulate even further. Evidently the priorities of the market end of educational planning may simply be incompatible with educational criteria. As one Head of PE in a secondary school lamented, the consequence of "having to sell our subject and school to win more pupils" may be an "over-emphasis on window dressing instead of getting on with teaching pupils". Requiring schools to address the levels of curricular provision they are making for PE, to ensure that it is 'broad and balanced', ought to have a positive effect on its provision in schools. LMS and Open Enrolment may, however, make this apparent commitment to a 'PE for all' extremely difficult to achieve.

V. Conclusion

Once we begin to look closely at the policy process (including the mechanisms for 'creating policy'), the discourses embedded in a policy context, and those that are marginalised or excluded, and how these interact with contexts in which teachers work, we begin to see how cautious we must be in advocating a view of policy which always is in a 'state of becoming'. Certainly, as a social process policy is always and inevitably being made and remade, but (to paraphrase Marx, 1969: p. 185)] not always in conditions of the actors' own making. Nor in the 'remaking' are all elements of a 'given' policy open to negotiation or contestation; they are not amenable to resistance or change. In this sense the policy process is not always like a game of Chinese Whispers in which the initial story line becomes increasingly and creatively more extravagant, expansive and altered as it is passed on from one person to another. As a text is relayed it may also be substantially reduced — the Chinese Whisper can distort and dilute too (Ingham, 1983). In the recursive flow of policy, creative activity may occur but the text and the conditions/contexts in which people work may constrain and narrow the possibilities for action. Certainly an emphasis on process in policy research is invaluable. It does help us avoid analytically an over-determined 'state control' or 'delivery model' of the curriculum, while emphasising that the State, LEAs and schools are differently empowered over time within the policy process (Bowe *et al.*, 1992). By viewing policy as a recursive flow of action and interpretation, attention is drawn to the way in which policy may be made and remade at different sites of educational practice. However, it is no more satisfactory to view policy as an unequivocal statement of a Government's intent (that will simply filter down through the quasi-state bodies and into schools, without adaption, contestation or resistance), than it is to see it as an 'open' resource providing unlimited opportunities for LEAs or teachers in schools.

Teachers will continue to 'make' their PE curriculum but in conditions which are neither always of their own making nor of their liking, and over which they may have diminishing levels of control. Certainly the key task for us now in our research is to grasp and demonstrate the significance of the NCPE as a policy text for the variety of contexts in which it is used and illustrate the possibilities and difficulties facing teachers and others as they endeavour to define the future of PE. In our study much remains to be done.

Note

1   This four-year research project began in September 1990. It is entitled *The Impact of the Education Reform Act on the Provision of Sport and PE in State Schools* and is funded by the ESRC (project R000233629), The Sports Council and the University of Southampton. We are grateful for their support.

References

Ahier, J. and Flude, M. (eds) (1983) *Contemporary Education Policy*. Beckenham: Croom Helm.

Ball, S. J. (1990) *Politics and Policy Making in Education*. London: Routledge.

Bernstein, B. (1990) *The Structuring of Pedagogic Discourse Vol.IV. Class, codes and control*. London: Routledge.

Best, S. and Kellner, D. (1991) *Postmodern Theory*. London: Macmillan Education Ltd.

Bowe, R. and Ball, S. J. with Gold, A. (1992) *Reforming Education and Changing Schools: Case Studies in Policy Sociology*. London: Routledge.

Buachalla, S. (1988) *Education Policy in Twentieth Century Ireland*. Dublin: Wolfhound Press.

Dale, R. (1989) *The State and Education Policy*. Milton Keynes: Open University Press.

Davies, B. (1988) 'Destroying teacher motivation? The impact of nationalising the curriculum of education process', *Working Papers in Urban Education*, 3. London: King's College.

CCCS (Centre for Contemporary Cultural Studies, University of Birmingham) (1991) *Education Limited*. London: Hutchinson.

DES (1987) *The National Curriculum 5–16: A Consultation Document.* London: HMSO.

——— (1989) *National Curriculum. From Policy to Practice.* DES Publications.

——— (1991a) *National Curriculum Physical Education Working Group. Interim Report.* DES/Welsh Office.

——— (1991b) *Physical Education for ages 5–16. Proposals of the Secretary of State for Education and Science and the Secretary of State for Wales.* DES/Welsh Office.

Evans, J. (1990) 'Defining a subject: The rise and rise of the New PE?', *British Journal of Sociology of Education,* Vol.11, No.2: pp. 155–169.

Evans, J. (ed) (1993) *Equality, Education and Physical Education.* Lewes: The Falmer Press.

Evans, J. and Davies, B. (1990) 'Power to the people? The great Education Reform Act in tomorrow's schools: A cultural and comparative perspective', in H. Lauder and C. Wylie (eds) *Towards Successful Schooling.* Lewes: The Falmer Press, pp. 53–73.

——— (1992) 'Equality and Physical Education', in J. Evans (ed) *Equality, Education and Physical Education.* Lewes: The Falmer Press.

Evans, J. and Penney, D. (1992) 'Investigating ERA: Qualitative Methods and Policy Orientated Research. *Research Supplement, British Journal of Physical Education.* No. 11, Summer 1992, pp. 2–7.

Evans, J., Penney, D. and Bryant, A. (1993) 'Improving the quality of Physical Education: the Education Reform Act 1988 and PE in England and Wales', *Quest* (forthcoming).

Foucault, M. (1980) *Power/Knowledge.* New York: Vintage Books.

Giddens, A. (1979) *Central Problems in Social Theory.* London: The Macmillan Press.

Hampshire CC Education (1991) The Use of Time in Secondary Schools — Timetabling the Secondary Curriculum. Unpublished paper: Hampshire CC Education.

Hargreaves, A. and Reynolds, D. (1989) 'Introduction', in A. Hargreaves and D. Reynolds (eds) *Education Policies: Controversies and Critiques.* Lewes: The Falmer Press, pp. 1—33.

Hill, M. (1980) *Understanding Social Policy.* Oxford: Basil Blackwell.

Ingham, R. (1983) 'The fate of a good intention: The "Football and the Community" Schemes', in A. Tomlinson (ed.) *Explorations in Football Culture.* LSA Publication No.21, Eastbourne: Leisure Studies Association, pp. 51–71.

Kirk, D. (1992) *Defining Physical Education.* Lewes: The Falmer Press.

Lawton, D. (1978) *The End of the 'Secret Garden'? A Study in the Politics of the Curriculum.* The University of London, Institute of Education.

Marx, K. (1969) 'The Eighteenth Brumaire of Louis Bonaparte' [1852], in *Marx-Engels Selected Works.* London: Progress Publishers.

McPherson, A. and Raab, C. D. (1988) *Governing Education.* Edinburgh: Edinburgh University Press.

NCC (1991) *Physical Education in the National Curriculum. A Report to the Secretary of State for Education and Science on the statutory consultation for attainment target and programmes of study in physical education.* York: National Curriculum Council.

Ozga, J. (1987) 'Studying educational policy through the lives of policy makers: An attempt to close the macro-micro gap' in S. Walker and L. Barton (eds) *Changing Policies, Changing Teachers.* Milton Keynes: Open University Press.

Penney, D. and Evans, J. (1991) 'The impact of the Education Reform Act (ERA) on the Provision of Physical Education and Sport in the 5–16 Curriculum of State Schools'. *British Journal of Education* Vol.22, No.1: pp. 38–42.

———— (forthcoming) 'Conceptualising policy. The development and "implementation" of the National Curriculum for Physical Education' in D. Edwards and B. Somekh (eds) *The Centrality of Values in Curriculum Research. BERA Dialogue.*

Ranson, S. (1988) 'From 1944 to 1988: Education, citizenship and democracy', *Local Government Studies*, Vol. 14, No.1: February.

Troyna, B. (1992) 'The hub and the rim: How LMS buckles antiracist education'. Paper presented to the 8th ERA Research Network Seminar (12th February 1992). Department of Education, University of Warwick.

Troyna, B. and Williams, T. (1986) *Racism, Education and the State.* Beckenham: Croom Helm.

PHYSICAL EDUCATION AND THE NATIONAL CURRICULUM: SOME POLITICAL ISSUES

Margaret Talbot
Carnegie Professor
Leeds Metropolitan University

I.   Introduction

This paper describes some of the political processes through and behind the construction of National Curriculum Physical Education, from the perspective of one member of the Department of Education and Science Physical Education Working Group. The descriptions are necessarily informed by personal and professional perspectives and interpretations, and by hindsight, since I have had the opportunity since March 1992, when the Final Orders (DES & the Welsh Office, 1992) were published, to reflect on the experience of being a member of this Working Group and on the political influences and pressures on the Group's decisions. It is worth bearing in mind that the members of the Working Group were asked to remain silent about the deliberations and progress of the Group, and about DES and Ministerial dialogue, from August 1990 until after the Final Report (DES, 1991b) was published in August 1991. This in effect prevented members of the Group entering into dialogue on the National Curriculum with colleagues inside and outside the PE profession, for a year of their lives.

My emerging thoughts about the political processes involved were given impetus by the course evaluations I received recently from two teachers who had attended an INSET National Curriculum Awareness course: the teachers accused me of being inappropriately "political". I had in fact represented the need for physical education teachers to be more prepared to marshal arguments, and more aware of the politics of education, so that they could better fight for the curriculum time and resources they needed to deliver the National Curriculum. I had argued that members of the physical education profession must be aware that PE's place in the National Curriculum was not indefinitely assured, that its current inclusion, especially after Key Stage 3, had to be fought for, and that its future place would need to be constantly established, protected and justified. Their discomfort at what they called this "overly political" approach, in turn disturbed me; the necessity for everyone in physical education to be informed about and to understand the nature of the struggle to ensure physical education's place in the National Curriculum seemed to me to be so obvious that I had not considered that professional colleagues might apparently prefer to know nothing of the vulnerability of their subject.

The purpose of this paper, then, is to provide some of the background to decisions and choices which were made by the Working Group (and of some of the choices which were effectively made for them!) and to make more accessible the kinds of tensions which had to be managed. The paper covers a range of different aspects:

* the inter-personal politics of the Working Group, and the extent to which these reflected different experiences, ideologies and agendas;

* the intra-professional politics of physical education, and the relative influences of the various interest groups;

* the inter- and intra-professional politics of physical education, sport and dance;

* governmental "official" policy in relation to the personal political agendas of particular Ministers;

* the tensions between government policy and/or directives, and professional belief, expressed in several contexts, including:
  — education;
  — local and central government relationships;
  — issues of control, accountability and standards in education, often expressed in official rhetoric, but having to be accommodated in reality;
  — long term processes and trends evident and reflected in HMI and DES reports, and the role and involvement of civil servants in the processes of educational policy making;
  — the personal politics of Ministers, major actors in these processes, who influenced the shaping of National Curriculum physical education in a variety of ways;
  — the peculiar status of physical education, in that it was the only National Curriculum subject whose development was overseen not only by the

Secretary (or Under–Secretaries) of State for Education, but also by another Minister, the Minister for Sport, who at that time had been recently relocated from the Department of the Environment into the Department of Education and Science, accompanied by the civil servants of the Sport and Recreation Division, now relocated in the Department of National Heritage.

By trying to trace some of these influences, I hope to show that the rationale given in the Final Report of the Physical Education Working Group (DES, 1991b), as a philosophical basis for the Group's recommendations, is a visible part of the ideology of National Curriculum Physical Education. However, it is possible to read too much into the Final Report. Various pressure groups within physical education have criticised the rationale for failing to make enough of the issues to which the pressure groups would give priority: thus, John Alderson (1992) has criticised the Final Report for its "failure" to give sufficient attention to sport. It is true that the term "sport" does not appear in the rationale: neither does "health", and for this omission I have already been taken to task by one of my own BEd students, during an interview for his final year dissertation. My response to him is the same as my response to John Alderson. Individuals and groups with their own agendas see and interpret things which are not necessarily meant. The Final Report could never meet the expectations and aspirations of every member or interest group within the physical education profession: it can be neither "all things to all people", nor the "Physical Education Principia" which some colleagues seemed to expect.

Without consideration of the terms of reference of the Group (see Appendix A, pp. 59–60), the task orientation which was imposed on the Group, the time constraints under which it worked, and the political context within which it worked, understanding will necessarily be partial and limited. I shall be using dance, equal opportunities and outdoor education as examples of "contested terrain", which vividly illustrate some of the tensions within and surrounding physical education during the production of the Interim and Final Reports of the Working Group.

II. Views of Physical Education

An issue which recurred throughout the life of the Working Group, and has continued since, is the lack of appreciation by many people outside the physical education profession, of either the breadth or the diversity of the subject. Related to this point is the common and vexed confusion on the relationships between sport and physical education: for many people, including ministers, physical education appeared to be sport. Yet this confusion was not supported by official documentation on physical education, which had long promulgated a progressive, pedagogically based, model of physical education which included activities like educational gymnastics and dance, as can be seen in *Physical Education from 5 to 16*, one of the HMI Series:

> Physical education in schools aims to develop control, coordination and mastery of the body. It is primarily concerned with a way of learning through action, sensation and observation. (DES, 1989: p. 1)

The document lists aims of physical education which include to "develop the capacity to express ideas in dance forms" and to "develop the ability to appreciate the aesthetic qualities of movement". This was the background to the "official progressive" view that physical education is incomplete without dance, and that physical education is more than sport, not only in terms of the activities covered, but also in terms of the educational intention and context of the subject. Further, many members of the profession were maintaining that physical education "needed" dance, not only as an activity category providing balance across the curriculum, but also to establish and protect the distinction of physical education from sport. As my colleague Anne Flintoff wrote:

> It is time for the outmoded, stereotypical attitudes towards dance held among some PE people to be banished once and for all, and for the profession to welcome dance, within its remit, rather than suggesting that it goes elsewhere. (Flintoff, 1990: p. 90)

However, the dance world itself was also questioning the location of dance within physical education: the rapid development of dance during the 1980s as a distinct and discrete activity within many schools, and the progress made in establishing examination awards in dance, had led those dance teachers whose background was not physical education, to assert dance's "rightful" place as being in the context of arts education (whether "performing" arts or "expressive" arts), rather than physical education. This point had been made repeatedly and articulately in the two years leading to the appointment of the PE Working Group, although there was also widespread acceptance that, given the precedent of the demise of drama as a discrete subject, dance was fortunate to have a designated place in the National Curriculum, even if it was under the umbrella of physical education! With this framework, pragmatists argued, dance should be seeking to articulate and develop its distinctive role within physical education, while retaining its links with the other arts in education (see Talbot, 1990).

At the same time, some criticisms of dance being included within physical education were being levelled, on the grounds of inappropriateness, from within the physical education:

> Since dance is a culturally valued form, it should be part of the education process in the same way music and art are. The difficulty lies in knowing how and where it should be located.
>
> ... physical educators have not proved to be the best people to promote dance ... it should be taught within departments of performing arts. We would reject the argument that if PE teachers don't do it, it will die altogether. Rather, the evidence suggests that in the hands of sport–minded physical educators, its death as an art form is ensured.
>
> Having said that, there may be a legitimate place for dancing in physical education either a) for young children during the development of those movement competencies that underpin involvement in the sport and art forms that require skilful action or b) in those dancing competitions that are sports in their own right. The term "p.e." should be abandoned in favour of "sport education". (Alderson & Crutchley, 1990: pp. 48–49)

This debate about the place of dance in physical education is not only about the grounding and conceptual classification of activity. It is also (although is rarely acknowledged as such) a debate informed and influenced by ideological differences in physical education which are part of the legacy of single sex teacher training and provision: it is a gender debate which is not only about the "suitability" of dance for boys and girls, but also about the history of the profession and about the struggle towards equity and the politics of gender within it.

It is common for dance educators to criticise physical education teachers (especially male physical education teachers) for their attitudes towards dance. It is certainly the case that several researchers (e.g. Evans, 1988) have observed that it is male physical education teachers who are least committed and even antipathetic towards equal opportunities and towards dance. The argument that dance (especially for boys) should not take up precious time "needed" for other aspects of physical education, notably team games often referred to as "national sports", has been heard both within and outside the profession, despite the criticisms made of these attitudes by multi–culturalists and others working towards equality of opportunity.

But dance teachers, too, can be seen to be unwilling to adopt a self–critical approach, which is essential for an educational service which meets the requirements of equal opportunities for pupils. How many dance teachers, for example, assume ability and capacity to benefit from dance education within the narrow range of stereotyped body shapes promulgated by some dance forms? Royston Maldoom, a London dance teacher, makes the point:

> There's the feeling from the top that 'this is what dance should look like, and this is what dancers should look like, and we'll do it for you'. Just as you can enjoy football, and play it, without becoming a professional footballer, so you can dance without becoming — or needing to look like — a professional dancer. Dance relates to life. (cited in Dougall, 1989)

The point is, to what extent are the activities within physical education presented as inclusive or exclusive, and how is their presentation by teachers (either unconsciously or by design) restricted by gender or other stereotype?

There are many teachers who claim to be espousing equality of opportunity by treating children "all the same". The criticisms of this approach have been well rehearsed elsewhere (see, for example, Talbot, 1990a), but it is worth reiterating the point that equal treatment is simply never done in practice, because to do so would be to ignore the fact that pupils differ in their abilities, interests, resources and previous experiences. In the context of dance these differences are grounded in gender and culture: to treat all children the same would be to ignore their individuality and limit the extent to which they might benefit from each others' various backgrounds, interests and abilities.

No effective teacher, in any case, treats all children the same. Classroom interaction studies show that teachers consistently give more attention to boys than to girls in mixed–sex teaching groups; that teachers' judgements of the same behaviour when displayed by girls and boys differ; and that such teacher–pupil interaction is similarly affected by ethnicity, social class and age. Teachers, even those committed to equal opportunities, find it difficult to accept that they are behaving in these ways, and when shown on video-tape or through interaction inventories, still find it difficult to change. The claim for equal treatment ignores the power and pervasiveness of gender in forming and reifying expectations of girls and boys, women and men. Nick May's (1987) research on engendered teacher education provides a vivid example:

> During the interview 'Mary' — who had last year been a school pupil and this year is a first–year undergraduate on the new degree in Education (with Teaching Certificate) — talked at some length, and with considerable feeling, about how her main frustration as a female pupil had been what she saw as her systematic disenfranchisement from influence over the content and process of the schools' curricula which she had pursued over the last thirteen years. Although she felt that all the pupils suffered this lack of influence she was convinced that girls suffered disproportionately. (Some time later in the interview), when talking about the 'teaching practice' she had recently completed, 'Mary' described how her 'music and movement' work had met with 'loud and disruptive' reaction from some of the boys in the mixed class of 7–8 year olds, even though the majority of children had clearly enjoyed and been engaged by the scheme she had designed. Faced with this rejection, and experiencing some anxiety about how the teachers and her tutor would assess her potential as a teacher if she was not seen to be exercising what they would count as 'good control' of the class, 'Mary' resolved her 'problem' by designing an alternative scheme which the few boys would not (and did not) reject. Although the girls had 'subsequently shown less interest', their quiet acquiescence to what she offered them reduced her anxiety about her assessment as a teacher. When she related her pupil experience to her teaching experience 'Mary' was dismayed to realise that she had 'reproduced for others precisely that frustration which (she herself) had experienced as a pupil'. (May, 1987: p. 79)

The ways teachers interact with colleagues and pupils reveal a great deal about their values and beliefs. In turn, children and possibly colleagues will attempt to measure up to perceived norms of behaviour and parity of treatment. There is considerable evidence that teachers will make more effort to accommodate boys' needs and demands in mixed sex groupings, than they will girls', partly because they are sympathetic to perceived "threats" to boys' gender identities, but also to avoid boys' disruptive behaviour. Boys' activities within physical education, as well as their behaviour, are often used as the norm against which content and presentation are measured for all children. This is certainly the case in mixed–sex groupings in higher education, where women students' achievement and development in dance and gymnastics are often limited, with collusion by staff, by the male students' responses, which range from total rejection, through negotiating optional participation, to disruptive or "hamming" behaviour during lectures which is frequently sufficiently severe to merit the description of sexual harassment of female students and staff (see Flintoff, 1993). I have previously (Talbot, 1990b) criticised the way such tensions have been described as "the gender problem", by asking the focus of attention to be shifted towards the narrow range of masculinities exemplified in boys' physical education. The popular images of physical education as "sport" both illustrate and help to perpetuate the problem. The issue of dance's place in National Curriculum Physical Education is part of a wider contested terrain, of the conventional uses of the term "physical education", and particularly its use in the press and by politicians.

The conventional nature of physical education, and the ways inequity is embedded within it, has resulted in practices which continue and reify inequalities for boys and girls, children from a range of cultural backgrounds, and children with disabilities. I hoped that the Physical Education Working Group would be able to identify and address the most important issues, and to provide guidance which would increase and improve the opportunities which all children could be offered in schools.

It was very soon apparent that some members of the Working Group did not share this concern. For example, early in our work, I was repeatedly challenged by one member of the Working Group over my advocacy for equal opportunities. I was told first, that there were no problems of this kind of any significance, and secondly that in making these issues visible, I was "making things worse", and that it would be much better to let things change "naturally". It was therefore a struggle at times to get equal opportunities on the agenda at all, although this did get easier when the Group was persuaded that we should adopt an inclusive view of equality of opportunity, including gender, race, culture and disability. There is no doubt that this strengthened and legitimised the case for equal opportunities, which was also considerably strengthened by the advocacy shown by Maggie Semple who, as a black woman, often made points to the Group far more effectively than I had been able to do: her lived experience made her contributions more powerful and persuasive. Points made by other members of the Working Group on the need to cater for children with special needs also were usually sympathetically received. One member was asked to take on the role of coordinating the information we needed to ensure entitlement for all children, regardless of ability, which also supported the overall approach we had taken.

This highlights a phenomenon which equal opportunities exponents often comment upon. While at least in public rhetoric, equal opportunities for people with disabilities (especially children) seems unarguable and racism is "wrong", there is commonly resistance to accept at all the existence of practices and structures which disadvantage girls and women, boys and men. While there was support from some other members of the Group, I was several times surprised by the apparent lack of awareness or commitment to equal opportunities from certain members, and by some of the statements which they made. One senior member of the profession actually gave the opinion that teachers should be careful about teaching contact sports to classes which had Asian members, because they were always smaller than white children and it might be dangerous!

The Group agreed on a short section on equal opportunities in the Interim Report (DES, 1991a), which was very well received and strongly supported by the physical education profession and by other agencies. The Council for Racial Equality (CRE, 1991), for example, expressed its delight that at last a subject Working Group had done more than pay lip service to the issue. Even so, the Secretariat and some members of the Group were still doubtful whether equal opportunities should be addressed in more detail in the Final Report than in the Interim Report. I was aware that many colleagues in the physical education profession felt that there was an opportunity for a real break through, if a properly argued section on equal opportunity could be included in the Final Report.

It was at this point that I telephoned the Schools Unit at the Equal Opportunities Commission, which had made no formal response to the Interim Report. I asked its representative whether the EOC would be making a response before the deadline and was told that because the Physical Education Interim Report (unlike most of the other subjects) had addressed the issue, they had not planned to do so. I asked whether the EOC was happy that physical education, as currently taught, catered adequately for girls and boys: I was already aware that the EOC Schools Unit had a growing list of complaints about physical education, and that the confusion of school sport and physical education caused recurrent problems in teachers interpreting (or choosing to misinterpret) the sex discrimination legislation. The response was that the EOC would like to see a more proactive approach being taken to equal opportunities by physical education, and that "if it would help", it would make sure that a response would be sent to the

DES. This was duly received, and provided considerable help in my efforts to ensure that the issue was visible and appropriately addressed in the Final Report.

The health related exercise (HRE) "lobby", too, had an effect: the high profile given to their argument that HRE was less "gendered" and offered a wider range of opportunities to children with disabilities and to children of a range of abilities, than competitive sports activities, helped to raise the awareness and enlist the support of key members in the Working Group. I was much encouraged also by support from the Chairman of the Working Group. During a discussion of the point that physical education, through encouraging boys to look beyond competitive sport, could help to extend boys' restricted perceptions of masculinity and masculine behaviour, the member who had earlier been so dismissive of equal opportunities, announced that he had no idea what we were talking about. At this point, Ian Beer intervened, saying: "I know exactly what they mean, and it's one of our biggest problems at Harrow": his experience as Headmaster of a residential boys' school with a strong and distinctive sports ethos had sensitised him to the difficulties which boys experienced who had other interests and qualities, outside the sport culture.

Support did also come from the physical education profession itself. The phrase eventually used to qualify the chapter on equal opportunities in the Final Report was taken directly from the contribution of the Physical Education Association of Great Britain and Northern Ireland (PEA, 1990): "Equal Opportunity: a Guiding and Leading Principle for Physical Education" was the sixth chapter of the Final Report. However, because of the Secretariat's concern about the length of the Final Report, a fuller account of equal opportunities, along with the sections on cross–curricular matters, partnerships in provision and a rationale for the programmes of study, were included only as annexes to the "main" report.

Whether this affected the fate of equal opportunities in the Final Orders (DES and the Welsh Office, 1992) (that is, that only the slightest mention was made of it) and the Non–Statutory Guidance (NCC, 1992) is impossible to assess. It is likely that the very obvious concern among the civil servants to present a Final Report which would be accepted by the Secretary of State, along with the equally obvious lack of commitment to equal opportunities issues at the National Curriculum Council, were more influential. The effect was the same: instead of national curriculum physical education providing an opportunity to challenge the structural and procedural inequities in physical education, the issues associated with equal opportunities were in effect rendered invisible.

III. PE, school sport and professionalisation

The struggle by the physical education profession over the last decade to persuade the public, Ministers and the media that physical education is "about more than sport" has been spectacularly unsuccessful, not least because Ministers change offices so quickly that as soon as arguments have been accepted by one Minister he [sic] is moved to a different appointment and there is another needing to be educated by the profession! It has also been the case that bodies like the Central Council for Physical Recreation tend to use the term "school sport" to the exclusion of "physical education": this was also the case with the all–party Select Committee on School Sport (Select Committee of the House of Commons, 1991) which sat during the life of the National Curriculum Working Group. It was therefore not surprising that the media and the public frequently confused the two groups, and that reporting on either or both in the press and on television tended to be fused or confused. The physical education profession does, of course, have to accept some responsibility for this confusion. As Elizabeth Murdoch has long argued, there is a lack of a "shared corporate conviction in our rationale" (Murdoch, 1986: p. 83), and "it (physical education) either has to declare itself with as coherent a voice as possible that it knows where it is going, or it will disappear." (*ibid.*, p. 85) In my Fellows' Lecture to the Physical Education Association in 1987, I too expressed the need for physical education to be more "professional" in its approach:

> Perhaps the most pressing need for those of us in physical education, is to learn to present our particular case effectively and with political impact, not merely to justify our own systems of values and practices as we believe they should be, but also, and equally importantly, to affect policy making and decision taking in the wider political arena. In other words, physical education policies need to be proactive, rather than reactive; for this to be achieved, there needs to be consensus, and there needs to be continuous appraisal, both of physical education practices and policies, and of the dynamic social context within which we all live and work. ... while it is easy to say what physical education is not, and that it is more than sport, we have to show that we can also say what it is, and how this informs and complements the place of sport in the lives of young people. (Talbot, 1987: pp. 1, 2 & 9)

These needs became even more apparent and acute during the debates on physical education's place and role in the National Curriculum, and the failure of the physical education profession to convey its message resulted in a series of retrieval operations for physical education which was a direct result of Ministers' and the media's views of physical education as sport. The success of these retrieval operations should be appreciated within the political context of the National Curriculum, and a number of political decisions and developments, some of which appeared to be at best arbitrary and at worst completely uninformed.

1. The Consultative Document on the National Curriculum published in 1987 had omitted physical education and dance altogether from the list of core and foundation subjects which it was proposed would be compulsory.

2. Physical education was finally included as a foundation subject in the Education Reform Act only after intensive lobbying from the physical education profession and from sports organisations.

3. The place of both physical education and the arts in the National Curriculum was effectively marginalised by their place in the order of subject development: music, art and physical education were the last three subjects for which Working Groups were appointed, and the last Final Orders to be implemented into schools. This meant that teachers of these subjects have had to fight for sufficient time on the curriculum, and that the greater share of centrally provided INSET funds were allocated to the subjects appearing first in the process — English, Mathematics and Science. Drama had already disappeared as a discrete subject, being subsumed within English.

4. Art, Music and Physical Education were differentiated from all the other National Curriculum subjects by the terms of reference (see Appendix A, pp. 59–60) given to their respective Working Groups. While the previous seven subjects had developed ten statutory levels of achievement to inform progress between and across key stages, the Working Groups for Art, Music and Physical Education were given the brief only to recommend statutory End of Key Stage Statements and Programmes of Study. Despite the Physical Education Working Group questioning this brief, on the grounds that End of Key Stage Statements would be far too general, and would necessarily be either too bland to be of use, or so prescriptive that large percentages of children would "fail", this brief was imposed on the Group. The Group was also not allowed to make any recommendations with regard to the time needed for delivery of National Curriculum Physical Education, despite heroic and repeated attempts by its members and its Chairman, Ian Beer, to

establish its right to do so, for example in the Interim Report. The secrecy within which the Group was forced to work meant that understanding of the effects of these imposed restrictions was limited among other members of the physical education profession, and among allies in the worlds of health, dance and sport. Indeed, we were frequently accused of "selling out" to the Government.

5. The relative lack of status of these last three subjects, already implied by the differences in the brief of their Working Groups described above, was emphasised just before they began their work by the request in July 1990 of the Secretary of State to the National Curriculum Council, to consider whether Art, Music and Physical Education should remain compulsory for pupils at Key Stage 4 (i.e., between ages 14 and 16).

On 5 August 1990 I wrote to John MacGregor:

Along with many other members of the physical education profession and the sports community, I was both disturbed and disappointed to read the reports of your speech in which you indicated that physical education, music and art might become optional for key stage 4, to make room for more flexibility for examinable subjects in GCSE. It was, to say the least, depressing to have the brief of the Working Group so radically changed from that of the other Foundation Subject Working Groups: it can only detract from the rationale and consistency of the Government's argument for a National Curriculum, and will almost inevitably give rise to second order categorisation of the very subjects of which young people, especially at key stage 4, are so in need. To remove art, music and physical education from the foundation education of young people at this age makes no sense, when they are constantly being criticised (by members of the current Government) for being uncivilised, unfit and uncouth.

Likewise, I do not understand the rationale that it will allow children to opt for a wider range of GCSE subjects, when one of the purposes of the National Curriculum is to ensure a balanced curriculum for all children from 14 to 16. To pander to the pattern of "collecting" GCSE subjects, at the expense of this fundamental element of the foundation curriculum, seems to me to be illogical and contradictory with National Curriculum policy. In pre–vocational terms also, this change in policy makes little sense to me! There are now more people employed in sport and leisure associated industries than collectively in the car industries and agriculture, fisheries and food: physical education can no longer be seen as irrelevant to widening vocational choice, particularly when so many days are lost from industry as a whole through illness from stress–related conditions and sedentary habits.

I therefore write to ask you to reconsider your intention to ask the Physical Education Working group to make recommendations on different criteria from the other foundation subjects. To do so will reduce the credibility, both of physical education's status as a founda-tion subject, and of the Government's consistency in formulating a balanced National Curriculum. (Talbot, 1990c)

I received a reply from Michael Fallon on behalf of the Secretary of State on 21 August, 1990 assuring me that:

The Secretary of State does not underestimate the value of art, music and physical education in the school curriculum. He expects that schools will provide for the great majority of pupils to undertake some form of PE at 14–16 and that there will be scope for the study of art and music. He takes the view that these are all subjects where valuable activity can take place outside as well as inside the timetabled curriculum. (Fallon, 1990)

He went on to say that "no decisions have been taken" and that the Working Groups should continue with their "task of drawing up recommendations in line with the terms of reference for each group". This claim that "no decisions have been taken" is a common one in political life: during my time as a member of the Working Group I came to realise that public representation is much less a part of decision making in our so–called democratic society than I had supposed. Instead, it became clear that the mythologies surrounding subjects, and the long–held opinions of Ministers and civil servants, were far more important in the arbitrary decisions which were taken, than reasoned and informed argument. The strength, source, visibility and publicity of representations were more important than their quality. Later, it also became clear that personal representation, when the "ear" of a Minister was available, was also very important. It was also clear that the Secretary of State never read the responses which were sent to the Interim Report: they were summarised by a member of the Secretariat, and analysed to produce a picture of the level of support/opposition for the various recommendations we had made in the Interim Report. The summary was indeed helpful to the Working Group in deciding which of its recommendations it would defend, explore further or concede, and it may have been that the attention of the Secretary of State was drawn to the weight of opinion shown by the summary. But the quality and thoughtfulness of so many responses had no influence whatever, as far as could be seen, on Ministerial decisions. A more thorough analysis of these responses would provide a unique insight into the state of mind of the physical education profession and its allies in health, dance and sport at that time.

In the case of key stage 4, it was clear that art, music and physical education subjects had already been assessed as in some way "less important" than the other National Curriculum subjects, and that the intention of balance within the Education Reform Act took less priority than the need to cater for pupils to do a second modern language or a second or third science subject in GCSE. In the tension between the official rhetoric of "a broad and balanced curriculum" and the very real problems of congestion of pupils' programmes at key stage 4, art, music and physical education were seen as expendable. The notion also that these subjects could somehow be catered for outside the official curriculum, underlined the view of physical education as school sport, and the implication that all three subjects were marginal and seen within a "play" or "leisure" context.

IV. The Working Group in action

The Physical Education Working Group, meeting for the first time at the end of August 1990, set the issue of its brief and the place of physical eduction at key stage 4 as its first discussion point. The Chairman agreed to challenge the terms of reference on behalf of the Group, and members also agreed a set of arguments with which to support the argument to include physical education in key stage 4. It is not possible to judge why physical education was successful in its efforts to maintain its place in key stage 4 when art and music were not. It may be that the harmony of the Working Group (in direct contrast to the early days of the Music and Art Working Groups), and the part played by some of the Physical Education Working Group members in rallying support among the profession and powerful allies in sport and health, may help to explain why in January 1991 the Secretary of State (by then Kenneth Clarke) was saying in his speech to the North of England Education Conference:

> ... art and music should be options at key stage 4. I do not believe it is right for the Government to use the law to compel every single pupil to

continue to do these subjects after the age of 14. From the start, it has
been the Government's policy that these subjects should have a much
more flexible National Curriculum regime. But all pupils will continue
to be required to take them up to 14 and I expect all schools to provide
appropriate opportunities right through to the age of 16. I expect that
the great majority will do an aesthetic subject as now. I have no doubt
that all pupils should be obliged to continue their physical education in
one form or another throughout their compulsory schooling, but there
should be a particularly flexible definition of physical education at key
stage 4. (Clarke, 1991: p. 8)

It was in the same speech that the Secretary of State announced that History and
Geography could be combined for key stage 4, also to make more room in
pupils' programmes for further examination subjects. In one way, this decision
strengthened the place of physical education vis–a–vis other subjects. The
National Curriculum Council's advice to the Secretary of State prior to his North
of England Speech (NCC, 1990) had been that, not only should physical
education remain compulsory at key stage 4, but that if physical education was
taken as an examination subject, "extra time should be found for it". In this case,
the difference in the terms of reference of the Working Group, that key stage 4
was not synonymous with GCSE, actually was an opportunity to maintain the
distinctive role of physical education for all children aged 14 to 16, and to
establish the right of children to take GCSE physical education in the extra
envelope of time which had been cleared by making art and music optional and
by merging history and geography. It is still doubtful whether this is fully
appreciated either by the Government, or by the physical education profession!
The arbitrary nature of the decision is reflected in the moral tone adopted — that
it was not "right" for the Government to compel all 14–16 year olds to do art and
music: in what way, therefore, was it "right" to compel them to do science,
mathematics, English, a modern language, etc.? The implication that the place
of "real subjects" was to be protected at all costs is clear.

This brief description of the context within which the Working Group
operated during the first few months of its life raises other questions about why
physical education survived these threats to its place in the National Curriculum,
especially when it was clear to many of us that the profession was in many
respects ill–prepared to counter these threats. During the year leading up to the
appointment of the Working Group, I had listed in a SWOT (strengths,

weaknesses, opportunities and threats) analysis (Talbot, 1989), the weaknesses of physical education I felt needed to be addressed if the challenges of the National Curriculum were to be met:

- lack of knowledge/preparation for National Curriculum (especially by secondary specialists);

- the need to retrieve curriculum time for physical education because of the prior implementation of other subjects;

- tendency in the profession to be inward-looking and conservative (sometimes arrogant!), and whether there was the capacity to respond to change;

- patchy practice and the shortage of well qualified PE curriculum leaders in primary schools;

- failure to establish balanced and focused PE programmes across the age ranges, and the dominance of, and dependence on, team games;

- lack of primary–secondary links;

- lack of investment, especially in facilities and staff development;

- failure of the profession to communicate a coherent view of physical education to the public;

- lack of political skills and "clout", failure to capitalise on allies;

- insecurity, especially in relation to status and control;

- lack of awareness of, or commitment to, equal opportunities issues;

- danger of spreading activities too thin: series of uncritical responses to demands beyond the school curriculum.

Given these weaknesses, with which most teachers with whom I discussed them agreed, the answer to the question, "Why *did* physical education survive in the National Curriculum?", in my judgement relates to three parallel developments, of which the members of the profession should be aware: the strengths of the sports lobby, and the health lobby, and the common approaches adopted by the various physical education organisations.

First was the strength of the sports lobby, which for the first time was using language complementary with and complimentary to physical education! In contrast to the professional polarities and hostility shown towards physical education in previous decades by sports organisations and interest groups, the case sports lobbyists were making on behalf of physical education supported claims of a distinctive contribution by physical education to the "physical literacy" of children, and to the unique opportunity for all children to learn the physical skills and knowledge required for later participation in sport and physical recreation. It was also evident that there was a much greater willingness to consult with members of the physical education profession on the most appropriate form of words to use in lobbying and advocacy. The Sports Council, at both national (English and Welsh) and regional level, were particularly helpful: several regional chairmen rang members of the Working Group or leaders of physical education organisations to ask them to help them with their responses. It seemed that there was a real recognition of the absolute need to protect the place of curriculum time physical education, as the basis for the whole provision of school sport and dance in this country. There were obvious exceptions to this: the distorted view of school sport presented by the CCPR/SHA report (1991) did little to clarify Ministers' or the media's understanding of the 'physical education'–'school sport' relationship, although the report may well, through the publicity gained, have raised Ministerial awareness of public interest during the crucial weeks when lobbying could have any effect.

Second was the strength and source of the health lobby. During a time of almost "moral panic" about the state of the nation's youth, the power of representations from the medical profession and health organisations (like the Health Education Authority) on the importance of physical activity for the physical and moral development of young people was significant. There is also no doubt that the power of the "Rugby Union Mafia in Harley Street" (my term!), stimulated by Ian Beer's contacts in the rugby world, was very significant indeed. At no other time had Government Ministers been assailed by so many letters on the National Curriculum from distinguished medical consultants, whose points they seemed loathe to ignore.

Third was the fact that, for the first time in my professional experience, the various PE organisations worked effectively together, using common arguments and coherent cases. They did not (as they have done since) fight amongst themselves for primacy: during this time of threat the possibility of a united physical education seemed nearer. It was certainly crucial during this period, and it was also noticeable that some of the most thoughtful and radical responses, for example, to the Working Group's Interim Report, were received from physical education organisations. It is regrettable that since this remarkable period of cooperation, individual vested interests appear to have taken precedence over professional unity and integrity.

Ironically, then, in this respect, physical education's failure to distinguish itself from school sport, or even sport, in the public's mind, operated to its advantage. The assault on the place of physical education for 14 to 16 year olds was seen implicitly as a threat to school sport: it became part of the "moral panic" about the nation's young people, and the profession's campaign was strengthened by support from quarters which had never previously spoken out in favour of physical education.

This fusion of "physical education" and "sport" had been reflected also in the membership of the Working Group, with two high profile sports*men* (John Fashanu and Steve Ovett) being included in the Group; and was very visible in the DES press announcements of the membership of the Group. It was not surprising, from the media coverage, that some members of the physical education profession had feared that "sport" was "hijacking physical education":

> The Working Group will be chaired by Ian Beer, the Head Master of Harrow School and a former England rugby international. It will include sportsmen such as the footballer John Fashanu and the athlete Steve Ovett as well as educationalists, academics and representatives from business. John Fashanu is a striker for Wimbledon FC and Steve Ovett, the Olympic gold medallist and former world record holder, is presently a writer and broadcaster on athletics. (DES, 1990: p. 1)

"Leisure Opportunities" (1990) headlined the same perspective more succinctly as "Ovett and Fash devise school sport". In the event, the personal influence of the two sportsmen on the Working Group was minimal, because of their lack of capacity to attend meetings, and despite the Chairman's best efforts to include them. They did, however, give much needed support at times of threat for the Group and vindicated the Group's decision to hold out for a broader approach at key stage 4 than the Secretary of State had requested in his response to the Interim Report.

V.   Policy and practice

The members of the Physical Education Working Group therefore not only had the task set for them by the DES in their terms of reference (see Appendix

A, pp. 59–60): there was also an advocacy task which the physical education profession itself had failed to address — to inform Ministers and the media what was the distinctive identity of physical education. Given the lack of previous knowledge, experience and expertise of several members of the Working Group itself, this was a task within the Working Group as well. This, along with the varied and high expectations held by their colleagues within the physical education profession, placed extra and difficult burdens on the physical educationists who were members of the Working Group. There were from August until December 1990 only four — none of them practising — full–time teachers of physical education. The two who were still in schools (Sue Jackson and Mike Thornton) were both deputy headteachers who maintained an element of physical education on their timetables; and the other two were myself and Elizabeth Murdoch, both appointed from our positions as Heads of well–known units of initial teacher training in physical education (Carnegie, Leeds Poly-technic; and Chelsea, Brighton Polytechnic, respectively). Anne Harris, a primary school head teacher, and Maggie Semple, dance education officer for the Arts Council, were the other "mainstream educationalists" on the Group, although after representation from the Group about the lack of an advisor member and the need for more primary expertise, Malcolm Brown was added to the membership in January 1991, bringing the number of physical educationists to five, within the total Group of fourteen including the Chairman. The Staff Inspector for Physical Education, B J Lewis, was "in attendance" at all meetings and made a full contribution to the deliberations of the Group, but was not formally a member. The Group was serviced by a team of four civil servants, two of whom had played similar roles with other subject groups and had chosen to be assigned to the Physical Education Working Group. Their role proved to be crucial and influential in our work.

They helped us, for example, in the delicate business of using the kind of terminology which Ministers would not find threatening. "Eggar–friendly" became one of the Group's own terms. (Tim Eggar was one of the Under–Secretaries of State.) They skilfully steered us through the minefields of Ministerial predispositions, and were able to advise us how radical we dared to be, from their previous experience with other National Curriculum subjects. In this respect, at least, there was a distinct advantage to being one of the last subject working groups to be formed: we could benefit from others' experiences and mistakes. The problem of the rapid turnover of Ministers (both Secretaries of

State for Education and Ministers for Sport), however, meant that this previous experience was not always shared by them, so that they in turn had to be "educated" to share our progress and conclusions. Physical Education was the only subject working group to be faced with the additional challenge of the close interest of the newly appointed Minister of Sport, Robert Atkins. At the same time as the formation of the Working Group, the Minister, along with the Sport and Recreation Division, was relocated into the Department of Education and Science at the end of 1990, as a response to the School Sport Forum Report (1988). As it happened, the Working Group's relationship with Robert Atkins proved to be at first our most serious challenge and later our greatest source of government support.

The Working Group's first meeting with the Minister for Sport was just after the publication of the Interim Report in February 1991, and the media coverage of the Secretary of State's hostile reaction to some of the recommendations, notably those which he perceived to carry resource implications. Kenneth Clarke had the previous day, during a TV interview, described the Working Group dismissively as "enthusiasts". He had also, in his formal response to the Interim Report, asked us to reconsider several elements of our recommendations (see Appendix B, pp. 61–63), the Secretary of State's response to the Interim Report of the Physical Education Working group). He had also set us an impossible task. "*I expect your recommendations to be realistically related to the general level of school funding which can reasonably be expected to be available.*" No guidance on these "reasonable expectations" was given!

It was, therefore, a somewhat bruised Working Group which met the Minister for Sport. It is perhaps worth explaining that the Working Group as a whole never met the Secretary of State until after it had presented its Final Report. The Chairman, Ian Beer, was summoned to meet him about the Interim Report, but he did not share with the other members of the Group how traumatic that meeting had been until much later. He deserves considerable praise for exercising this restraint, since the Group was not put under such intense pressure as would have been the case had all members known just how hostile Kenneth Clarke had been to the Interim Report.

Robert Atkins began the meeting by explaining to us that he wanted to see the status of physical education teachers elevated, but that in his view we (the Working Group) had gone the wrong way about this: our approach was "far too academic" and there was "not enough about doing". Our language was "over elaborate" and he had found much of the Interim Report "incomprehensible": while he agreed with our objectives, the methods and construction of the curriculum were "over the top". It became clear that one of his objections related to the use of terms like "attainment targets", "programmes of study" and "personal and social development" [PSD] — all terms in everyday usage within and around the National Curriculum. He had not been briefed about, and was totally unaware of, either the terms of reference of the Group, or the requirements of National Curriculum subject development. He underlined the Secretary of State's doubt about the place of outdoor education in the school curriculum, the place of swimming in primary schools and the place of dance in any part of the curriculum, especially for older boys. He urged us to remember that physical education was "not just a subject" and that surely we "did not want just any old teacher taking physical education in primary schools, we needed to bring coaches in". When it was pointed out that some primary school children were as young as five years old, he commented that he thought they began school at nine!

At this point, it was clear that his knowledge and appreciation of the place and purpose of *physical education in state schools* was shaped and led by his belief in and experience of the place of *sport in public schools*. It was also clear that he was under the impression that hardly any primary schools already taught swimming, that dance was disco–dancing, and that outdoor education had to be taught through costly expeditions to mountains, seas and lakes. While his reputation as a cricket fan was well known, it still came as a shock that he apparently valued team games (especially cricket) to the exclusion of almost all other forms of sport, and that he had accepted so uncritically the rhetoric of "character building" and so on which surrounds male contact sports.

Most members of the Group were deeply shocked by this experience, although one member did have the temerity to say: "With respect, Minister, men of your age and background perhaps don't know much about state school physical education". To his eternal credit, Robert Atkins responded: "Well, then, show me". He subsequently attended parts of two of our Working Group meetings, including presentations on outdoor education by leaders of the outdoor education profession and children from Durham Road Junior School, Newport; and a visit to the Ackers Trust (an inner city outdoor education centre) in Birmingham. He also accepted invitations to a series of school and community dance groups. Through exposure to these experiences, through the representations of his staff and through the vehement public responses he received to some of his more extreme statements (for example, being quoted as saying that dance was suitable only for overweight pupils who could not benefit from team games!), the Minister for Sport gradually was won round. He began to use (if not understand) terminology like "physical education is more than sport", and was persuaded to issue a statement (see Appendix C, p. 64) on the Government's recognition of the part played by dance in schools.

Later still, in August 1991, he presided at the launch of the Secretaries of State's Proposals for National Curriculum Physical Education (DES, 1991b) at Old Trafford Cricket Ground in Manchester (his constituency), presenting with enthusiasm the recommendations in the Final Report alongside the Chairman Ian Beer. He described the event as a "major landmark in the provision of physical education in schools", and announced that: "I am very glad to say that we have been able to accept the recommendations of the PE Group almost in their entirety as a basis for what will be included in the National Curriculum". This was a far cry from the Secretary of State's response to the Interim Report. There is not space here to map the ways in which Robert Atkins' views (at least in public) changed between the publication of the Interim and Final Reports. I am convinced, however, that this "sea–change" is attributable to a series of political processes:

1. Skilful manipulation of the Minister's encounters with the Working Group, by the Chairman, with the "businessmen" being briefed to "work on him" over dinner etc.

2. The strength and coherence of the support for the Interim Report shown by the 200 responses, reflected in the summary prepared by the Secretariat.

3. The consistent efforts of DES and Sport and Recreation Division civil servants to provide information and arguments to the Secretary of State and the Minister for Sport, at times and on occasions when they felt it would be most persuasive. They were also conscientious in their resolve to protect the members of the Working Group from the more extreme of their Ministers' opinions.

4. The Select Committee on Sport in Schools (1991), which had been sitting during the life of the Working Group, published its report to the House of Commons in early summer 1991; one of its main recommendations mirrored that of the Working Group in the Interim Report, that all children should learn to swim at primary school. While this was one of the Working

Group recommendations to which the Secretary of State had responded most vehemently, being apparently under the impression that the Group was suggesting something new, which would cost a great deal to implement, the Select Committee making the same recommendation had a strong effect. As an all-party Select Committee, it had a currency which was difficult to ignore. It was also supported by several high profile MPs, international sportsplayers and by comprehensive media coverage, coordinated by the "Swim for Life Campaign".

5. It is possible that this press coverage helped to maintain public interest and interventions by well–known sports personalities, in the press and on television, during the period between the presentation by the Working Group of the Final Report and the Secretary of State's response to it. Certainly press speculation continued during the summer of 1991, and a Commons debate on sport also helped to keep the issues alive.

6. The Minister for Sport did seem to be influenced by the personal contact he had with children and other participants during the Spring of 1991. The compelling nature of presentation by the children from Durham Road School, Newport on their outdoor education experiences, and the obvious enjoyment, exercise and social benefits being gained by the group of largely Asian secondary schoolgirls at the Ackers Trust outdoor activities centre in Birmingham, seemed to extend the range of physical activities in which he had confidence: in these cases, seeing *was* believing.

VI. Conclusion: Dinner with the Minister

It is not known how much the Minister for Sport and the Secretary of State conferred about national curriculum physical education, or whether there were any major disagreements between them, although we were aware that Kenneth Clarke was less antipathetic to dance than Robert Atkins. It became clear during the Spring of 1991 that Robert Atkins had eventually decided that national curriculum physical education was "a good thing" for his political career, and that he wanted to be associated with it being successful. It was certainly congruent with "ethics in sport", which was one of the issues which he espoused during his first year as Minister. It is also interesting that the PE Working Group was the only working group to be given an official Government dinner, hosted by Robert Atkins at Lancaster House: we did wonder whether this was a gesture of rapprochement for the bad beginning to our relationship, although he assured us that it was a "thank you" for a job well done! Whatever the motive, the gesture showed a degree of identification with the Working Group which could not possibly have been predicted at that first meeting!

The style of this dinner was in direct contrast to the somewhat graceless reception for the Art, Music and Physical Education Working Groups hosted by Kenneth Clarke and his under–secretaries of state. In his speech of thanks, the Secretary of State referred to the members of the three working groups as "the hearties and the arties". Perhaps it is not surprising that these three subjects have had to fight so hard for their continued survival as national curriculum subjects?

References

Alderson, J. (1992) Physical Education, Sport Development and Leisure Management, paper presented at British Sociological Association/Leisure Studies Association Seminar, Chelsea School, Brighton Polytechnic, June, published in this volume, pp. 73–84.

Alderson, J. & Crutchley, D. (1990) 'Physical Education and the National Curriculum' in N. Armstrong (ed) *New Directions in Physical Education Vol. I.* Rawdon, Human Kinetics Publishers, pp. 37–62.

CCPR/SHA (Central Council for Physical Recreation/Secondary Heads Association) (1991) *Sport in Schools.* London, Central Council for Physical Recreation.

Clarke, K. (1991) *Secretary of State's Speech to the North of England Conference,* 4 January, Leeds.

CRE (1991) Response to the Interim Report of the DES Physical Education Working Group on the National Curriculum, London.

DES (1989) *Physical Education from 5 to 16. Curriculum Matters 16.* HMI Series, London: HMSO

——— (1990) 'John MacGregor announces Physical Education Working Group', *DES NEWS* 11 July.

——— (1991a) *National Curriculum Physical Education Working Group. Interim Report.* DES/Welsh Office.

——— (1991b) *Physical Education for ages 5–16. Proposals of the Secretary of State for Education and Science and the Secretary of State for Wales.* DES/Welsh Office.

DES and the Welsh Office (1992) *Physical Education in the National Curriculum.* London: HMSO.

Dougall, D. (1989) 'Youngsters in a Popular Movement', *Sunday Times* 15 January.

Evans, J. (1988) 'Introduction: Teachers, Teaching and Control', in John Evans (ed) *Teachers, Teaching and Control in Physical Education.* Brighton: Falmer Press, pp. 1–20.

Fallon, M. (1990) Personal correspondence with Professor Margaret Talbot, 21 August.

Flintoff, A. (1990) 'Physical Education, Equal Opportunities and the National Curriculum', *Physical Education Review* Vol. 13, No 2, pp. 85–100.

———— (1993) "One of the Boys?": An Ethnographic Study of Co–education and Initial Teacher Education in Physical Education. PhD Thesis, The Open University.

Leisure Opportunities (1990) July.

May, N. (1987) 'Engendering Teacher Education', *School Organization* Vol. 5, No 1 pp. 79–87.

Murdoch, E. (1986) 'Future trends in the physical education curriculum', *British Journal of Physical Education* 17, pp. 83–86.

NCC (National Curriculum Council) (1990) *The National Curriculum at Key Stage 4,* Advice to the Secretary of State, York, 7 November.

———— (1992) *Physical Education Non–Statutory Guidance,* York: National Curriculum Council.

PEA (1990) Submission to the DES Physical Education Working Group on the National Curriculum, London.

School Sport Forum (1988) *Sport and Young People: Partnership in Action*, London: Sports Council.

Select Committee of the House of Commons (1991) *Report on School Sport,* London: Her Majesty's Stationery Office.

Talbot, M. (1987) 'Physical Education and School Sport into the 1990s', Annual Fellows' Lecture, Physical Education Association, London; unpublished lecture.

———— (1989) Are we ready for the National Curriculum? Address to Annual General Meeting, Leeds, Physical Education Association, March.

———— (1990a) 'Equal Opportunities and Physical Education', in N. Armstrong (ed) *New Directions in Physical Education* Vol. I, Rawdon: Human Kinetics Publishers, pp. 101–120.

———— (1990b) Gender — a Cross–Curricular Dimension, paper presented at NATFHE Dance Section Conference, London.

———— (1990c) Personal correspondence, 5 August.

Appendix A

National Curriculum Working Group on Physical Education

TERMS OF REFERENCE

Background

1. The Education Reform Act 1988 provides for the establishment of a National Curriculum of core and other foundation subjects for pupils of compulsory school age in England and Wales. The Act empowers the Secretary of State to specify, as he considers appropriate for each foundation subject, including physical education, attainment targets and programmes of study. Taken together, these attainment targets and programmes of study will provide the basis for assessing a pupil's performance, in relation both to expected attainment and to the next steps needed for the pupil's development.

The Task

2. The Secretary of State intends that, because of the nature of the subject, the objectives (attainment targets) and means of achieving them (programmes of study) should not be prescribed in as much detail for physical education as for the core and other foundation subjects. He considers that schools and teachers should have substantial scope here to develop their own schemes of work. It is the task of the Physical Education Working Group to advise on a statutory framework which is sufficiently broad and flexible to allow schools wide discretion in relation to the matters to be studied.

3. The Group should express an attainment target in terms of what is to be expected of pupils at the end of key stages. This expectation should take the form of a single statement of attainment in broad terms for each key stage which may comprise components covering different aspects of the subject. Each statement should represent what pupils of different abilities and maturities can be expected to achieve at the end of the key stage in question. These statements are intended then to form part of the statutory Order for the subject. The statutory assessment arrangements for physical education will not include nationally prescribed tests (except in the case of GCSE examinations at the end of key stage 4).

4. In addition, the Group should make recommendations for non-statutory statements of attainment calibrated into ten levels. It is intended that these should form part of guidance to teachers to help them to plan for continuity and progression and to identify both high attainers and those in need of extra help, including pupils with special educational needs. It will be necessary for these 10 levels to be defined in such a way that they can be used consistently with the statutory statements for the end of key stages.

Appendix A (cont.)

Submission of Reports

5.   The Working Group is asked to submit an interim report to the Secretaries of State by 31 December 1990 outlining and, as far as possible, exemplifying:

   i)   the contribution which physical education (including dance) should make to the overall school curriculum and how that will inform the Group s thinking about attainment targets and programmes of study;

   ii)   its provisional thinking about the knowledge, skills and understanding which pupils should be expected to have attained and be able to demonstrate at key stages and the profile components into which attainment targets should be grouped; and

   iii)   its thinking about the programmes of study which would be consistent with the attainment targets provisionally identified.

6.   By the end of June 1991 the Working Group is to submit a final report to the Secretaries of State setting out and justifying its final recommendations on attainment targets and programmes of study for physical education.

Approach

7.   In carrying out its task the Group should consult informally and selectively with relevant interests and have regard to the statutory Orders on mathematics, science, English and technology and to the reports of the other subject groups – history, geography, and modern foreign languages. The Group should in particular keep in close touch with the parallel music and art groups. Additionally the Group should take account of:

   i)   the contributions which physical education, including active physical recreation, competitive sport and dance, can make to learning about other subjects and cross-curricular themes including, in particular, expressive arts subjects (including drama and music), health education and Personal and Social Education and which they in turn can make to learning in physical education; and

   ii)   best practice and the results of any relevant research and development.

Appendix B

ELIZABETH HOUSE YORK ROAD LONDON SE1 7PH
TELEPHONE 071-934 9000

The Rt Hon KENNETH CLARKE QC MP

Ian Beer Esq   19 February 1991
The Head Master
Harrow School
Harrow on the Hill
Middlesex HA1 3HW

Dr M B...,

1.   Thank you for your letter of 21 December with which you
enclosed a copy of the interim report of the National Curriculum
Working Group on Physical Education. I am replying on behalf of
both David Hunt and myself.

2.   We shall be publishing the report today, with this letter.
We are most grateful to the Working Group for the hard work which
we recognise has gone into the preparation of the report, and for
the amount of ground you have been able to cover in the
relatively short time available. I do, however, have a number of
comments on the report which I should like you to take into
account in your work towards your final report.

Structure of the attainment targets

3.   I see that you have proposed three attainment targets:
planning and composing; participating and performing; and
appreciating and evaluating. I am not at all convinced by this
structure, particularly for an essentially active subject such as
PE. I see that you consider the attainment target which covers
performance to be the single most important element. I therefore
ask you to reconsider the structure with a view to coming up with
a single attainment target for physical education which reflects
the practical nature of the subject. In the course of your
reconsideration, I should be grateful if you could ensure that
the active element is predominant.

4.   I recognise that the Group wishes to avoid using jargon and
other language that is comprehensible only to the specialist. I
am afraid that I am not convinced that you have succeeded in your
aim. I ask you to continue your efforts in this direction,
particularly in the non-statutory statements of attainment, many
of which will, at the lower levels, be delivered by non-
specialists. I am aware also that you have given careful thought

Appendix B (cont.)

to the titles of the attainment targets, but I do not consider
that the words used are satisfactory. I attach importance to
titles which will be readily understood by non-specialist
teachers, parents and pupils.

End of key stage statements

5.   The Group has done a substantial amount of work on the
statutory end of key stage statements. While I recognise your
reservations about the different regime which is operating for
PE, art and music, I see no reason to change this now. I
believe that your report has demonstrated that statutory end of
key stage statements and programmes of study, supported by the
non-statutory levels of attainment which will be available to
schools, can form a good basis for raising standards in these
subjects.

6.   I should like the Group to continue to work on the end of
key stage statements with a view to ensuring that they are short
and general in character. They should relate to each key stage
as a whole and, it seems to me, should be less clearly
identifiable with particular statements represented in the non-
statutory levels.

Programmes of study

7.   I look forward to seeing the results of your further work on
the programmes of study. I remind you that these should focus on
the active side of PE, should not be too detailed and should
contribute to a sensible non-prescriptive statutory framework
for PE. I should be grateful if you could in particular consider
whether inclusion of all six areas of activity can be justified
in all of the first three key stages, and especially in key stage
3, where I should be inclined to suggest that schools might
choose, say, four out of the six areas. I shall be looking for
convincing arguments on these matters and for clear evidence that
you have had regard to the resource implications.

8.   I agree that outdoor education and a residential experience
are often very desirable parts of a child's education. However,
for practical reasons, I have to say that I do not consider that
a residential experience should be an obligatory part of the PE
curriculum - or for that matter a compulsory element of any part
of the statutory curriculum. I should also like you to
reconsider the feasibility of compulsory inclusion of outdoor
education in the statutory PE curriculum

Practical implications

9.   I note the Group's firm recommendations on swimming. This
and other of your recommendations - for example, for the teaching
of dance and outdoor education - would have serious practical
implications for many schools. I shall need to consider them in
the light of what you and those commenting on your report have to
say about their feasibility. I am glad that you intend to pay
further attention to this aspect in your final report. It is
not part of the Group's remit to make recommendations for the
resources to be provided for PE. I expect your recommendations

Appendix B (cont.)

to be realistically related to the general level of school
funding which can reasonably be expected to be available.

Curriculum time allocation

10. You express some anxiety about the curriculum time available
for PE and say that you intend to do further work on a minimum
curriculum time allocation. I am as concerned as you that
schools should offer pupils a balanced PE programme. The
statutory attainment targets and programmes of study will in fact
achieve this. I have no power to specify time allocations for
any subject: indeed, I am specifically proscribed from doing so.
Schools are free to decide their own curriculum time allocations
for each subject in the light of the statutory requirements of
the National Curriculum and of their decisions in respect of the
rest of the curriculum. I therefore see no need for you to
pursue the matter of a time allocation, except in the sense that
you should have regard to what is likely to be practicable within
the constraints of school timetables and the rest of the
curriculum.

Key stage 4

11. You will of course be aware of my decision that PE in the
National Curriculum at key stage 4 should have a particularly
flexible definition. By "a particularly flexible definition" I
mean that pupils should have a wide choice of activity at key
stage 4, of a more flexible kind than you are recommending. I
envisage that they should be required to keep fit and active by
participating in some sport or other PE activity of a sensible
kind. I have it in mind that pupils should have a choice of two
or even one of the areas of activity. More should of course be
available for pupils who want them and choose to specialise in
PE. The end of key stage statement for key stage 4 should
reflect this greater flexibility. There will still be scope in
key stage 4 for sensible combinations of subjects - such as dance
with music and drama in a performing arts course for those who
want this - and I should like you to pursue your intended
discussions with the Music Working Group to this end.

KENNETH CLARKE

Appendix C

STATEMENT FROM MR ATKINS ON DANCE IN SCHOOLS

"The Government fully recognises the important part dance
can and does play for many pupils in schools, either within
physical education or as part of a performing arts
programme. That is why dance was specifically included in
the terms of reference of the Physical Education Working
Group. What it should not be seen as however is a substitute
for all other forms of physical activity. We believe that a
comprehensive programme of physical education throughout a
child's time at schools should be wider than this.

In his response to the interim report, the Secretary of
State pointed out the programmes of study for PE should not
be too detailed, and should focus on a sensible non-
prescriptive statutory framework. This applies to dance in
the same way as for any other area of activity. The
Secretary of State also pointed out the practical
implications of dance being a compulsory part of PE. By this
he meant in particular the need to ensure that teachers are
properly trained to meet the requirements of the National
Curriculum. It would be irresponsible of us not to take
these factors fully into account, but it should not be taken
as in any way as undervaluing the importance of dance. We
look forward to seeing what the Working Group and others
have to say about this. "

EDUCATION, SPORT AND LEISURE: COLLAPSING BOUNDARIES?

Elizabeth B. Murdoch
Chelsea School Research Centre
University of Brighton

I. Introduction

Partnerships and networking are concepts that are becoming increasingly popular in current discussions among professionals in the fields of physical education, sport and leisure in relation to Youth Sport. There is a strongly growing commitment to developing coordinated provision for sport for young people from all those who are involved. It is, therefore, possible to give an initial, affirmative response to the question of the title of this paper. Barriers are collapsing as all agencies attempt to rationalise and coordinate their resources for the benefit of young people in sport. The issues involved merit more detailed consideration. This paper will focus on three major factors in the building of successful partnership — people and attitudes; structures and institutions; and resources.

It is important to set current developments in context. Interest in youth sport was raised in 1986 when the 'great media debate' was initiated in the press. An attack was made on Physical Education for letting down the nation, in the failure to provide, through the schools' programmes, an adequate base for the emergence of international sportsmen and sportswomen.

This controversial publicity for physical education, however, led to some very positive action. The two Government departments DES and DoE jointly, in an unprecedented show of cooperation, commissioned a Desk Study. This study was worked from the remit to report to the respective Ministers of Education and Sport on the state of physical education and sport in schools in England and Wales. The resulting document, entitled "Sport in Schools" (Murdoch, 1987), carried a number of recommendations and was the stimulus to the setting up of a School Sport Forum. Membership of this working group included representatives of all agencies involved in the provision of sport for young people of school age. The report of the Forum was presented to the respective Ministers in both departments in 1989 and produced a published Government response outlining the extent of Government support. This ultimately led to consideration of the state of physical education in schools by a Select (all party) Committee of the House of Commons. By this time the media reports had been answered by reasoned debate and published materials from the appropriate professional bodies. While it was acknowledged by all that the provision for children was far from adequate, it was conceded that the physical education profession could not alone carry the responsibility for the total experience offered to young people. The call for the setting up of partnerships was strong.

The establishment by ERA in 1988 of the National Curriculum, and the inclusion of Physical Education as a Foundation subject, permitted the physical education profession to make clear policy statements about the place and role of the subject in support of the nation's sporting needs and to place this in context of the total educational needs of children. At the same time the Sports Council reviewed its policy and extended and confirmed its support of Youth Sport as a strong arm of its work. The National Coaching Foundation confirmed its intention to review and strengthen its provision for the coaching of children. All of the above supported the idea of the teacher as the key provider and facilitator.

> Each of these major agencies declared that it was not possible for them to make appropriate provision alone so there has never been a better time or context for the collapsing of boundaries and the formation of partnerships.

II.   People and attitudes

One of the greatest barriers to cooperation has been a misunderstanding that is prevalent among very influential people, of the difference between physical education and sport. Among significant policy makers, a considerable confusion still exists in clarifying not only the difference between physical education and sport but also the relationship of one to the other.

It is acknowledged that this is due, in part at least, to the failure of the physical education profession to communicate clearly exactly what physical education is and what it offers to children. The work of the National Curriculum Subject Working Group in Physical Education, with subsequent publications, has gone a very long way to redress this lack. Much productive thinking still has to be done to clarify even more the central contribution of physical education to children's development and performance in sport. John Alderson in his paper in this collection suggests that we should be addressing Sport Education instead of Physical Education and immediately this raises a question about Leisure Education. All of these aspects of 'physical education' feature in the National Curriculum proposals. The problem is greater, however, than simply the name and there are conceptual issues still to be addressed. People's beliefs and attitudes are very significant in this and members of the physical education profession are sometimes unwilling to concede that theirs is a specific and significant role that goes beyond both sport and leisure in the education of children.

A critical issue in efficient communication by the physical education profession has been the complex and involved structure of the separate professional associations that promote the subject. Many calls have been made for the profession to unite under one association which focuses on what the profession believes and stands for. These calls are being heeded and negotiations are well advanced towards a 'united' profession.

Discussion about partnerships has given rise to the problem of the professional relationship between teachers of physical education and coaches of sport (School Sport Forum, 1988). Many educators see the influence of coaches as a threat to their professional autonomy and to the nature of the work given to children. There is need for a clear delineation of roles and specific acknowledgement of areas of responsibility. The significant number of fairly recent 'new' posts has markedly increased the potential for sport development in local communities. The employment of Sports Development Officers is still expanding at a remarkable rate. There is no intention in the sporting community to effect a 'take-over' of physical education. On the contrary, all the public statements of policy place the teacher as the central decision-maker in the coordinated provision for children. Teachers are asked to assume a role that is akin to the 'management' of the child's learning and its context. The major question must be whether teachers are willing and properly equipped to assume such key roles. It is critical that teachers do step forward, realise the significance of what they can and must do and take it on.

Parents are a very significant force in the experience offered to children in sport. The image that some parents have of appropriate sporting activity for children is often very different to that of educators and, since many parents act in the capacity of voluntary coach, there can be real conflict of interests. The move to approach individual sports through modified versions is not always understood or accepted by parents who see only the value of full-sided, conventional versions. The educational approach adopted towards 'games making' can often be treated with derision as a 'soft option'. There is much parent education to be done to avoid confusion for the children. The inclusion of high level sporting figures in the National Curriculum Subject Working Group was in part to reinforce the credibility of the group to some of the sporting fraternity and to parents.

There are increasing numbers of groups being set up within regions and counties to create local policy, and plan for coordinated provision of sport for young people. To have all interested agencies sitting round the same table will see the collapse of boundaries largely through sensitive understanding of respective beliefs and roles and the willingness to put the child at the centre of proposals and make relevant compromise. Official support was not forthcoming from the Government response to the call from the School Sport Forum (1988) for local Youth Advisory Groups. It is encouraging to see these groups being formed through local initiatives. The results will undoubtedly be better through this internally stimulated development.

III. Structures and institutions

At Government level there have been a number of changes in the locus of control since 1988. The welcome move by DES and DoE to work jointly led to a move of the Minister of Sport from the DoE to the DES with a remit for physical education and sport. This offered the potential for collaborative planning and provision and was a significant force in strengthening the many partnership debates.

A characteristic of the 1980s and 90s is the short life of significant structures and institutions and the constant change in the locus of control. The most recent reshuffle in Government has resulted in the formation of the Department of National Heritage. Since there is now no single Minister with remit for sport, focus on a coherent policy of collaboration at this level has been reduced. The significance of renaming the DES as the Department for Education has yet to be monitored. It is interesting to note that, since the introduction of the National Curriculum, there have been no fewer than four Secretaries of State for Education. The National Curriculum Council and the Schools Examination and Assessment Council, which up to the present have had separate responsibility for the implementation of the national curriculum and its assessment respectively, are soon to be combined. The Sports Council is being redefined in relation to central and regional influence. The result of all these changes in structures is uncertainty, especially at a time when there is more and more central control of education.

One significant national initiative, which is an example of partnership and collaborative planning, is now nearing completion of a first phase. *Champion Coaching* (NCF, 1992) has produced a monitoring report of its work so far. The success was mixed but where real partnerships were effected the results were highly satisfactory. The initial impetus came from the National Coaching Foundation which, supported by a grant from the Government, harnessed the support of local education authorities, schools and physical education teachers, departments of leisure and recreation, national governing bodies of sport, sports clubs and parents and families, to provide schools of sport. The next phase, as a result of monitoring phase one, will concentrate on training of staff to manage and promote the schools of sport.

A large range of initiatives is also in evidence at local level, and these are varied and unique to each area. One such that is proving successful is in East Sussex where there has been a deliberate attempt to bring planners and providers together into the same physical environment. Day-to-day informal meeting as well as the easily managed formal meetings of a variety of different people from the Local Authority, Higher Education, Sports Council, National Coaching Foundation and specific groups such as British Sports Association for the Disabled [BSAD] is proving very effective in the harnessing of resources and in the capitalising on expertise.

IV. Resources

One of the most interesting developments in the provision of physical education and sport for children will be the process of implementation of the Statutory Orders in the National Curriculum. One of the more significant boundaries is that between the legislative text that has been produced as Government policy and the "context of its location", as John Evans puts it in his paper in this volume. The process that has been used to produce this policy has involved both professionals and lay people with the intention of ensuring that the text was accessible to the person in the street — that the human agent would have a role. The final report from the Physical Education Subject Working Group, subsequently adopted by the Secretaries of State as their proposals for the curriculum, was full and definitive and provided the statement about physical education that has been long awaited by a number of agencies (Murdoch, 1987). Statutory Orders inevitably reduced this to a bare minimum as the statutory requirement. The National Curriculum Council was then charged to provide non-statutory guidance for teachers to assist in the implementation of the Orders. It is evident that this process can, and does, result in a loss of detail of material and also a loss of quality. It is critical that, in order to fully appreciate the spirit and the content of the National Curriculum proposals, teachers and others make reference to all stages of the production of these and contextualise the development.

The next, and final, stage is that of the teachers translating all this different material into a workable curriculum. With a system that is so strongly centrally driven there has been little opportunity for teachers to play a part in the thinking about and production of initial policy texts. To progress implementation of these texts, therefore, it is essential that there is a well-structured in-service programme and that appropriate materials are made available. There are real problems in this on both counts.

No direct provision has been made for the implementation of a 'national' in-service programme despite recommendations for this from the School Sport Forum and a recognition also from the National Curriculum Subject Working Group for Physical Education of the necessity of such consistent support. In-service will be the responsibility of each school and budgets for this are being targeted at the core subjects of English, Mathematics and Science rather than the later subjects to be implemented. Any money for implementation of the Physical Education curriculum is being used to monitor the implementation and not to support it. This leaves Physical Education with very limited resources indeed to mount what is an essential programme of INSET courses for teachers, particularly those in Primary schools. The irony is that any money that may become available for such courses could come from the Sports Council which has acknowledged the importance of the Foundation stage of educational provision and its role in youth sport.

In relation to the supply of support materials, the situation could be difficult for teachers in that many different materials are being offered and little help will be forthcoming in estimating the value of these materials. Many will be produced for financial, commercial gain and will not necessarily advance the cause of education. Attractive and clearly presented materials, where they are available, will be used by teachers. The effect of the well presented documentation in the development of Health Related Fitness in the schools is a good example of this. Materials will be influential especially in the Primary sector as many teachers here feel a great need for support for a woefully inadequate structure for training in the teaching of physical education. Teachers will need to be able to discriminate and be carefully selective.

A significant, collaborative initiative in the provision of resources was that of the British Council of Physical Education, Sports Council and the National Coaching Foundation in which National Governing Bodies of Sport collaborated with educational consultants to produce teachers' materials for the teaching of games to children of 5-11 within the National Curriculum. The teaching book was due to be published in early 1993 and it is hoped that it will receive a wide circulation. As a result of this cooperation there is now a much clearer and shared approach to the teaching of games in which sport and education have agreed the appropriate materials and teaching approaches for children of this critical age group. The level and quality of this collaboration will ensure very much more coherent support for teachers and coaches and give them a common agreed base from which to progress.

One very significant structure in the provision of sport and physical education for children has been the Local Education Authority Advisory/Inspectorial Service. Recent policy in the devolution of responsibility to individual schools and the gradual reduction in the influence of Local Authorities has meant the loss of a substantial number of these posts. The loss of support, also, from the LEAs to schools is yet to impact but the steady erosion of Local Authorities will mean that schools may be forced to seek grant-maintained status to survive at all. The full effect of this, coming as it does in conjunction with the increase in sports development posts, is yet to be assessed but there is a concern expressed by many that the role of the teacher of physical education could be compromised by what could be seen by Head Teachers and Governors as an attractive alternative in the form of the qualified sports coach who may be able to work what is perceived to be a financially more efficient hourly contract. The apparent boundary between teachers and coaches should be crumbling as both have more opportunity to understand the needs of the other and to work out a fair strategy that will harness resources in favour of the children. Each partner needs to establish independent strength in order that the integration will be as strong as possible and yet unthreatening.

There is good evidence of significant developments in coach education which will serve to strengthen the career prospects of what is an emerging profession. Posts such as Youth Sport Managers and Youth Sport Officers placed within Local Authorities will make the administration and implementation of Youth Sport policies a more likely proposition. The increasing number of Sports Development Officers (SDOs) is providing a range of different posts the remits of which vary from county-wide to specific sport development briefs.

The establishing, in East Sussex, of a new post of Curriculum Development Officer (CDO) has markedly increased the quantity and quality of support for teachers in the Primary sector. Funding for these innovative but fixed term posts is shared by Sports Council and LEA.

All of the above posts will interact with teachers and schools towards an integrated provision for young people. In the main policy documents for both sport and education it is stated very clearly that the role of the teacher is critical when the target population is school children. This is recognised by all parties in collaboration. It is to be hoped that teachers rise to this challenge to act as the 'managers' of children's learning and find the time, from within an already very busy timetable, to be influential in what is provided for children. Many boundaries are being removed from between the schools, sports clubs and voluntary groups in the Youth Service and with such a collapsing can come insecurity and threat as well as good working partnerships. Personal ideologies may have to be sacrificed for the sake of a common, shared policy and its implementation. Collapsing boundaries will be seen in:

- the central to peripheral emphasis in policy and administration;
- willingness of providers to relinquish specific and personally held roles;
- setting up of local initiatives;
- shared values being made explicit — the role of human agency;
- joint professional development/courses/seminars/conferences.

V.   Conclusion

Each of the above is happening now with different degrees of success. These are critical issues that will affect decisions underpinning good policy. Similar developments are taking place in many parts of the world where sport and education are attempting to forge links and relationships. We have much that we can learn from countries such as New Zealand and Australia where there are well-developed youth sport programmes. The strength of the National Curriculum in Physical Education in Great Britain is not matched in these countries as yet, so there is potential for mutual benefit through discussion on the policies to be developed for youth sport and education.

This is a time of unprecedented change in education and in the development of policies for sport. The will is there in all parties to create partnerships and networks of provision but this will take much ingenuity against both a diminishing support base from central funds and the dismantling of central services as a result of central Government policies.

References

DES and Welsh Office (1992) *Physical Education with National Curriculum.* London: HMSO.

Murdoch, E. (1987) *Sport in Schools — Desk Study*, Department of Education and Science/Department of the Environment.

NCF (National Coaching Foundation) (1992) *Champion Coaching — a Report.*

Read, B. and Edwards, P. (1992) *Teaching Games to Children 5–11*, National Coaching Foundation/British Council of Physical Education/Sports Council.

School Sport Forum (1988) *Sport and Young People: Partnership in Action*, London: Sports Council.

PHYSICAL EDUCATION, SPORT DEVELOPMENT AND LEISURE MANAGEMENT

John Alderson
School of Leisure and Food Management
Sheffield Hallam University

I.   Introduction

The motivation for offering a paper to this workshop arises from the fact that my colleagues and I are involved in the undergraduate training of PE teachers through the 4-year B.Ed. route, and of leisure managers through a 3-year honours route, inclusive of a period of industrial attachment and work-based learning. As such, we are well aware that there are controversies and issues abroad in the area of education, sport and leisure, reflected in the title for this workshop.

The preparation of this paper has afforded me an opportunity to try to clear my head and bring some order to my own confused thoughts about *physical education*, *sport development* and *leisure management*. The confusion is in part brought about by the changes in the way that the delivery of higher education is funded, in the way that students themselves are funded, in the way that quality control systems are to be funded (or not, in the case of CNAA and the Inspectorate), in the way in which teachers are trained, in the future role of CATE, in the way that schools are funded and managed. Collectively, these changes pose questions for the curriculum team of which I am a member, which must be mirrored in our sister institutions, like Brighton Polytechnic's Chelsea School here in Eastbourne.

Specifically, questions arise as to *how* we should train the future generation of Physical Education Teachers, and *what* we should train them to do.

We are aware of the attractiveness to some potential students of a non-B.Ed. first degree in the leisure area that also confers QTS, and of the pressure that is mounting to shorten degree courses — particularly, perhaps, 4-year ones like the B.Ed. Our undergraduate programme already offers strong perspectives in community recreation and sport development: a new modular structure offers flexibility in the packaging of study units to suit specific needs; hence the potential for integrating PE training into a broader leisure management programme is now with us. However, there are, currently, quite clear differences in the approach and structure of the two forms of training: it is unlikely that these could happily co-exist within a single programme.

Of necessity, the answers to questions about the preparation of future PE teachers depends upon one's view of the purpose of education in schools and of the nature of the school curriculum. The recent Physical Education National Curriculum document clearly gives, as it were, 'the official view' which should inform an approach to questions relating to the future training of PE teachers. However, we should also bear in mind that to a certain extent, and of necessity, the PE National Curriculum Working Group's efforts were politically constrained and that the document provides a good deal of scope, both for interpretation and for evolution.

II.   Leisure, and Education for Leisure

It is surely generally accepted that the education of young people is intended as a *preparation for adult life*, within the opportunities, constraints imposed and value structures operating within a given society. In this country, among others, formal education has traditionally been conducted through the agency of schools and scholarly activity: namely, pupils' immersion in a variety of academic disciplines.

There has been much controversy in recent years about a lack of success in schooling. The government clearly blames teachers and new-fangled teaching methods for poor standards, and appears to want to preserve the academic discipline approach in secondary education. However, there are contrasting opinions. For example, Hewlett (1987) expressed the view that the "ologies" model of education fails to work because it wrongly assumes that children will be able to apply the intellectual training and discipline-specific knowledge they receive in school to the situations, issues and decision requirements that they meet in real life. In order to be effective in this sense, Hewlett argues, the school curriculum should be explicitly concerned with the realities of life: for him the curriculum should consist not of academic subjects which, at best, can only be *implicitly* related to the real world, but rather of *explicit* 'regions of application' such as work, leisure, the home and self.

The argument here is that within a society such as ours, pupils should be *explicitly* prepared through their schooling to make quality judgements and decisions about their lives and to have the competencies to operate effectively within a society that is constantly changing, and not necessarily for the better. Focusing on the leisure dimension of life, Hewlett's view would suggest that education should develop in young people the skills and competencies that will enable them to use leisure time in a satisfying way, to be discerning in their choice of leisure activities, to appreciate the need to budget for leisure spend and to use their vote wisely in terms of local leisure provision.

In short, education/schooling should be responsible for producing well-informed leisure consumers who can make autonomous decisions about leisure value, including *'value for money'*.

It seems to me that this is a crucial notion for educators, since the private sector of the leisure industry is evolving rapidly to meet perceived increases in 'demand' and is busy inventing new leisure products by the minute. There may not be many in this room who have yet played 'paint-ball', or 'quasar', been to a legal (or, for that matter, illegal) 'acid house party', or experienced 'virtual reality'. The private sector seems increasingly determined to relieve customers of their money, sometimes with scant regard to concepts of service, or even ethics. I refer, for example, to the leisure product provided by the 'Chippendales' (to name one of the classier acts of that genre) and to the legalised sale of Ecstasy at public raves in Holland! It is perhaps relevant to note that many of the new leisure products are specifically targeted at young people, either of school, or of immediately post-school, age.

At the same time, the public sector of leisure is increasingly short of money to provide traditionally subsidised forms of leisure provision, including physical recreation and sport. Ever since the time when philanthropic Victorian industrialists first provided slipper baths for the unwashed work force, the general public has enjoyed 'bathing' — and later, other recreation opportunities — on a subsidy basis. The £55 million Ponds Forge Sports and Swimming complex recently opened in Sheffield seems a far cry from the 17 yard long rectangular puddle in which I used to do my schoolboy swimming. I took that facility for granted then and I guess a lot of people take their new leisure pools with waves, flumes and jacuzzis for granted now. Currently, there is certainly no formal, systematic way in which school pupils are introduced to these kinds of notions about their personal involvement in leisure pursuits. Compulsory competitive tendering (CCT) is a mechanism seemingly introduced to facilitate the removal of subsidy from local authority leisure operations, perhaps heralding a period in which public sector users will be forced to re-evaluate, if not actually evaluate for the first time, this form of provision and its cost to their leisure budget. There are of course, deeper philosophical and social questions about whether or not a modern society should provide subsidised leisure services. Hewlett would no doubt argue that their debate should feature within a senior pupil's education too, but there is not the time to dwell upon them now in the context of this paper.

If one were to accept the view of a need for *explicit* leisure education, then the question arises as to how it should be delivered. Given the absence of Hewlett's curriculum model, should leisure education be a cross-curricular theme, should it be part of a PSD programme or should it be the responsibility of good old PE? Currently, leisure studies is almost exclusively found in further and higher education rather than in the secondary school. However, were it to be included in the school curriculum, which professional association should champion the cause of leisure education and guide its development as a school subject?

III. Sport and Leisure

The fact that leisure is usually defined as 'time free from obligations' is probably largely responsible for its absence from the school curriculum. Instead, the curriculum has included certain 'subjects' which people can relate to their use of leisure time in a satisfying way — sport and the arts being the most obvious examples. The justification for the inclusion of these subjects in the curriculum is that they introduce children to valued cultural forms, transmitting heritage to the next generation at the same time as facilitating the acquisition of participation skills (see Parry, 1989; and Almond, 1989 who also reports White, 1982).

There is no doubt that sport is also a major leisure product, with two distinct forms of consumption: namely, 'active participation' within the wide variety of sport activities; and various forms or derivatives of 'spectating'.

That sport has a cultural value and significance is demonstrated in Nicholas Ridley's comment in the (1988) School Sport Forum document:

> Sport plays a vital role in everyday life. We recognise its importance to people in the national and international scene. At home, sporting activity provides a healthy and enjoyable leisure pursuit; sport promotes civic and national pride; it can assist social and community aims; it has a significant impact on the economy. Internationally, sport can extend British influence and prestige and promote trade and stability.

The range of sports activities implicitly represented in this paper is perhaps best represented by reference to an earlier publication (Alderson & Crutchley, 1990) which offers the following typology:

a. *Organised Competitive Activities:* Activities in which participants strive for ascendancy (to win!) within an agreed, but arbitrary, rule framework. The essence of all these activities, at whatever level they are played, is the contract that participants enter into with one another to try to win. We would offer the following major sub-categories:
Gymnastic Sports ... in which the winners are those whose movements are deemed the best in qualitative terms ...
Athletic Sports ... in which the judging procedures seek to determine which performance is the fastest, longest, highest or strongest in quantitative terms ...
Game Sports ... in which the scoring procedures determine which player or team achieves territorial domination through goals, runs, touchdowns, target sport and so on.

b. *Conditioning Activities:* These activities are designed to promote physical power, endurance and mobility, and/or mental discipline. These activities are not by nature competitive in the sense that one participant seeks to beat another.

c. *Adventure Activities*: These activities are essentially concerned with overcoming natural obstacles and journeying over wild terrain/water.

d. *New Games*: This group contains activities that have a point or purpose and a form of rule structure designed to promote co-operative rather than competitive experiences. (They are relatively new within the British sport culture).

IV. Sport Education and PE

It would therefore appear that there is a strong case, not only for including sport within the school curriculum, but for emphasising its place through the use of a title such as 'Sport Education'. This idea is not new. Jake Downey, ex-PE teacher and lecturer, now Director of Coaching of the Badminton Association, and Geoff Gleeson, then General Secretary of the BANC made the suggestion in the early 1980s, followed by Len Almond in 1989.

There is no need for something called sport education, many might say, because sport in schools is ably catered for by the PE profession. PE clearly *is* the route through which most school pupils are introduced to sport, and particularly to a *range* of sport activities, though given that, it seems to me that there are a number of problems with the way in which it is currently envisaged we introduce school pupils to sport within physical education.

1.   Sport does not feature in the rationale for Physical Education in the recent National Curriculum Document

The following is abstracted from para 3.1 of the NC document rationale:

Physical Education educates young people in and through the use of the body and movement. It:

- develops physical competence and enables pupils to engage in worthwhile physical activities;
- promotes physical development and teaches pupils to value the benefits of participation in physical activity...;
- develops artistic and aesthetic understanding within and through movement;
- helps to establish self esteem through the development of physical confidence; ....

This is, of course, a perfectly valid rationale for physical education, *if* one adopts a process-oriented view, with body management, physical competency and healthy lifestyle as one's major aims. However, the stated rationale excludes sport education as a major aim of the physical education curriculum. The word "sport" does not appear once in the rationale section of the document: reading it, and knowing PE's obvious association with sport, I am left with the impression that the word can only have been quite deliberately written out.

However, the rationale is followed by a (longer) section entitled "Physical Education & Sport". Seemingly paradoxically, it is stated here that "sport, including competitive games, is an essential part of any programme of physical education" (para 4.1). Paras 4.2—4.4 define sport as a range of physical activities, conceptually differentiated from PE, which is defined as "a process of learning, the context being mainly physical" (para 4.5).

The general tenor of this section of the document would seem to be that sports are physical activities to be employed as media for the higher order learning process of physical education.

Para 4.8 states that "physical education teachers do their best to establish a sound value system for young people in their charge..." but that these efforts can be undermined by professional sportsmen and women in ways which have been presented to young people as unacceptable". The authors then urge NGBs and the media to be more responsible about the images of sports behaviour which they allow to be presented. There are implicit moral assumptions in this kind of statement: for example, that a professional foul is 'a bad thing'. Given that spectator sport is big business and positively valued by substantial numbers of leisure consumers, it is at least arguable that the professional foul is inevitable, and possibly even acceptable, *within* the context of professional sport. Surely what pupils need is the opportunity to 'chew over' these sorts of arguments, to investigate the concept of rule breaking within amateur and professional sport, so to arrive at personal conclusions about the moral issues involved. This kind of sport education would have potential application for their future sport consumption, both as active participants and as spectators.

Whether or not one agrees with these approaches taken in the national curriculum document, it must surely suggest that the PE curriculum is not the place where children are intended to learn *explicitly* about sport as an important part of their culture, with a view to their future use of sport as autonomous, informed leisure consumers.

2.   The PE Curriculum presents too narrow a view of Sport

a. *The range of activities.* As far as sport is concerned, the PE curriculum tends to focus on traditional competitive activities with which there is a common association of elitism and national identity in international competition.

Despite the positive intent expressed in the National Curriculum PE document, for a variety of reasons which include resource availability, pupils rarely experience a balanced education in terms of the four categories of sport defined earlier, though the NC document has done what it can to protect Outdoor Education and basic swimming.

b. *Consumer role.* As we have just seen, Physical Education is clearly focused in physical competency and learning through performance development in physical activities. This focus does little to facilitate education for other sport consumer roles, such as that of official, coach or administrator, not to mention that of the whole spectating dimension of sport — yet surely the basis for the whole range of sport consumer roles should be laid down in school.

c. *Networking.*   Currently, there is a lack of networking between schools and other agencies responsible for the provision of sport to the community, whether NGBs, local authorities, private or voluntary sector agencies, or national sports centres. The PE National Curriculum document does recognise this problem in its section on the relationship between PE and sport (para. 4.9). However, I am left feeling that a fundamental objective of a sports education curriculum would be to ensure that as many pupils as possible would be assisted in the process of progressing from school-based sport into an appropriate community sport opportunity *before* they left school. This would be an *explicit* stage of sport education, not merely the recognition that a problem currently exists.

3.   PE lacks scholarship and any real conceptual underpinning for Sport

PE has always, unashamedly, been about participation in physical activities, including many sports. The notion of studying in sport has, until recently, been unacceptable as legitimate curriculum PE. The introduction of GCSE PE and of 'A'-level Sport Studies and Physical Education syllabuses has begun to change that view, though the national curriculum document still presents GCSE as a bolt-on to the 14+ PE subject in the 11–16 national curriculum.

It is my view that the PE professional has never really differentiated fully between the role of offering/facilitating extracurricular opportunities for recreation including the networking just referred to, and the education for recreation/leisure that should occur in curriculum time.

If pupils are not encouraged to learn about sport, in an intellectual as well as an experimental sense, it makes sense to me that their potential for informed consumption thereof after leaving school, both as participants and spectators, is unlikely to be maximised. To take a simple example, it is clear that children can only be introduced to a limited number of physical activities within curriculum time, if that exposure is wholly dependent on practical teaching in the activity context. How then, are pupils to be informed about the wider range of sports and other newly developed leisure activities available to them, if this is not done in a condensed, essentially intellectually-based way? The obvious answer is through learning activities which focus on a cognitive appreciation of family groupings of activities, their organisation, their rule structures/conventions, the equipment needed, the cost of involvement, their environmental impact, etc. Such learning can be practical, if not necessarily performance-based, involving new technology and investigative project work. The activity groupings or family resemblances introduced in this way can then be exemplified by performance-based learning, the selection of specific activities being made on the basis of student and/or staff preferences and resource availability.

Almond (1989) put it like this:

> I would like to propose that teachers consider the idea of sport education instead of teaching a wide variety of discrete sporting activities. The task for the teachers is two-fold:
>
> 1. Initiate young people into a range of sporting activities which illustrates their significance as important aspects of cultural life.
> 2. Demonstrate how engagement in sporting activities can enrich people's lives and improve its quality so that they are able to illuminate their understanding of what to do with their lives and how to spend their time.
>
> Thus it is important that teachers go beyond simply providing the opportunity to engage in a variety of sports. Instead, they should sample and select activities which are representations of distinctive types of sport because of the vast range of sporting possibilities; there is also a need to teach much more than just engagement in physical activity. (p. 23)

V. The Notion of Sports Development

In recent years the phrase 'Sports Development' has come into currency, much influenced by the model, first suggested by the Sports Council for Wales, which defined the foundation, participation, performance and excellence levels of people's active involvement in sport, represented as a pyramid with excellence at the top.

It is generally recognised by the sport agencies that the foundation level, the essential introduction of people to sport, is the responsibility of the PE profession. Thereafter, other agencies have a role to play, whether Sports Development Officers, community recreation workers, NGB development officers, NGB coaches or organisations like the British Olympic Association and BSAD.

In a strictly logical sense, it seems strange that the PE profession, whose rationale in the NC document says nothing about sport, and states that the primary use of sport is for instrumental reasons associated with physical development and physical competency, should be seen as the crucial foundation level for this pyramid of sport development. This form of instrumentalism, in my view, belongs to a past era of education and does little for sport education specifically, or leisure education more generally.

If one takes the view that sport is a valuable aspect of our culture to be transmitted in an enlightened way to future generations so that they can share in its development and take satisfaction from their consumership as active participants or informed spectators, then the notion of sport development, it seems to me, could in itself be developed in the following way.

I envisage an evolution of the Sports Council model for Sports Development, from the two-dimensional triangle to a triangular pyramid (see **Figure 1 opposite**). The horizontal levels remain the same, from foundation at the bottom through to excellence at the top: but the three faces of the pyramid could be seen as representing different aspects of the management of the sport development process for individual members of society.

One face of the pyramid represents the influence of sports leaders, development officers and coaches, whose job is to provide a face-to-face development role with individuals. The precise nature of that role changes with respect to the level of the pyramid at which a leader/development officer or coach is working with a particular individual or group.

A second face of the pyramid represents the influence of the recreation resource manager, who controls and programmes the resources which make the sport development experiences possible. Such a person may be the chair of a voluntary sector sports club management committee, a public sector leisure centre manager, a national sports centre manager, a private sector leisure facility manager, or PE teacher managing a school's recreation facilities in extracurricular time, whether on a local school management basis or not. Again, facility managers need to be sensitive to the different levels of the sports development pyramid for which they are organising sport development opportunity.

The third face of the pyramid represents the influence of sport education. Education is a cradle-to-grave process, not only the province of the professional teacher. Clearly the PE teacher has a crucial role to play here, especially at the foundation level and within the school curriculum. However, the educative role extends beyond both the school and the foundation level of the pyramid. Sports

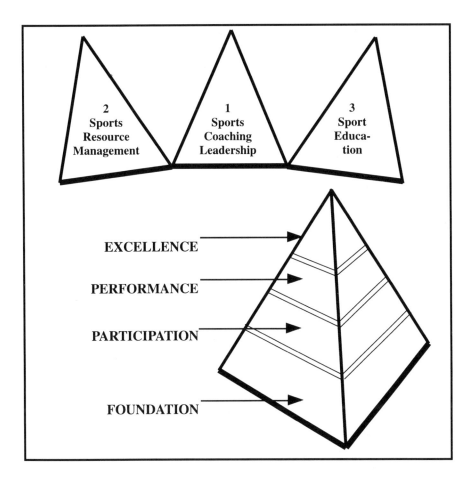

Figure 1: 3 Aspects of Managing the Sport Development Process

and community development officers, sports leaders and coaches all have a potential educational role which again would be tailored to the needs of the individual or group concerned at their particular stage of sports development.

I like this model of sports development because it identifies a single, continuous process for the individual sports activity consumer. At any age, that individual may need a particular combination of teaching, leading/coaching and resource management. The faces of the pyramid represent facets of a process, not insular job descriptions for individual employees within the education and sports professions or the leisure industry.

Rather, the model implies a plasticity allowing overlap between these roles: a specific job description will tend to emphasise one facet, but at the same time offer opportunities to be involved with the others.

The model also implies that the training of these professionals should be rounded, that they should have an appreciation of the sport development model as a whole and complementary expertise in more than one facet of it.

Therein lies a potential solution to our curriculum development problem of how to train the next generation of PE teachers and whether or not that generation can be integrated with the next generation of leisure managers, especially those with sports development and community recreation interests.

VI. Conclusion

1. Given the nature of our society and the way in which it is changing, should education for leisure feature formally in the school curriculum?
2. There is a strong case for 'Sport Education' as a facet of a broader notion of leisure education.
3. Physical Education, as it is currently practised in schools and intended in the PE National Curriculum document, may well not fully meet the needs of 'Sport Education', as envisaged here.
4. One can conceive of an elaborated model of 'Sport Development' which identifies complementary roles for sports teachers, sports leaders/coaches and recreation resource managers.
5. That model implies complementarity in the training of these 'leisure professionals'.

References

Alderson, J. and Crutchley, D. (1990) 'Physical Education and the National Curriculum' in N. Armstrong (ed) *New Directions in Physical Education Vol. I*, Rawdon: Human Kinetics Publishers, pp. 37–62.

Almond, L. (1989) 'The place of Physical Education in the Curriculum' in L. Almond (ed) *The Place of Physical Education in Schools*. London: Kogan Page, pp. 13–36.

DES (1991) *Physical Education for ages 5–16. Proposals of the Secretary of State for Education and Science and the Secretary of State for Wales*. DES/Welsh Office.

Hewlett, M. (1987) 'The explicit curriculum', *The Times Educational Supplement* January 2: p. 13.

Parry, J. (1989) 'Physical education, justification and the National Curriculum', *Physical Education Review* Vol. 11: pp. 106–118.

School Sport Forum (1988) *Sport and Young People: Partnership in action*. London: HMSO.

White, J. (1982) *The Aims of Education Restated*. London: Routledge & Kegan Paul.

INTERROGATING THE POLICY TEXT

Alan Tomlinson
Chelsea School Research Centre
University of Brighton

I. Introduction

In any open or aspiringly democratic society policy is not merely imposed; rather, it is progressed via open debate, consultation and negotiation. And it is through such processes that new orthodoxies emerge, consensus evolves or directions and meanings are struggled over. As policy actually emerges in a move from speculative proposal to legislative action, the openness of the debate is transcended, and accepted and transmitted meanings become more fixed and closed. Policy which once was openly debated then assumes a momentum of its own, claiming an a-priori legitimacy or a consensual 'voice'.

There are instances in which policy is challenged at an early point, with policy communities (Houlihan, 1989) laying bare the tensions within them. In such cases sub-groupings within those communities oppose proposed policy directions. The Conservative Administration in Britain met such opposition over a proposed Football Member's Bill. After widespread reports of hooligan behaviour by England's soccer fans at the 1988 European Championships in Germany, the Government proposed its Football Members' Bill, designed "to enforce compulsory membership for all football supporters" (Taylor, 1992: p. 109). The Working Party established to consider this did not include any representative of supporters or supporters' organisations. The National Federation of Football Supporters' Clubs, standing up against any form of compulsory membership, opposed what was becoming known as the "I.D. Card Scheme"; petitions were organised at football grounds throughout the country; and in the wake of the tragic deaths of football supporters at the Hillsborough disaster in April 1989 the proposed Bill was withdrawn. It will never be certain that the

93

opposition to this policy proposal would have been successful if the tragedy of Hillsborough had not swayed public and then political opinion. But without such organised debate, lobbying, opposition and protest the policy could well have assumed an unstoppable momentum. The policy could have become part of a "discursive formation" which lent legitimacy to the terms of the policy itself.

The concept of discourse is helpful here, referring as it does in the work of Foucault (1974) to "ideological clusters or 'discursive formations' which systematically organize knowledge and experience, and repress alternatives through their dominance. In this context questions arise as to how discourses can be challenged from within and alternative discourses emerge" (Meinhof, 1993: p. 161). Disputation in the making of policy is a reminder that discursive formations do not come ready-made; they represent particular interpretations and interests. Disputation in the implementation of policy is more difficult, as an established policy may well have become a discursive formation itself, laying claim to the setting of the agenda, and the moral high ground of the particular policy territory. Also, the discursive formation may provide the interpretive frameworks for general understanding of an area, and the language and terms in which the area is understood. This can be seen in the way in which early policy statements can become the dominant frame of reference for how particular policy communities then communicate. For example, what were proposed to be the "fundamental principles" underlying the school curriculum in 1985 — principles which could be widely disputed — are, some years on, the conventional wisdom (to use the phrase coined by Galbraith) of the professional discourse. This kind of process can best be understood by subjecting influential and formative policy texts to rigorous scrutiny. Revisiting such texts can remind us of how the particular discursive formation began to emerge. Revisiting them not just as the friendly relation or old chum, but as the interrogator, can show how policy formation proceeds from more open debate to an informal foreclosure of any debate, and so to the marginalisation of alternative interpretations.

So much for the theoretical excursus; now to a single and particular example, that of the Government's White Paper entitled *Better Schools* (HMSO, 1985), and the languages inscribed in that text. The principles espoused in *Better Schools* now have an everyday currency. The view that the curriculum should be broad and balanced is almost a professional truism; at the very least, professional exchanges assume a shared understanding of what this means. It is prominent in strategies and development plans across the schooling sector, so that the strategic development plan of a former VIth form college can claim that "recent developments have seen ... a continuous emphasis upon 'breadth and balance' in each student's programme" [Strategic Development Plan: April 1993 — Spring 1996, Varndean College, Brighton]. Modular programme involvement, general educational provision, tutorial support and guidelines, and work experience opportunities are cited as the means whereby such a development is activated.

It is used too by professional communicators — Mr. Do, Deputy Editor of the *Times Educational Supplement*, in critiquing particular aspects of governmental policy on education and schooling, prefaced his remarks by noting that 'breadth and balance' in a curriculum is a good thing [address to Year 11 Awards Event, Varndean School, January 21 1993]. In this volume too its professional currency is reiterated (see, for instance, chapters by Elizabeth Murdoch, John Evans *et al.*, Margaret Talbot).

But what does broad and balanced mean? Let us go back to 1985 and, with the policy text to hand, interrogate it for the political meanings which motivated it. For these purposes the text itself must be recalled.

II. The Text

This section extracts from *Better Schools* those parts concerned centrally with the "purposes of school education" and with "a number of fundamental principles" of the curriculum which are bound up with such purposes. The *Better Schools* document (pp. 14–15) proposed that the purposes of school education were:

(1) to help pupils to develop lively, enquiring minds, the ability to question and argue rationally and to apply themselves to tasks, and physical skills;

(2) to help pupils to acquire understanding, knowledge and skills relevant to adult life and employment in a fast-changing world;

(3) to help pupils to use language and number effectively;

(4) to help pupils to develop personal moral values, respect for religious values, and tolerance of other races, religions and ways of life;

(5) to help pupils to understand the world in which they live, and the inter-dependence of individuals, groups and nations;

(6) to help pupils to appreciate human achievements and aspirations.

There is room for legitimate disagreement about the priority to be attached to each element in this list, and the relationship between them. LEAs and schools have generally reflected the content of this list in their own formulations of basic aims. The Government takes that as evidence that, at the most general level, there is very little disagreement that these are indeed the purposes of school education.

45. The Government believes, and its belief is embodied in certain national programmes, that these purposes require that the curriculum offered to each pupil, from whatever background, should reflect a number of fundamental principles. Those set out below have commanded widespread assent during the consultations of the last 12 months:

(1) the curriculum in both primary and secondary schools should be broad: as a whole and in its parts it should introduce the pupil to a wide range of areas of experience, knowledge and skill. The HMI surveys *Primary Education in England* and *Curriculum and Organisation of Primary Schools in Wales* both pointed conclusively to the fact that the teaching of language and mathematical skills in isolation or in a purely theoretical way was less effective than when they were associated with a wide-ranging programme of work which also included art and craft, history and geography, music, physical education, and science. This principle applies in respect of every pupil: it leaves no room for discrimination in the curriculum on grounds of sex;

(2) the curriculum should be balanced: each area of the curriculum should be allotted sufficient time to make its specific contribution, but not so much that it squeezes out other essential areas;

(3) the curriculum should be relevant: all subjects should be taught in such a way as to make plain their link with the pupils' own experience and to bring out their applications and continuing value in adult life. Related to this is the need for a practical dimension to learning, reflected both in the balance between subjects and in the content and teaching of subjects themselves. Most pupils take well to practical and other work which they believe will help them to get on in the modern world, whose technology they find stimulating rather than daunting. The curriculum should be devised and taught so as to harness such excitement and enthusiasm. These requirements are at the heart of the Technical and Vocational Education Initiative (TVEI [...]), which explores how what is learned at school from age 14 can be more effectively related to the demands of working life; and of the Microelectronics Education Programme, whose aim is to

help schools to prepare pupils for a society in which the new technology is commonplace and pervasive. The Government thinks it important that the relevance of the curriculum should also be enhanced, as is happening increasingly, by local initiatives which bring schools and employers together in shared activities;

(4) there should be careful differentiation: what is taught and how it is taught need to be matched to pupils' abilities and aptitudes. It is of the greatest importance to stimulate and challenge all pupils, including the most and least able: within teaching groups as well as schools the range of ability is often wide. The Cockcroft Report (*Mathematics Counts*) pointed to the "seven-year difference" at age 11 in attainment in mathematics, and similar differences may be expected in other subject areas. Such differences need to be reflected in classroom practice. The Government is supporting development work to promote this principle through the Lower Attaining Pupils' programme, which investigates how differentiation is best developed and applied across the curriculum for pupils within the chosen target group. It is thus closely concerned with teaching approaches. Similarly, for pupils (including the most able) aiming for the 16+ examinations and beyond, the General Certificate of Secondary Education (GCSE [...]), with differentiated papers and questions, will encourage and test success at different levels of attainment.

46. A curriculum founded on these principles will, in the Government's view, serve to develop the potential of every pupil and to equip all for the responsibilities of citizenship and for the formidable challenge of employment in the world of tomorrow. It is vital that schools should always remember that preparation for working life is one of their principal functions. The economic stresses of our time and the pressures of international competition make it more necessary than ever before that Britain's work-force should possess the skills and attitudes, and display the understanding, the enterprise and adaptability that the pervasive impact of technological advance will increasingly demand. This applies equally to those who will be employed by others and to the many who may, for part or all of their working lives, be self-employed. The balance within the curriculum and the emphasis in teaching it now need to alter accordingly." *[HMSO, 1985]*

III. The Interrogation

There are some interesting points in this text. The purposes of school education
are not seen as in need of discussion. The phrase "there is very little disagreement" claims a consensus around the purposes. And before the principles are set
out the reader is told that they have "commanded widespread assent during the
consultations of the last 12 months". We are not presented here with a set of
questions for debate, then; rather, this is presented as a representative text,
speaking with the common voice and in the common or general interest. At the
same time, "the balance within the curriculum and the emphasis in teaching it"
must change: these "need to alter" in the light of social and economic factors and
political interpretations of the impact of these. So general principles are
espoused, but they are politically driven. Enterprise, self-employment, vocationalism — these central tenets of Conservative philosophy of the time constitute
the underpinning of the text. The text needs to be understood as a specifically
political statement, embodying the political principles of the time. It would be
a misreading to see it as a non-partisan professional statement. One of the
fascinating aspects of the history of such texts is, though, that they often become
read in such ways, partially retold and in a sense bowdlerised, as the potted
version takes its place in the emerging discursive formation.

It is particularly interesting to concentrate the interrogation on the four
fundamental principles, and to prise out of them the implications of the 1985
formulation.

First, *"the curriculum in both primary and secondary schools should be
broad"*. Perhaps there really is widespread agreement on this, other than among
the most elitist specialists (who, of course, in the public schools have not been
subject to the pressures of government policy — nor for whom, it seems, are
initiatives around 'education for leisure' perceived at all necessary; for public
school pupils perhaps education for leisure has a well-rehearsed pedigree on the
playing fields of the schools and in established cultural networks). But broad
could also mean superficial, and this very worthwhile principle could be
reinterpreted at will by any government more interested in crude performance
indicators such as examination results, and contrasted unfavourably with other
principles — such as depth perhaps. And how broad should the curriculum and
parts of the curriculum be? The application of the principle to particular aspects
of the curriculum, too, reminds any specialist that a true acknowledgement of
breadth would lead to impossible demands on the time available in and for any

curriculum. So it is a seductively appealing principle, worthy but rhetorical. Some of these complexities behind its formulation should be more widely acknowledged whenever it is reiterated.

Second, "*the curriculum should be balanced*". The key question here is "Who decides" precisely what constitutes balance, particularly when it is concerned with time-allocation? For time-allocation is about status and value, and most of the dynamics concerned with this principle of "balance" have really been about hierarchies of subject-status and traditional prestige claimed by different subjects and disciplines.

Third, "*the curriculum should be relevant*". This principle is framed in terms of pupils' own experiences, potential applications and practical dimensions said to be valuable for adult life. It prioritises what one might call techno-relevance and the real world, at the expense of any principles of, say, liberal education. Relevance is framed too in terms of particular pupil experiences, and the transformative aspiration of education is all but lost.

Fourth, "*there should be careful differentiation*". This sounds very sensible, sensitively matching the content and method of teaching to children's varied ability and aptitude. The sub-text, though, is about the recognition of differences on a level of selectivity and selection. In practice, the matching is likely to reaffirm divisions and justify elite approaches. Whilst the third principle talks of the connection between the worlds of work and education, but does so in a way which targets a relatively low-status potential workforce, this principle recognises that classroom practice can of course vary. This principle legitimates practice which may not fit easily with the other principles. It is a realistic acknowledgement that there are differing levels of ability and aptitude; in practice, though, it is an escape clause for anyone arguing for more specialist or elite provision — differentiation is a euphemism for selectivity.

Overall, then, sceptically scrutinised and interrogated, the *Better Schools* text might be seen as premised on four principles of:

- superficiality
- hierarchy
- para-vocationalism for the masses
- selectivity

rather than the principles of breadth, balance, relevance and differentiation. A professional discourse which reiterates the principles in the commonsense language of professional practice glosses over the political specificity of the formative moments in the making of the definitive policy text. Ball has observed that "the issue in discourse analysis is why, at a given time, out of all the possible things that could be said, only certain things were said" (Ball, 1990: p. 3). What was, and is, said in the name of 'better schools' is revealing in the politics of the time. Interrogation of the policy text is not just an ivory-tower game or an iconoclastic indulgence. It is a reminder of where we came from, of how discursive formations actually evolve; and a basis for reflection upon and debate about the professional dimensions of the policy process.

References

Ball, S. J. (ed) (1990) *Foucault and Education — Disciplines and Knowledge*. London: Routledge.

Houlihan, B. (1989) 'The politics of sport policy in Britain: The examples of football hooliganism and drug abuse', *Leisure Studies* Vol. 9, No. 1, pp. 55–69.

Taylor, R. (1992) *Football and Its Fans — Supporters and Their Relations with the Game, 1885–1985*. Leicester: Leicester University Press.

Foucault, M. (1974) *The Archaeology of Knowledge*. London: Tavistock Publications.

Meinhof, U. (1993) 'Discourse', in W. Outhwaite and T. Bottomore (eds) *The Blackwell Dictionary of Twentieth-Century Social Thought*. Oxford: Blackwell.

HMSO (1985) *Better Schools*.

III.

THE CURRICULUM CONTEXT —
DELIVERERS AND USERS

EDUCATION, ART AND THE PHYSICAL: THE CASE OF THE ACADEMIC STUDY OF DANCE — PRESENT AND FUTURE

Graham McFee
Chelsea School Research Centre
University of Brighton

I. Introduction

Dance has an anomalous place within — or perhaps not within — physical education: if included (as in the National Curriculum in the UK), it is arguably the only art-form within the compass of physical education. Moreover, dance is a major leisure-time activity, both for spectators and participants. So in that way too it is a topic suitable for discussion here. Although I am very interested in the *educational* possibilities of dance (McFee, 1989), this paper approaches such questions 'from the other side': from the perspective of dance *as an academic discipline*. For a proper assessment of the academic credentials of dance will require us also to gauge the degree to which the project of dance-study may be conceived of independently of concerns of education or of leisure.

The title of this paper already provides two clues to the importance of the topic. First, I shall be speaking of dance *as an academic discipline*: that is to say, not about other ways of involving dance in education. So that I am not invited to address some kinds of dance training (for example, that which goes on in the Royal Ballet School) where (roughly on a parallel with choir schools for music) pupils receive a sound scholarly (academic) background, but also give time to technical development and performance in the art-form. Instead, my context is dance in higher education, at least first and foremost. Notice, by the way, that this focus on dance as an academic discipline does nothing to decide whether or not any such study requires practical participation in dance, as parallel cases make clear. The academic, disciplinary study of visual art is (largely) the province of art historians, who need not themselves be painters or whatever. By contrast, the academic, disciplinary study of music —

say, in musicology — is seen as requiring a level of practical participation in music-making.

The second aspect of my title requires the consideration of the *present and future* of dance as an academic discipline. It is revealing to note that its *past* is excluded. I have heard it urged that dance as an area of academic study is a 'come-lately', whose place at the academic 'feast' must be *argued*: that it has to elbow its way to the table, as it were (say, compared with music). Here the big point — that the credentials of dance still need to be justified — is what I'm hoping to get to. For it provides a *context* for the issue I shall address: that dance study does not have an *established* and *recognised* disciplinary way of proceeding, and that it *needs* one if its claims to *academic* status are to be widely accepted.

As a kind of summary way of making that point about acceptance: at the institutional level, it might consist in getting UFC (HEFC) funding for all students, at fees all of which will be paid by LEAs.

Again, we are reasonably familiar with what — apart from *mere* academic prejudice — might stand in the way of such acknowledgement: related doubts about disciplinary methodology and about objectivity. It is such doubts that I shall also be addressing. As a result, I shall have little or nothing to say about ways dance study might extend beyond the rather 'un-ivory' tower of higher education: in particular, nothing about how to make it appealing to sponsors.

II.   The nature of academic disciplines

I begin with three general points about the nature of academic disciplines. The first is that academic disciplines require, for their thriving, an undergraduate base and a research base. By this, of course, I do not just mean that there must be undergraduate courses in the area. To mention my own discipline, I imagine that philosophy would thrive even if the only undergraduate courses in philosophy were those at Oxford University, which are always philosophy as part of some mixed degree. What I mean, though, is that the kind of understanding characteristic of undergraduates is essential to the flourishing of a discipline. And that is so because, put very roughly, such undergraduates represent an audience with some insight into the research in respect of that discipline. Hence they represent the broad-based disciplinary understanding.

The second general point is that, although academic disciplines require both an undergraduate base and a research base, the research base is the most important, and in three ways: first, because the knowledge that the under-graduates have is, to some degree or other, knowledge provided by the research; and, second, because it is methodologically structured by the methodologies of the research. Again, this means that, in typical cases, what one is doing as an undergraduate is a kind of scaled-down version of what the researchers do. In that way, one begins to learn disciplinary methodologies and, also, some background knowledge. So these are two ways in which the research aspect is primary.

A further consideration derives from viewing the undergraduate from the teacher's perspective. Here I want to introduce the idea (from Lawrence Stenhouse, 1975: Ch. 10) of teacher-as-researcher: that is to say, that the teaching process is, again to some degree or other, a research process. This is an important point in my thinking, to which I will return when I discuss "reflective practice".

Those two general points about academic disciplines explain why much of my discussion will seem to be about the research side, but why, in effect, it has implications for the undergraduate base, and hence for a general project to recognise the status and potential of the academic study of dance..

A third general point about disciplines is implicit in thinking that dance as an academic discipline has a *present*: it exists. So whatever I say cannot be radically revisionary of current practice. It may involve changes of emphasis, some inclusion, some exclusion, from what presently goes on under the heading of dance study in, say, specialist research and teaching institutions; but it cannot realistically be urged that the academic discipline of dance should simply involve rejecting all that is presently going on and replacing it with, say, study of the collected works of Graham McFee. This would be a conceptual mistake. I would have missed the point that, in order to count as dance study, an activity must have a close relation to what is being done at present.

III. Academic credentials for dance study?

The present more global picture is not encouraging for the establishing of academic credentials for dance study. The humanities areas are not being widely supported. Moreover, the positions of arts activities – such as dance – seem especially problematic. For general questions of objectivity surround the arts: and the arts in the UK are in a parlous state at present. They are under threat, both from forces external to the art world, and from internal forces. When considering the first category, the external, we should remember that totalitarian regimes have regularly seen the arts as a threat, either censoring artists (as in Soviet Russia in the 1950s) or defending the 'True Art' against its 'degenerate' (that is, challenging) counterpart (as in Hitler's Germany [Chipp, 1968: pp. 474–483]). Now, these regimes had a point: art is important and (potentially) challenging. Thus regimes which reject the very idea of challenge might be expected to respond in these ways.

In contrast to the seriousness manifest in such examples, the government in the UK has recently treated the arts as something trivial, as mere amusement, or of no great significance. This indictment of the present situation in the UK is sharply put by the late Peter Fuller, who writes against general Thatcherite values as they apply to art, considering the specific example of Charles Saatchi, an art collector as well as Mrs. Thatcher's former media orchestrator. Fuller (1988: pp. 79–80) comments:

> I believe Saatchi has been a catastrophe for art in Britain... because, as far as art is concerned, Saatchi has no taste or discrimination — one reason why he prefers to buy works of art by the baker's dozen.

Fuller's point — which he takes Saatchi to exemplify — is that there is an attitude which sees "...no merit whatever in the old spiritual and aesthetic idea of art as a 'disinterested' pursuit" (Fuller, 1988: p. 63). Given such an attitude, one might predict two things; first, "...the transformation of fine art courses into courses orientated towards the new technologies, design and mechanical processes" (pp. 63–64). A second prediction might be that holders of this attitude would have "...starved the museums and galleries — and we might add 'dance companies and theatres' — of resources" (p. 64). This is exactly what has happened in the UK recently.

Within the art world, things are not much better. So that, looking to our second case, from art's defenders we find many misty claims masquerading as analysis. Thus David Best (1990: p. 5a) perceptively comments on the extent to which, instead of a vigorous argumentative defence of the value of art, we encounter "...vague and soothing soporifics from supporters". Applied to education, these 'soporifics' typically take one of two forms. First, an 'argument' is advanced to the effect that, in schools, classes in the arts represent 'the other side of the coin', light relief in contrast to the serious intellectual business of mathematics or physics. Second, there is the blithe assumption of aesthetic value — which means that one is not required to say anything about the arts, their value being self-evident. In either of these variants, this is simply a commitment to a reprehensible form of subjectivism.

In this context, realism about a *bright* future for dance as an academic discipline cannot — in the short term — be genuinely warranted: indeed, some pessimism seems justified. But any such future — perhaps any future at all — will depend on establishing the *academic* credentials of dance study. I do not propose to sketch the present state of dance as an academic discipline, but I want to make five comments which help us to see its present position, and also to work productively towards the future.

1. The first thing to note is what I shall call the 'ologies' of dance. They are not, of course, all ologies — sociology of dance, anthropology of dance are; dance history is not — but the idea is clear enough: areas where dance is studied from the perspective of some established academic discipline. A kind of index of this sort of work at the research level is that a good researcher, and perhaps the best kind of researcher, would be somebody whose undergraduate background was in the ology in question. So that, for example, having learned the methodology of history in an undergraduate course, a history graduate might undertake studies in dance history. And this might be the most favoured background for graduate research.

Those ologies are clearly very productive. I do not want to say much about them beyond *that*, except to notice the fragility of dance as an academic discipline if it consisted solely or primarily of such ologies. The parallel with the present parlous state of education studies makes the point exactly. Some of Kenneth Clarke's pronouncements when he was Secretary of State for Education cast doubt on the value of the sociology of education and such like. In that sense, education is seen as something which goes on independently of the ologies: they are therefore dispensable. In this way, if dance as an academic discipline centres on, or is justified by, the ologies, it looks fragile. So while the ologies are important in the present, and indeed in the future, of dance as an academic discipline, it would be a mistake to put undue weight on them.

2. The second thing to talk about is the position of what might be called "product development". I have in mind here cases where artists, in dance or in the visual arts, speak of "research", meaning an investigation of materials, of situations, to act as a stimulus for composition — with lots of provisos around the word "stimulus". I want to suggest that, in the sense in which we have been using the word "research", this is not research. Of course, the discussion is not

intended to make a verbal point. The research and development departments in business companies do just the same kind of product development; but (and equally on the parallel) I think we are happy to distinguish research in that sense from research as we think of it in academic disciplines. So when we look for the research base to support our undergraduate base for dance studies, it cannot be that kind of 'research', because for our purposes that is not research at all. Again, this is not merely a verbal distinction. What we are looking for, for our research base, will not be provided by that kind of study.

3. The third thing to note about the present state of dance studies is the importance of what I shall call the "highly specialised" (for want of a better expression): so that, for example, there is good dance research going on which involves the description of dances (perhaps even of other activities) through notation systems such as Labanotation or Benesh, and the subsequent analysis of relationships between body parts or between dancers or some such through the study of the notation. I note here that while this might be perfectly good research in its own right, it is clearly not a major basis for the undergraduate programme. Of their nature, such complex notation systems are, at least, not the sorts of thing an undergraduate comes in with at a sufficiently developed level to operate in this kind of way. A parallel (or, rather, non-parallel) case makes the point: the student of, say, French is required to have mastery of French before entering the undergraduate programme, because that aspect will not be explored in the programme, and the mastery of French, at a certain level at least, will simply be a tool for the whole of the student's under-graduate programme. By contrast, our dance student is being required to do a large number of other things. So it would be unrealistic from the intellectual point of view (even if it were realistic practically) to require, on entry to the undergraduate course, a great deal of mastery of these 'specialised' aspects.

This point may usefully be filled-out in two ways. For there is an oddity in using expressions such as "dance-literate" to describe those who have a mastery of such notations-systems. For such expressions share with the expression "computer-literate" the wholly misleading impression that mastery of notation (or of a programme) is *equivalent* to mastery of language. But this is not so. The ability to conceptualise (and also to make) dance precedes such 'literacy' — we can readily imagine successful choreographers who understand dance without such knowledge. [My own powerful commitment to the importance of notation, via the Thesis of Notationality (McFee, 1992: pp. 97–99), does nothing to modify this point.] In this sense, to become "notation-literate" (like becoming "computer-literate") is to become master of a *tool*. To be *literate*, by contrast, is as much to be able to conceptualise as to be able to record that conceptualisation (Winch, 1987: pp. 197–198). As such, literacy goes hand-in-hand with conceptual mastery. Again, the contrast with the place of the French language for the undergraduate student of French is exact: what is studied there *presupposes* mastery of the French language. The student of dance, however, could for example study the activities of choreographers by observing dances. Possession of a notated score is not *essential*. Indeed, the central case of investigating dances must be through perceiving the dance themselves (rather than perceiving a recipe for them [McFee, 1992: p. 88]).

A further (and related) consideration involves recognising that notation systems embody methods of analysis or conceptualisation. As Suzanne Youngerman (1984: p. 101) puts it:

> Notation systems are more than tools for documentation; they are systems of analysis that can be used to illuminate many aspects of the phenomenon of movement. Notation scores embody perceptions of movement.

That is to say, scores are not so much neutral objects which can *then* be analysed, as objects which *have been* analysed — as, say, when we have chosen which are the key aspects of a pattern of movement.

4. As a fourth point, notice, though, that this does suggest something useful. That there may be a kind of analysis not dissimilar to that sophisticated, 'specialised' analysis of the dances which *might* be done. It will consist in observing dances, perhaps in reality and perhaps through video or something similar, and analysing them for just such relationships. What should be noted, though, is that this kind of thing is done, though perhaps less 'scientifically', in dance criticism. So making this thought a key one for our analysis of dance will be extending the role of what we might summarise as dance criticism. As we will see, this is a rather important idea.

5. Finally in this section, I want to comment on a danger, one which comes in a variety of forms: the danger of subjectivism. It is very easy to think that the value of dance is self-evident, and therefore to begin one's account of dance study on the uncritical assumption of such value. But this is something to be combated. I will offer three remarks here: the first concerns the difficulty of pro-

ducing a plausible academic discipline if one slips into subjectivism. For, as described by a *subjectivist*, dance study will be an area where 'anything goes', where everyone is entitled to his or her own *judgement*. But, if this were true, dance study would be *ruled-out* as a candidate for producing knowledge: hence, as an academic discipline. How can I come to *understand* X if my judgement before the activity is as relevant, perspicacious, etc. as my judgement after? How can I *know* anything about X (and you not know it) if your judgement and mine are *automatically* of equal worth? In both cases, I cannot. And this is the heart of my rejection of subjectivism in dance study: if what it urges is true, the questions about methodology and objectivity can never be answered.

As a second remark, note the way in which subjectivism leads to a denigration of dance as an area of study by not allowing knowledge and so on. That is to say, if dance study does not generate knowledge or understanding – and if, moreover, we cannot explain its value — then it will be easy for a sceptic to dismiss it. The third remark — which I won't expand now — concerns the *relativism* inherent in such a view.

Briefly, explaining what I mean by subjectivism in dance study involves pointing out the way in which the term "subjective" is used not only dismissively by opponents of dance, but also 'supportively' by defenders of dance, on a parallel with work in the other arts as mentioned previously.

Let us drag together the five major points in this section. I have urged that the centre of dance studies cannot be the ologies, although they are important; that it must not be treated in a subjectivist fashion; that another important area, the sophisticated or 'specialised' studies (of which I gave notation as an example), also take us only so far; but that at least one centre for dance studies rests in what I called, rather loosely, dance criticism.

More precisely, it rests in the idea of understanding dance. This is a particular theme of mine, a hobby-horse if you like, but it begins to define the centre of dance studies. That is to say, dance as an academic discipline focuses centrally on dance as an object of understanding: what makes it so; what traditions and conventions support it; how the understanding works; how meaning in dance works; and, by extension of that idea beyond our informal criticism, on the work of professional critics.

I want to meet one imaginary objection at this stage, before looking — in the next section — to the future.

The imaginary objection is that, contrary to what I said initially, we are now back with the ologies: that what we are looking at is the philosophy of dance. At one level, it is difficult for me to oppose such an interpretation — after all, that's how I got into it. But in another way, there is something slightly misleading about that. Philosophy here is not taking us away from an examination of the dance itself, or at least not primarily. We really are considering dances. And in two ways. First, we are considering the *nature* of dance — primarily, dance as a performing art, with associated questions about the relationships of particular performances to other performances and to the dance itself, about the place of technique, about dance's contribution to human thought and feeling; but, further down the line, dance as a popular-cultural form. Second, we then have the tools to confront individual dance works, to explore them (rather as critics do) but from an *informed* background.

I suggest that this emphasis on *understanding* is crucial for any academic study of dance worth the name: and that is what we should look to for a future.

IV.   A future: dance studies for understanding

Finally, I want to say more about the future, under four headings designed to accommodate the points just made. First, dance studies should be seen as fulfilling two fundamental principles (Baker, 1977: p. 24; McFee, 1992: pp. 313–314). These are (a) the autonomy of artistic enquiry into dance: that the concepts and statements used in our discussion of dance are not logically equivalent to any non-artistic concepts or statements; (b) the reality of artistic enquiry concerning dance — that it is possible to give genuine explanations of the concepts and statements used in discussion of dance.

These two principles, which resemble those which might be articulated for an enquiry such as jurisprudence, focus on "the increase of understanding, not of knowledge; the generation of new insight, not the discovery of new facts" (Baker, 1977: p. 24). They are fundamental just because, without them, dance study would collapse into some other study — for example, study of the biology of dancers, or the economics of arts activity, or the sociology of the 'consumption' of dances — or would be reducible to some other activity. These principles are therefore of a piece with our commitment to understanding: and they pick-up the sense in which it is dance *as an artform* that generates the primary 'object of understanding'. Our discussion of the artistic character of dance will serve both to distinguish the arts from other areas of human experience and also to distinguish dance from within the arts. In this way, the concepts that we use to understand dances are importantly different from (although not unconnected with) concepts we use in other places.

Second, I want to say something about research into the social implications of dance — or, rather, I want to say almost nothing about it, except that this is standardly where our ologies, perhaps supplemented by educational investigation, come into play. There are plenty of appropriate ologies with which to investigate the impact of dance on particular communities, to study ways of developing dance for particular communities and particular purposes.

All of that investigation, though, is predicated on an understanding of why anybody should want to do any of those things, beyond some kind of vested interest in dance. Here is a need for dance *research*, and not just research which is essentially history or sociology simply taking dance as its subject. My aim is to insist on the need for research into dance *itself* and not merely into its history, consumption, or the physiology required for its delivery. While not exhaustive, certainly a major element of this research will be philosophical in character.

That takes me to the third area. The future of dance studies, I've suggested, involves elaborating the central idea, the idea of understanding dance. It has to involve exploring what is distinctive about dance; that is, what is involved in investigating dance as an art form. For that is an area where dance is an object of understanding. Of course, the ologies too might investigate other dance forms. But what is distinctive about dance as an academic discipline will be its investigation of dance as an art form. In a similar kind of way, what is distinctive about visual art as an area of academic study is that it (typically) looks at (for example) the paintings that are art — and of course some that approach art and so forth — but the centre of its interest is on the art dimension.

What is that investigation going to be like? It is certainly going to develop along the lines of philosophical understanding of the nature of dance. If that is the research base, how is that going to feed back into the undergraduate teaching? It feeds back in a way which has implications for the research element too. If we accept that dance is an object for understanding (when the dance is an art form), and if our focus is on the nature of that dance understanding, an important way to come to understand that understanding is by exploring, say, choreography, and exploring it both as an observer of the choreography of others (what I call masterworks), but also in doing some oneself.

The point is not to turn one into a choreographer — although of course that may be a valuable spin-off — but to turn one into someone who *understands* choreography. And this, of course, is what takes us beyond the research and development (or as I called it earlier, the product development) aspect. One isn't studying the choreography in order to make choreographies, even in order to be able to know how to make choreographies. One is studying it to gain insight into dance understanding.

Fourth, and finally, there is a kind of research project which is very dear to my heart, which I take to be fundamental to the future of the research base of dance as an academic discipline. For practice both of dance study and of dance teaching are what Donald Schön (1983; 1987) calls "reflective practices": people who do these are "reflective practitioners". As a result, they have acquired the habits of the practice, held in place by values. An important area for dance research is research into those values: the practice-values of the dancer and dance teacher. Yet more than just asking is required. Professional teachers or trainers (call them what you will) who are operating as reflective practitioners may well be unable to articulate their knowledge, insight, or understanding, in speech or in writing. Indeed, some of the worst material I have ever read about the nature of dance has been composed by people who, through their practice, clearly know an awful lot about what dance is and how it works. So a research strategy is required.

In order to move forward on that basis, we must rethink our understanding of the nature of knowledge. We must think of it in a way which privileges the kind of knowledge which has always gone on in dance studies: a kind of knowing through doing. For at the centre of Schön's notion of *reflective practice* is a view about knowledge (and a related view about *understanding*): that knowledge is *essentially* connected with action and with practice, rather than peripherally or accidentally so connected. And that sort of knowledge feeds-back into what goes on at the undergraduate level because, of course, we are there beginning to describe the sorts of values and other commitments which the undergraduate needs in order to proceed into the world of dance.

To identify the dance teacher as reflective practitioner, we should consider the extent to which dance practitioners possess *craft-knowledge* of a kind which might be investigated by viewing dance educators as reflective practitioners. As Schön (1987: pp. 65–69) argued, reflection-in-action is central to the design process. At first, in his writing, this point is exemplified through an actual case of design. Then it is generalised. Thus Schön (1987: p. 175) remarks, 'Musical performance is a kind of designing'. Musical performers, then, are a good example of the kinds of professionals who can be reflective practitioners. Given the affinities between dance and music (both are performing arts), the extension to dancers seems natural. Moreover, Schön (1987: pp. 182–201) explicitly considers the case of teaching music by using a *masterwork*: the pianist teaches both a particular musical work (Schubert's *Wanderer Fantasy* Opus 15) and musical understanding more generally. So here too the comparison with dance is promising.

Moving on, we notice the task of the dance educator as constrained in just the ways Schön (1987: pp. 208–215) suggests. For pupils must undergo *induction into craft-knowledge*. The pupils must be led to grasp both the designing of performance and the performance of design.

The upshot of following-through Schön's discussion of the teaching of music is to see two related areas for dance research: for both dancer and dance teacher may be reflective practitioners, in the sense articulated here. Of course, it would be wrong to suggest that no research previously undertaken fitted this mold. However, none that I know of does so *explicitly*: and explicitness is essential if one requirement is a reformed view of knowledge. It would be equally mistaken to predict what such an investigation might yield. I suggest only that it offers a promising research route, both for dance education and for dance study more generally. For we are invited to show what we can do, rather than just telling what we can say. So we have identified one of the tasks to be undertaken — the fuller articulation of the 'reflective practice' picture of knowledge. Moreover, we have implicitly identified a disciplinary base for that enquiry: it is philosophy.

V. Conclusion

Central to our conclusion is the need for a *clear* and *revealing* account of dance study, explaining its methodological structure and justifying its objectivity. We have noted how major problems for the present include:

* the fragility of the justification, if the 'ologies' are invoked;

* if not, often (that is, in the literature), subjectivism in some way.

We need an account of dance as an academic study more perspicuous than, for example, one which stresses "choreography, performance and critical appreciation" (Adshead, 1981) as key concepts. Such an account is alright as far as it goes, but it remains descriptive: it does not *yet* explain three central matters. First, why are these key concepts?; second, what point is there to investigations depending on them?; and, third, what methodologies do such investigations employ? These three issues amount to saying that we do not *yet* see how these concepts *cohere* to form an academic discipline ... nor how practitioners could *learn* 'ways of proceeding' (ways to be a reflective practitioner) which might hold the discipline together.

We should recognise five points, seeing dance study as:

- concerned with understanding ... and therefore inflected methodologically, towards dance understanding. I do not think we can now — if we ever could — sustain the claims of an academic dance-study if very much of the emphasis is given to the doing of dance as such. Weight must be given to dance as a vehicle for understanding. So that if, with Adshead (1981), we were to take choreography, performance and critical appreciation as basic concepts for dance as an area of academic study, we would justify their several places by reference to their contribution to dance understanding, and to understanding more generally.

- inflected by craft-knowledge, with the idea of the reflective practitioner – and the associated view of knowledge. That notion seems fruitful for research into the craft-knowledge of the dance teacher, but also of the dancer. The key characteristic has been to locate a dance research, rather than one depending on disciplinary perspectives on dance (history of dance, sociology of dance etc.).

- an 'artistic' account — that is, centred on the art-form. This view builds on the artistic/aesthetic distinction to find the justification of dance in its artistic possibilities.

- obedient to our two 'principles' — the autonomy and the reality of dance study.

- against subjectivism in dance — this whole sermon is part of the polemic against subjectivism. It highlights the numerous places where the temptation to subjectivism is presented to the dance educator.

At each stage, it is important to see how the subjectivist position undermines the claims to understanding, to learning, to art-status, or all of these! Doing so will have clarified (some of) what are and what are not issues for the academic study of dance.

The future for dance studies is non-revisionary in terms of practice: so we won't really be doing anything different: any radical difference here would be a way of denying that we are doing dance studies, for there is a real (if limited) contemporary life to the idea of dance studies.

This is not to say that nothing follows from the account of dance studies here: the primary difference operates at the level of justification. But this is just what we need for dance as an academic study: that is, we need to justify, first, its objectivity; second, its methodological unity; and third, its institutional or 'professional' viability. In this sense, what I am describing is less a misty vision of the future of dance as an academic discipline than a clear sight of both the key questions for such a future and the major constraints on any satisfactory answer.

Now, if we ask what this might mean for the use of dance in, say, the National Curriculum, our answer will have two dimensions, reflecting different aspects of the use of dance. First, and for me of least importance, reference will be made to dance as a physical activity — to its health impact, for instance. In this mode, dance is merely one physical activity among others in physical education. Second, though, reference will be made to intrinsically educational properties of dance: these provide its distinctive justification. Of course, I will not here say much about the *answer* to be arrived at. But that answer is a topic for the academic study of dance, in two ways. For we must establish what, when dance is an object of understanding, renders it uniquely educational. Further, we must consider the place, if any, of the academic study of dance in the formal education of the young; for example, through A-levels — where it seems to have a clear place! Indeed, one could be forgiven for thinking that this might be the conceptual centre for a truly educational dance in education. All this, though, remains in need of an elucidation not tainted with subjectivism, and recognising that there are real questions here; that the answers are not self evident. But that is precisely a call for work in the academic study of dance.

References

Adshead, J. (1981) *The Study of Dance*. London: Dance Books Ltd.

Baker, G. P. (1977) 'Defeasibility and meaning', in P.M.S. Hacker and J. Raz (eds) *Law, Morality and Society*. Oxford: Clarendon Press) pp. 26–57.

Best, D. N. (1990) Arts in Schools: A Critical Time, Birmingham Institute of Art and Design [NSEAD Occasional Paper].

Chipp, H. B. (ed.) (1968) *Theories of Modern Art.* Los Angeles: University of California Press.

Fuller, P. (1988) *Seeing Through Berger.* London and Lexington, KY: The Claridge Press.

McFee, G. (1989) 'The concept of dance education', in G. Curl (ed) *Collected Conference Papers in Dance* Vol. 4, London: National Association of Teachers in Further and Higher Education, pp. 15-37.

——— (1992) *Understanding Dance.* London: Routledge.

Schön, D.A. (1983) *The Reflective Practitioner.* New York: Basic Books.

——— (1987) *Educating the Reflective Practitioner.* San Francisco: Jossey-Bass Publishers.

Stenhouse, L. (1975) *An Introduction to Curriculum Research and Development.* London: Heinemann Educational.

Winch, P. (1987) *Trying to Make Sense.* Oxford: Blackwell.

Youngerman, S. (1984) 'Movement notation systems as conceptual frameworks: The Laban System', in Maxine Sheets-Johnstone (ed) *Illuminating Dance: Philosophical Explorations.* Cranberry, NJ: Associated University Presses, pp. 101–123.

ETHNICITY AND THE PHYSICAL EDUCATION CURRICULUM: TOWARDS AN ANTI-RACIST APPROACH[1]

Scott Fleming
Chelsea School Research Centre
University of Brighton

I.   Introduction

In the last few years the sporting experiences of Britain's minority groups have been the focus of considerable media attention through television documentaries (*cf.* BBC TV, 1990, 1991, 1992; C4 TV, 1991), and the lively debates that these have generated in the press (*cf.* Glanville, 1990; Wilson, 1990) and elsewhere (*cf.* McNab, 1990; Semple, 1992). Yet the school-based sporting experiences of young people from minority groups have been largely neglected; and I would argue, are often misunderstood. The importance of these experiences should not be underestimated, for as I have suggested elsewhere (Fleming, 1991), these significantly shape attitudes and perceptions, and therefore directly influence participation patterns in physical education (PE) and sport. In this paper I hope to demonstrate that minority groups have not been well served by PE, and that it is time for physical educators to adopt an explicitly 'anti-racist' approach to their work in order to offer real 'equality of opportunity' to all pupils.

II.   From monoculturalism to multiculturalism

The discourse that has surrounded the issues facing PE in a multi-ethnic and multi-cultural society during the last 30 years has, in the main, been concerned with the ideology of assimilation and the practices of monoculturalism. This inevitably meant a 'colour-blind' approach to PE curricula and pedagogy, and an articulation of the view that: "Children 'want to be treated the same, not differently'" (cited in Bayliss, 1989: p. 19). The message, as Troyna and Carrington (1990: p. 2) observe, was clear: "Forget the culture of your parents, discard any affiliation to your ethnic background and blend in". Moreover, in the general climate of assimilation, this view became widespread and deeply embedded. The implications, with the considerable benefit of hindsight, were abundantly apparent:

> Treating all children the same means treating them all like white children and probably like white middle class children. This will inevitably mean that all children's needs are not being equally met. (Williams, 1989: p. 163)

In one sense this attitude is rather paradoxical for there was some recognition of the 'differentness' of some particular minority groups. For example, Field and Haikin (1971: p. 57) were clearly concerned about some of the difficulties faced by recent arrivals from the Indian sub-continent:

> The Asian child must feel himself [sic] to be an island, surrounded by a raging torrent of a sea, formed by new and frightening sounds — of children chattering in an unknown tongue, of weird music and piano, and the boisterous bouncing on wooden floors in physical education.

But this attitude was symptomatic of what became the "problems approach" to the physical education of minority groups, and about which Tony Bayliss (1983, 1989) has argued most cogently: that is to say, seeing the pupils of minority groups as the 'problem', rather than inappropriate curricula and teaching methods.

Physical education and sport in Britain have been somewhat resistant to change generally, and slow to react to wider ideological influences and political pressures (Leaman & Carrington, 1985; Hargreaves, 1986). Indeed it was not until the latter half of the 1980s that there was a change of emphasis in terms of multiculturalism and equal opportunities in PE — though not a change in the underlying ideology. The new approach adopted by the PE profession was different in that it was concerned with a multicultural approach to PE, and was based on the belief that:

> Introducing multi-cultural perspectives into the curriculum is a way of enriching the education of all our pupils. It gives pupils the opportunity to view the world from different standpoints, helping them to question prejudice and develop open-mindedness. (National Curriculum Council, 1990: p. 3)

No doubt the intentions were good, and there is real evidence of the recognition that young people from minority groups were no longer treated as "immigrants", but were "our pupils". Yet multicultural education is not without its critics, and multicultural PE may be especially problematic.

III. Multicultural Physical Education: a brief critique

Multicultural education is based on the fundamental premise of assimilation of minority groups (Cole, 1986; Donald & Rattansi, 1992). It is upon this ideological stance that the first criticisms of multicultural education can be made. For it is clear that within an assimilationist stance — as Chris Mullard (1985) has argued — there is an implicit notion of cultural and even 'racial' superiority. It implies a universally shared set of values to which all should assimilate; and also acts as a means of coercion and control.

Indeed more specifically than this, Mike Cole's (1986) analysis of multicultural education indicates further issues that need to be considered:

> Traditionally multicultural education has been seen (overwhelmingly) as 'teaching' children about other cultures, thereby instilling respect for such cultures by white indigenous children and improving the self-image of non-white immigrant and indigenous children, partly as a result of the positive images thus engendered. It was also expected to have the spin-off of generating tolerance and understanding between minority groups. (Cole, 1986: p. 124)

As a critic of multicultural education, Cole's description might be seen as an over-simplification, but in it he does identify some of the basic elements of its rationale. Some of these relate directly to PE. First, multicultural education focuses on what Cole (1986, p. 124) calls "safe cultural sites". The clearest example of this in PE is the way in which dance is often touted as a vehicle through which awareness and tolerance of minority groups might be increased (*cf.* Kansara, 1984; Todryk, 1988; Gajadhar, 1990); and there are claims that it develops a greater understanding of minorities' cultures of origin (*cf.* Leaman, 1984; BAALPE, 1990). Yet without the necessary depths of cultural insight into the subject matter being taught, material is delivered in a contextual void — what Judy Katz (1982, p. 13) has called "The Tokenism Game: Let's Dress Up and Eat Chinese Food". In the absence of a full socio-historical cultural context, the effect is that material is made to seem tokenistic and exotic: the 'three S's syndrome

— saris, samosas and steel bands' (Carrington & Troyna, 1990; Donald & Rattansi, 1992). The implication is that when safe cultural sites are presented to pupils, they might — at best — only lead to a distorted understanding of the material being presented; but at worst, might easily create acute misunderstanding and exacerbate ethnic antagonism.

Second, there is an important and bogus assumption that Cole (1986) identifies: that multicultural education will necessarily enhance the self-esteem of the members of the minority groups. It presupposes, of course, that such an enhancement of self-esteem is necessary and possible. The visions of the pathological 'black youth in crisis' — so heavily criticised by Errol Lawrence (1981) — would appear to be the basis for this analysis. However, even if it were possible and desirable to enhance the self-esteem of minority groups, it is not easy to see how this might occur. It is much easier, on the other hand, to see how the opposite effect might take place; and this is the third point. By teaching pupils about ethnic and cultural 'differentness', it is both possible and likely that cultural distinctiveness might be reinforced, racist stereotypes might be consolidated, and ethnic antagonism exacerbated (Fleming, 1992a; 1992b).

Fourth, it is important to recognise the importance of relevance in the curriculum, and in relation to dance in particular, This is an issue that has only recently been examined with any real understanding of the demographic changes affecting Britain's minority populations (*cf.* McFee, 1993). In essence, Britain's school-aged minority populations are increasing, yet many of the young people from minority groups are British-born. To illustrate the point, the 'safe cultural sites' of first generation South Asians may have little relevance for their British-born children and grandchildren[2]. As Vitesh Chandra[3] remarked to me: "My family does about as much Asian dance as the average English family does Morris dancing".

Fifth, and this is perhaps the most important point of all, a multicultural approach to PE fails to acknowledge and address the centrality of racism in the experiences of young people from minority groups. The evidence for the impact of racism is becoming increasingly overwhelming. From early work conducted by Cashmore (1982) it was clear that young black people were subjected to various forms of racism at school[4], and subsequent work by other researchers corroborates this (*cf.* Carrington & Williams, 1989; Fleming, 1991, 1992a).

IV. Multi-racist Physical Education

The case for adopting an anti-racist stance in the teaching of PE rests, in part, on the frequency, regularity and seriousness of racist incidents. One of the criticisms levelled at multiculturalism is the failure to adequately address racism, and it is a criticism for which multiculturalists have neither a convincing nor a satisfactory answer. For the purpose of this discussion, it is helpful to distinguish — as Abercrombie *et al.* (1984: p. 173) do — between individual racism: "involving individual acts of oppression against subordinate racial groups or individuals"; and institutional racism: "involving structural relations of subordination and oppression between social groups".

Personal racism includes a most explicit and directly offensive set of behaviours, and because it is overt and blatant it should be relatively easy to monitor and act upon. Yet in PE verbal abuse is sometimes accepted as 'part of the game', and physical violence is legitimised through the contact element of certain activities. The following examples from my own study of the sport-racism-ethnicity relation (Fleming, 1992a) are illustrative:

> I was tackling Mark and he didn't want me to take the ball off him, and by mistake I pushed him, so he started swearing at me, very rude — "You 'Paki', bastard, idiot, get back to your own country". [Aslam]
> If I am a goalkeeper and I let in a goal, people say "Look you fucking 'Paki', you can't do anything". That happens even at school. [Naresh]

On a more subtle level, it is clear that myths and stereotypes exist about particular minority groups (Leaman, 1984; Hill, 1989, Williams, 1989), and that these are often very damaging both to members of those specific groups, and to others. In 1979 Stephen Kew observed that the sport-ethnicity dynamic was not understood beyond the level of crude stereotypes: "'The Welsh love rugby, the Chinese are good at table tennis, West Indians are all mad about cricket' etc." (Kew, 1979: p. 31).

All of these, it can be argued, are valid generalisations about particular socio-cultural groups of people. Yet the dangers arise when such stereotypes become the basis of conventional wisdom founded on fallacious logic. Troyna and Carrington (1990) have reflected on the perils of false syllogisms, and nowhere is their point made more effectively than in relation to PE. Consider the following:

The Chinese are good at table tennis,
'X' is Chinese,
ergo, 'X' is good at table tennis.

This is clearly a flawed proposition. Yet this kind of understanding has been the basis upon which curricular choices have been made. The PE curriculum has often attempted to provide activities within a PE programme that appeal to minority groups (Craft & Klein, 1986). Yet in order to make such judgements about material for the curriculum, stereotypes have been adopted. It has further been assumed that these are not only valid (which as generalisations they may be), but valid for *all* pupils from a particular ethnic group (which they most certainly are not).

The further danger of such flawed logic is apparent when stereotyped assumptions associated with so-called 'natural ability', become the basis for physiological and psychological causal links to explain particular phenomena. For example:

Pakistanis have dominated world-class squash for many years,
Pakistanis are good at squash because they're Pakistani,
Pakistanis are physiologically and psychologically better equipped for squash.

The implications of such analyses have been abundantly clear from the earliest studies of minority groups in sport. The much-publicised view that black footballers "haven't got the bottle" for the physical aspects of the game was accepted as coaching and management lore for many years (*cf.* Hill, 1989; C4 TV, 1991). The whole concept of 'natural ability' associated with particular ethnic groups *because* of their ethnicity has been discredited by Lashley (1980) and Cashmore (1982) amongst others, yet the entrenched views have remained largely intact, and have resisted evidence to the contrary.

To illustrate the absurdity of the argument of causality based on natural ability, consider the following type of argument:

The French make good red wine,
The French have natural ability at making red wine,
The French are genetically better equipped to make red wine.

This analogy is, of course, a caricature of the parallel syllogism for natural ability in sport. But it emphasises the key point that such a position ignores: the importance of culture and environment.

In spite of these concerns and reservations about 'natural ability', clear analytical thinking has been confused by discourse based on 'argument by example'. The people who advance the view that, for example, Afro-Caribbeans have 'natural ability' at sprint events in track and field athletics, offer evidence that Afro-Caribbeans are proportionally over-represented... "so it must be physiological and psychological". The implication is clear: they *do* because they *can*. That is to say, the reason why Afro-Caribbeans run fast is because they are able to; and the reason why other ethnic groups don't is because they are not able to.

The logical extension of this argument is especially worrying, and goes beyond mere participation in sporting activity. For if it is accepted that people do because they can (and don't because they can't), the implication, for example, from academic achievement statistics would lead to the bogus conclusion that some groups are 'naturally' more able academically and intellectually than others. This, of course, is arrant nonsense.

The impact of such stereotypes on the practice of the PE profession has been well documented. Afro-Caribbeans have been channelled into sport and away from academic study (Lashley, 1980; Cashmore, 1982). Conversely, and conforming to the prevalent stereotype of the non-sporting South Asian, many South Asians have been channelled towards academic study and away from sport.

Furthermore, in addition to channelling of minority groups, there has also been a process of funnelling in operation; whereby young people from particular ethnic groups have been directed towards certain sporting activities and away from others. For example, Afro-Caribbeans have been encouraged to pursue sporting interests in track and field athletics, football, and even boxing; whilst South Asians have been funnelled into cricket, hockey and squash.

V.   A way forward: anti-racist Physical Education

The reality is that multicultural PE does not address racism, and instead focuses on issues concerned with culture — albeit often lacking a full socio-cultural context for so-doing. But as Godfrey Brandt (1986) indicates, it is naively optimistic to concentrate on culture and hope that racism will go away. Indeed as I have argued above, the opposite may in fact be the case. Hence my concern here with an explicitly anti-racist approach to PE, that confronts overt racism, challenges stereotypes and places the issues of racism at the heart of pedagogy and practice. In order to do so, I draw upon the work of Godfrey Brandt (1986) more fully, and adopt the framework for analysing the curriculum that he advanced.

(i) The curriculum

In view of the damaging stereotypes that exist about certain cultural groups, it seems clear that a reappraisal of current curricular content is both desirable and necessary. In simple terms, such a reappraisal — as Brandt (1986) suggests — should be an attempt to eradicate ethnocentrism. It is time for the PE profession to rid itself of the fixation with the 'problems approach' to minority groups, and replace it with a recognition of cultural pluralism in tandem with a commitment to the understanding of pupils as individuals. Therefore the profession needs to be disabused of the prevalent and enduring stereotypic notions associated with different cultural groups.

It is perhaps an inopportune time to talk about a re-examination of the PE curriculum, especially given the amount of work and endeavour that has gone into the preparation of the PE in the National Curriculum documentation at its various stages. But in view of Maggie Semple's (1992) comment [as much advocacy as comment, perhaps: see pp. 41–42 in Margaret Talbot's article in this volume] on the centrality of the principle of equal opportunities in the deliberations of the National Curriculum Physical Education Working Group, it is surprising that there is not a more forthright statement about the need to confront inequality:

> We are using the term cultural diversity to embrace the racial, ethnic, cultural and social and religious heritage brought by children to physical education. These factors give rise to a range of shared identities which provide rich opportunities for physical education to be more multi-cultural. However, they **may also** focus on prejudice, stereotyping and exclusion — which must be challenged. (DES & WO, 1991: p. 58; emphasis added)

Moreover, it is quite clear that access does not equate with opportunity, and the failure of PE to deliver *real* equality of opportunity to all ethnic groups is a cause for real concern.

It is apparent that it is in 'games' (rather than other areas of the PE curriculum) that stereotypes are perpetuated and reinforced most strongly. Robin Grinter (1990: p. 217) expands on this proposition suggesting an innovative alternative to current practice:

Competitive team games as group activities often reflect the divisive effects of these stereotypes. The power of these stereotypes where they have not been questioned demands a quite fundamental reassessment, and a restructuring of PE and sport onto a more individualistic basis from which to explore the reality of differences and skills behind the stereotypes.

The prevalent stereotypes associating particular ethnic and cultural groups to particular levels of competence in specific sporting activities, however, are not necessarily negative. Some are very positive, but because of the flawed logic of ascription to stereotypes upon which they are based, these must be confronted and challenged just as strongly as those that are founded on more negative assumptions.

(ii) Curriculum material

If the PE curriculum is to be reappraised in the way that is necessary, the material and balance of the curriculum must be subjected to close inspection and scrutiny. Brandt (1986: p. 131) posits that:

> It seems clear that materials used ... must reflect our diverse society and in a positive light. They must relate to the experience of the pupils while aiding the transition or extrapolation to a global perspective. They must also be the basis for challenging the stratification and inequitable distribution of society's 'neutral' to the notion of material which can be useful in challenging inequality, injustice and in challenging racism.

There are two further implications from Brandt's analysis. First, that cultural neutrality in the curriculum is impossible to attain. There is a theoretical point here about the notion of neutrality, and it would be difficult to construct an argument advancing a 'culturally value-free' curriculum, since social behaviour and the values associated with it are products of the cultural context in which the behaviour occurs. But with sensitive and imaginative curriculum planning, it should be possible to devise PE curricula that facilitate cultural equality (or at the very least, overtly discourage cultural inequality).

The second implied assertion from Brandt's argument is that cultural equality through PE is incompatible with challenging inequality, injustice and racism. Yet whilst facilitating cultural equality in PE, it should be possible — and even necessary — through a culturally balanced curriculum to do all of these things.

Anne Williams (1989, p. 163) notes that:

> A narrowly focused games curriculum may reflect on white middle class culture in contrast to a curriculum which introduces children to a variety of game forms and in so doing offers **something** with which children from many different cultures can identify. [Emphasis added]

The important point is that it would be an impossible (not to mention soulless) task to design a PE curriculum in which all activities were culturally neutral in themselves. (Indeed such an approach would attempt to disregard the cultural context in which activities are pursued, and would assume some sort of social void in which sport could take place.) But a package of activities that created a culturally balanced curriculum should be much more possible. To extrapolate Williams' suggestion, the entire PE curriculum should offer *something*, though not everything, with which children from many different cultures can identify. Furthermore, if the PE curriculum content has been sensitively planned, the sense of identity experienced by one particular ethno-cultural group should not occur at the expense of others.

(iii) The 'hidden' curriculum

Many of the institutional procedures of the organisation and administration of PE are potentially racist (Rattansi, 1992). The widespread nature of these subtle forms of discrimination is clearly evident from Bayliss' (1983, 1989) analyses of the 'problems approach' to PE; and for many of the so-called 'problems', there is an explanation that has its basis in the inherent racism of the hidden curriculum.

There is, for example, "indirect discrimination" in the compulsory nature of PE clothing (Rattansi, 1992: p. 23); and also in the "procedures and expectations" of the physical educator (Williams, 1989: p. 169). These too are matters for re-examination and re-evaluation. In order to combat this type of inherent inequality, the hidden curriculum must be made explicit and accountable so that racist practices can be identified, understood and deconstructed.

VI. Concluding comments

It is clear that many of the experiences that young people from minority groups have of sport in the widest sense are often characterised by intolerance and a lack of real understanding. Sports providers and policy-makers have at last recognised the 'gaps in their knowledge' and some attempts have been made to plug such gaps (*cf.* Verma *et al.*, 1992). There is a temptation, however, to adopt white, middle-class and male values in the understanding of sport, and apply typically Eurocentric models to the full range of culturally diverse groups in Britain. It is critically important to recognise that equality of opportunity does not necessarily require equal participation. Neither does it necessarily mean participation at the same time, in the same place, and in the same way.

For physical educators, there are enduring stereotypes, and even prejudices to be challenged; and as the current generation of black professional footballers is finding, this is likely to be a slow process (*cf.* BBC TV, 1991; C4 TV, 1991). When prejudices become the basis for conventional 'wisdom', they are not easy to shake — despite the weight of evidence. It is true that there is an increasing awareness of the issues that face PE in a culturally pluralist society; and it is also true that attitudes are beginning to change. But it is not yet the time for the profession to step back in self-congratulation and watch as the process of greater equity in PE and sport develops. On the contrary, it is now time to redouble efforts in an attempt to accelerate the rate of change. To this end, an explicitly anti-racist approach to PE is advocated here.

The key principle that underpins the whole of the discussion above is that all pupils should experience genuine equality of opportunity in PE, and all pupils must be granted real dignity in a climate of mutual and general respect. At the risk of over-simplifying the situation, it is vitally important that particular individuals and groups are not oppressed in any way because of their cultural values, ethnicity and physical appearance. The main thrust of my argument is that whilst multicultural PE might be well-intentioned, it seldom delivers what it intends to. Moreover, it fails to confront the disrespect and loss of dignity that is a product of the racism that permeates sport generally.

The main difficulty in the adoption of an explicitly anti-racist approach to PE, however, is that 'race relations' is a sensitive area. The rhetoric of anti-racism is often the language of conflict and confrontation, and people are often quite understandably offended by assertions that they are racist. Grant Jarvie's (1991) article entitled 'Ain't no problem here' points out the view taken by many sporting bodies about their treatment of minority groups. In my own research I was surprised (though I shouldn't have been) by the number of people who prefaced their remarks to me with the words: "I'm not racist but...", and then proceeded to recount any number of stereotypes, factual inaccuracies and worse.

Indeed people engaged in bringing these issues to the fore-front of collective public consciousness are often treated with suspicion and hostility. There is a view that anti-racist policies (and those who espouse them) 'stir up more trouble than they cure'. Daphne Griffith (1988) quite correctly dismisses such a view as ill-informed and offensive, but some sections of the community still believe it.

The reality is that racism is a matter for white people to address, though the symptoms of it are experienced by minority groups. This is a bitter pill for some people to swallow, and typically some white people reject many of the issues raised by anti-racists, claiming one of two things.

First, that "It's all a lot of fuss over nothing"; and there can be great difficulties in convincing the people that hold this view that their position is problematic. The issues of racism and anti-racism are very clearly not a lot of fuss over nothing, but very often white people can not (or will not) appreciate them, and/or further appreciate how certain other people are affected by them.

To shed some light on this position, it is important to recognise that it is not necessary to experience a phenomenon to understand it. (As a colleague once reminded me "I've never been to the North Pole, but I know it's bloody cold!") Neither is it necessary to have experienced a phenomenon in order to empathise with those that have. There may be many issues that white people do not 'experi-ence' themselves[5], but that does not prevent them from recognising that there are issues, and showing respect to those who suffer or are offended by them.

The second response of many white people to the issues raised by anti-racists is that: "I treat everyone the same". The adoption of a colour-blind approach to issues of equal opportunities generally, and 'race' and ethnicity in particular, is also fundamentally problematic, for quite simply people are not 'all the same'. There are, of course, complex political (and Political) concerns with regard to the concepts of 'affirmative action' and 'positive discrimination'; but these need not concern us here. The real point is that recognition of cultural diversity is necessary to offer real equality of opportunity. For it is only when diversity is acknowledged that many of the crass assumptions about the sport-ethnicity relation can be challenged or avoided. It is also essential to appreciate that certain groups in society suffer from multiple disadvantage, that their access to opportunity is restricted, and that their needs can only be understood in the context of these disadvantages and restrictions. To treat everyone the same is to disregard these fundamental facets in the lifestyles of many different groups of people.

It is time, however, that physical educators 'grasped the nettle'; acknowledged that current practice in physical education is, in effect, denying real equality of opportunity to all pupils. An anti-racist approach to PE, if implemented with tact and sensitivity, would significantly alter for the better the experiences of many otherwise oppressed individuals from all sections of Britain's minority populations.

Notes

1. I would like to express my thanks to Barry Copley, John Evans, Pauline Fancourt and Margaret Talbot for their contributions to stimulating and lively discussion when a version of this paper was first presented; and to Lesley Lawrence for her comments on an earlier draft. The final product is, of course, my own responsibility.

2. I am not suggesting here that there is a constant dilution of cultural values with successive generations. Rather, there are certain 'cultural sites' that may become less important. My point is that for many second and third generation South Asians, traditional cultural dance forms are examples of this.

3. The empirical findings reported here were gathered in collaboration with the Greater London and South East Regional Sports Council. Pseudonyms have been used throughout.

4. Cashmore's early work in this area is concerned exclusively with black sports**men**, and this is one aspect of the study to which Carrington (1986) draws attention in a perceptive critique. A second key point is that Cashmore's sample is atypical insofar as it is a collection of elite sports performers, and therefore not representative of the wider population of black people. The fundamental issue that Cashmore does not address, is the effect of the racism experienced by his sample upon a more 'typical' population of black people.

5. There are occasional moments when the roles are reversed, and such moments can be very enlightening for those that experience them. Former England football captain Bryan Robson explained:

   "Just this week [on the way to a European Cup Winners Cup tie in Poland], Paul Ince was sitting on the coach and he's going: "You know Danny's [Wallace] not here, and Viv's [Anderson] left the club, and I'm sure I'm the only black in Poland at the moment!" And until he said it I hadn't even thought about that. But obviously something had clicked in Paul's mind ... And there's only one evening I can remember, where we were playing in a 5-a-side competition in London. Lenny Henry had come across to watch the game; and Cyrille [Regis] and Brendan [Batson] and Lenny Henry said they were going to take me out. So, of course, 'yea — let's go out for this night out in London'. The next minute we go into this night-club. We walk in this club, and it's a black night- club; and they haven't told me that they're taking me to an all black night-club ... And I walk in, and I'm the only white in the place. And the looks I'm getting ... The shoe's on the other foot ... And I'm standing there next to Cyrille, and I'm going: "When you go to the toilet, I'm going to the toilet. 'Cos I'm not going to the toilet without you!!" (C4 TV, 1991)

References

Abercrombie, N., Hill, S., and Turner, B. S. (1984) *The Penguin Dictionary of Sociology*. Harmondsworth: Penguin.

BAALPE (British Association of Advisers and Lecturers in Physical Education) (1990) *Perceptions of PE*. Dudley, BAALPE.

Bayliss, T. (1983) 'Physical education in a multiethnic society', *Physical Education*. London: ILEA.

———— (1989) 'PE and racism: making changes', *Multicultural Teaching* Vol. 7, No. 5, pp. 18–22.

BBC TV (1990) *Inside Story — The Race Game*. BBC1.

———— (1991) *Black Britain*. BBC1.

———— (1992) *Standing Room Only*. BBC2.

Brandt, G. (1986) *The Realization of Anti-Racist Teaching*. Lewes: Falmer.

Carrington, B. (1986) 'Social mobility, ethnicity and sport', *British Journal of Sociology of Education* Vol.7, pp. 3–18.

Carrington, B., and Williams, T. (1988) 'Patriarchy and ethnicity: the link between school physical education and community leisure activities', in J. Evans (ed) *Teachers, Teaching and Control in Physical Education*. Lewes: Falmer, pp. 83–96.

Cashmore, E. (1982) *Black Sportsmen*. London: RKP.

C4TV (Channel 4 TV) (1991) *Critical Eye — Great Britain United*. C4.

Cole, M. (1986) 'Teaching and learning about racism: a critique of multicultural education in Britain', in S. Modgil *et al.* (eds) *Multicultural Education — The Interminable Debate*. London: Falmer, pp. 123–148.

Craft, A., and Klein, G. (1986) *Agenda for Multicultural Teaching*. York: Longman.

DES and Welsh Office (1991) *Physical Education for ages 5–16. Proposals of the Secretary of State for Education and Science and the Secretary of State for Wales*. DES/Welsh Office.

Donald, J., and Rattansi, A. (eds) (1992) *'Race', Culture and Difference*. London: Sage.

Field, F., and Haikin, P. (1971) *Black Britons*. London: Oxford University Press.

Fleming, S. (1991) 'Sport, schooling and Asian male youth culture', in G. Jarvie (ed) *Sport, Racism and Ethnicity*. London: Falmer, pp. 30-57.

Fleming, S. (1992a) *Sport and South Asian Male Youth*. Unpublished Ph.D. thesis, CNAA/Brighton Polytechnic.

——— (1992b) 'Multiculturalism in the Physical Education Curriculum: The Case of South Asian Male Youth, Dance and South Asian Dance', *Multicultural Teaching* Vol. 11, No. 1: pp. 35–38.

Gajadhar, J. (1990) 'Dance brings down barriers', *New Zealand Journal of Health, Physical Education and Recreation* Vol. 23, No. 4: p. 16.

Glanville, B. (1990) 'Black players still suffer the taunts of morons', *The Sunday Times* 7th October, p. 2.3.

Griffith, D. (1988) 'When in Rome...' *Education* Vol. 172, No. 22: p. 532.

Grinter, R. (1990) 'Developing an Antiracist National Curriculum: Implementing Antiracist Strategies', in P. D. Pumfrey and G.K. Verma (eds) *Race Relations and Urban Education*. London: Falmer, pp. 217–230.

Hargreaves, J. (1986) *Sport, Power and Culture*. London: Polity.

Hill, D. (1989) *"Out of his skin" The John Barnes Phenomenon*. London: Faber & Faber.

Jarvie, G. (1991) '"Ain't no problem here"', *Sport and Recreation* Vol. 32, No. 5: pp. 20–21.

Kansara, B. (1984) 'Indian dance in London schools', *Impulse* (Summer) pp. 22–24.

Katz, J.H. (1982) 'Multicultural Education: Games Educators Play', *Multiracial Education* Vol. 10, No. 2: pp. 11–18.

Kew, S. (1979) *Ethnic Groups and Leisure*, London: Sports Council and Social Science Research Council.

Lashley, H. (1980) 'The new black magic', *British Journal of Physical Education* Vol. 11, No. 1: pp. 5–6.

Lawrence, E. (1981) 'White sociology, black struggle', *Multiracial Education* Vol. 10, No. 1: pp. 3–17.

Leaman, O. (1984) 'Physical education, dance and outdoor education', in A. Craft and G. Bardell (eds) *Curriculum Opportunities in a Multicultural Society*. London: Harper & Row, pp. 210–222.

Leaman, O. and Carrington, B. (1985) 'Athleticism and the Reproduction of Gender and Ethnic Marginality', *Leisure Studies* Vol. 4, No. 2: pp. 205–217.

McFee, G. (1994) *The Concept of Dance Education*. London: Routledge.

McNab, T. (1990) 'The Race Debate', *Athletics Weekly* 23rd May, p. 12.

Mullard, C. (1985) 'Multiracial Education in Britain: From Assimilation to Cultural Pluralism', in M. Arnot (ed) *Race and Gender*. London: Pergamon, pp. 39–52.

National Curriculum Council (1990) *The Whole Curriculum*. London: NCC.

Rattansi, A. (1992) 'Changing the subject? Racism, culture and education', in J. Donald, A. Rattansi (eds) *'Race', Culture and Difference*, London: Sage, pp. 11–48.

Semple, M. (1992) 'Cultural diversity, physical education and dance', *British Journal of Physical Education* Vol. 23, No. 2: pp. 36–38.

Todryk, D. (1988) ILDTA Conference Speech — 'Multiculturalism and dance', *Impulse* (Summer), pp. 20–21.

Troyna, B., and Carrington, B. (1990) *Education, Racism and Reform*. London: Routledge.

Verma, G.K., MacDonald, A., and Darby, D. (1991) *Sport and Recreation with Special Reference to Ethnic Minorities*. Manchester: University of Manchester.

Williams, A. (1989) 'Physical Education in a multicultural context', in A. Williams (ed) *Issues in Physical Education for the Primary Years*. Lewes: Falmer, pp. 160–172.

Wilson, N, (1990) 'Blacks Playing Racists' Game', *The Independent* 2nd May, p. 30.

FEMININITY, PHYSICAL ACTIVITY AND THE CURRICULUM*

Beverley Miller
Thomas Bennett School, Crawley, Sussex

I.   Introduction

This paper outlines the methodology and some of the results and conclusions of an investigation into teen-aged girls' perceptions of femininity, particularly in relation to themselves and also in relation to significant others in their lives, and the effect these perceptions have on their active lifestyles. Interest in the topic arose out of popular images portrayed of girls and women dancing and playing sport where appearance and traditional feminine characteristics seemed to command at least as much attention as the quality of their performance; perhaps it was more acceptable to girls, in terms of feminine image, to dance than to play sport? I wondered what pressures contemporary active school students felt in relation to the influence of various perceptions of femininity.

a)   The interview schedule

The interview schedule was perhaps the most important tool of the fieldwork; it was the key to successfully extracting the relevant information to answer the research question. These were: primarily, *are there conflicts or ambiguities between perceptions of femininity and a commitment to an active lifestyle for teen-aged girls?*; and secondarily, *do students with a commitment to dance have a different perception of femininity from students with a commitment to sport, and what effect do these perceptions have on their expectations?*.

Great care was taken not only to construct the right questions and unbiased cues, but also to ensure that the schedule was logical; 'user friendly' in terms of use of language; logical in sequence; relevant to the students' experience; and interesting. It was important to reflect upon issues raised in the earlier desk study, tempered by the craft knowledge of the experienced PE teacher/researcher. The preferred style of questioning about issues was to immediately elicit examples and anecdotes from the students which expressed evidence of belief or opinion rather than merely unsubstantiated direct opinion. This was possible by carefully designing cues and questions based on a depth of knowledge and understanding of the literature. It proved to be a successful style of interviewing.

b)   The format and conduct of the group interviews

The selected students were grouped in 11 like-minded groups (dance, sport or both dance and sport) of 4–6 students from among those who responded to a questionnaire completed by 346 girls in 2 comprehensive schools in a town in Sussex. Groups of students from the 2 schools were interviewed in their own schools at mutually convenient times. The nature of the interviews was semi-structured. There were definite issues which needed investigating, hence the interview schedule, but at the same time dialogue was important. Semi-structured interviews would allow for both.

The interviews were between 50 minutes and 65 minutes long, varying according to which school I was in, interruptions, punctual arrival of students, and so on. These were conducted in the Spring of 1991. All groups were asked the same questions, except when an issue was particularly relevant to sport or dance separately. The interviews were tape recorded (with the students' permission) as unobtrusively as possible, on a small portable audio cassette recorder. This did not seem to interfere with the quality of the interviews.

II.   Evidence, observations and an analysis of the interview material

A wealth of material was collected both on tape and in extended note form from the 11 group interviews conducted. The task of analysing the material in relation to the research question involved a degree of interpretation on behalf of the researcher, who was in a favourable position to do so. She was confident that the interview schedule had been rigorously cross-referenced with a quality literature review and endorsed by her craft knowledge as an experienced PE teacher. She was also confident that the responses made by the students would allow for systematic analysis and evaluation in terms of the issues.

The design of the group interviews had a remarkably stimulating consequence. The students were able to feel confident enough to express quite personal information and anecdotes. There was an atmosphere of trust and tolerance within each group both between researcher and respondents and between respondents themselves. This was shown by the students' candidness and by the open discussion within each group, often turning the interview into an 'action research' style of investigation with my questions sparking off discussion, cross-questioning and suggestions for change amongst the students.

The group interviews also had the happy consequence of being mutually beneficial. I recognised from the outset that I was setting up the interviews for my own purposes, but was pleased with the unexpected opportunity to pay back the students' interest. Most of the students found the interviews useful in their own personal development and learning. These students do not very often have the opportunity to talk for an hour about themselves and things which are important to themselves (especially dance and sport) and be listened to by an interested adult within a non-threatening, supportive group.

There now follow two examples of many issues raised with the students, showing some of the students' responses and the analysis of them by the researcher.

Issue 1   Activity role models

Family role models are still quite apparent particularly for dancers, although friends are by now far more so. Other members of the family, especially mothers and sisters, were also involved in or keen dancers both in formal and informal ways, although one 'both' respondent admitted regretting giving up dance classes just because her friend left. Male members of the dancers' families were often described as 'sporty' with examples of sports commitments. Interestingly, several Year 12 sports respondents felt their families still encouraged them in sports and that not many of their school friends shared their interest in sport, so they positively sought 'sporty' friends out of school:

> "My friends tend to be related to sport anyway. Not in school because we're looking to the future now we're in the Lower 6th — especially girls. When I say about my friends tend to be sporty, they tend to be boys anyway."

> "Yes, you can tell by the [low] number [of girls] who go to the leisure centre. We're hopeless!" [*conversation between Year 12 sports respondents numbers 002 and 003*]

These two students obviously perceive themselves as different from their own-age girl friends in respect of their sporting interests, but perfectly in keeping with boys of their own age.

The other source of role model investigated was the media's portrayal of sports and dance stars. When asked if the students could name any famous sports people or dancers, there were some interesting, quantifiable results. Firstly, evidence from sports respondents is shown. One group named 14 men and 2 women; another named 11 men and 7 women, naming all the men first; another group named 20 men and 1 woman, although they did name the woman first!; another group named 16 men and 6 women; another group named 11 men and struggled to name 4 women:

> "The one with the long finger nails, Jo someone ... and the other one; the white one ... what's her name? Davies isn't it? And another black runner [suggestions offered] ...no ... she's English, I know that." [*sports respondent number 009*]

There were only 14 individual sportswomen named at all, all tennis players and athletes except 2, a horsewoman and a snooker player. There were 47 individual sportsmen named, from the sports of football, tennis, skiing, athletics, snooker, golf, rugby, swimming and boxing. Gazza, Daley Thompson and Fatima Whitbread were the most often quoted. All sportspeople named appear on television in sports with high media profile. When asked whom they admired the most, very few interviewees picked a woman.

Perhaps the most significant factor arising from this aspect of the investigation was the lack of unprompted consciousness of the overwhelming imbalance of the representation of male and female sports stars. Only one student appeared to notice, without prompting, that there were many more sportsmen being named than women, though recognition of reasons why were forthcoming later:

> "The men get more TV coverage, don't they? Status. Though it depends which sport — swimming doesn't exactly get loads of coverage [argument]." [*sports respondent numbers 003 and 004*]

> "The programme planners reckon that during the week, most women are supposed to stay at home so daytime TV during the week is for women; and therefore at the weekends sport is for the men." [sports respondent number 147]

When the rest of this group were asked if they agreed with this view, they said:

"This may be the case, but I can't agree to that ... I think that's why they do it, but I still don't agree to it. Anyway, they don't put sport on for women on daytime TV anyway; it's childcare and Australian soaps ... Men would be outraged if they showed women playing football on a Saturday afternoon instead of men! [giggles]." [*sports respondent numbers 143-147 inc.*]

Students did however recognise that some progress had been made in the portrayal of women on television, especially newscasting. However, some students felt that certain programmes were still usually presented by women; e.g. breakfast TV and certain programmes by men; e.g. documentaries. TV adverts came in for the strongest criticism of gender role stereotyping, e.g.:

"They're very idealistic; not true to life. You always get the woman doing the washing powder adverts and men doing the gardening. Traditional." [*'both' respondent number 166*]

To summarise, the evidence shown in this section shows that the sports students are aware of the media presentation of women in general and sport in particular, but needed their consciousness prompting and supporting in order to be able to express their understanding. This suggests that their awareness is usually suppressed and that feminism does not come easily to them.

Secondly, evidence from dance respondents in relation to media role models, is shown. It is not the case that the media is seen as such a strong gender-image maker for dance as it is suggested for sports.

When dance interviewees were asked if they could name any famous dancers, many groups struggled to name many. This could probably be explained by the lack of dance coverage on television, the most widely viewed aspect of the media, in relation to sport. They all named Michael Jackson, Madonna and Wayne Sleep and all named one or two contemporary dance companies (such as Phoenix, Images) with whom the students from both schools had recently participated in workshops. There were several inaccuracies in naming famous Russian ballet stars. The 'both' groups admitted to finding dancers much more difficult to name in abundance than sports stars. There was, however, generally a balance of male/female dancers named by most groups.

Since all groups managed to name pop star dancers (although some admitted assuming I would not be interested in 'that sort' of dancer) it can be reliably predicted that these have the strongest influence as role model dancers for these students. Evidence to support this also comes from the fact that many of the dance students take seriously their own disco dancing and take classes and compete regularly. Two students had become disco dance teachers at their school's youth wing and trained the younger students for competitions. Again, a significant feature of the discussion was the lack of apparent consciousness that although students were able to name men and women dancers who had become famous, their own dance experience had been almost entirely female. The 'penny did not drop' without significant prompting. In many respects, this was similar but in reverse to the lack of apparent consciousness held by the sports–players in recognising the male dominance of the media and how that did not match up to their own experience in playing sport. The 'both' groups demonstrated each of these aspects of slowness to recognise certain dissonance, which they could comment on with ease once the 'penny had dropped'.

It would also be relevant to note that the Asian students in the dance interview groups had very different role models throughout their lives to Western students. In relation to dance, their extended family still provided dominant role models. In their families, mothers, cousins, sisters and brothers also danced regularly — sometimes just the males. Muslim women who danced were traditionally associated with prostitution. This was explained by one student:

> "In our culture it's not alright for women to dance or play sport. No-one should really dance, especially women. Men get away with anything in our culture; women don't." [*'both' respondent number 164*]

This student also expressed her dissatisfaction at women's place in her culture, sometimes quite aggressively, several times during the interview e.g.:

> "I've been to Pakistan 3 times — I hated it all the time. It's a bit of a sexist country out there. The girls do the cooking and stuff like that. The city's not so bad but the country's awful." [*'both' respondent number 164*]

This student is having difficulty finding a role identity which she is comfortable with within her culture which is very domineering.

Issue 2   Self image and femininity: physical appearance

When asked what their wardrobes were full of and what they wore mostly, all of the students except 5 initially overwhelmingly reported jeans, jackets and jumpers, leggings and tops, trainers or basketball boots (heels for work) and the occasional skirt for weddings and family outings. Some students added refinements, on reflection, admitting a greater variety e.g.:

"Sometimes I feel I want to dress up and want to wear a skirt [giggles] ... I love dresses though I haven't got one. If I go into clothes shops I try on loads of dresses." [*'both' respondent number 166*]

Also frequently mentioned were items of men's clothing like men's jackets — one sports student said nearly all of her clothes were men's:

"Teenage girls clothes are frumpy in general — skirts and blouses." [*sports respondent number 011*]

Two students wore traditional Asian dress. There was little significant difference in the way sports and dance people dressed except that skirts were least popular, and sometimes hated, amongst sports groups. They were not very popular with any groups, just a few individuals.

There was as much variety in the wearing of jewellery and make up as there were students. Questions about jewellery and make up caused some amusement in one interview since it was against the school rules to wear either, and most students clearly didn't adhere to the rule! These students felt confident enough within the interview to be able not to worry about getting 'told off' for being open about this. Similarly, the students paid varying amounts of time and attention to their hair, either getting rid of it where they didn't want it or styling it where appropriate, although no students were completely unbothered about hair. Comparing sports and dance students' responses, no pattern that suggested a discernible difference between them was to be found.

Questions about their own body image could have caused embarrassment to individuals in a less supportive atmosphere. However, most students seemed able to be open about how they felt in relation to their own bodies, and needed little prompting in recognising and describing gender stereotypes in others and androgyny in themselves. Following initial giggles, the first reaction of someone in every group without exception was to describe themselves as fat e.g. 'flabby — disgusting!', 'fat and ugly!', 'overweight — too many curves', 'fat legs', 'big bum', 'fat', 'plump'. There then followed typically an argument amongst the group as to whether the other students agreed — they usually did not. Then some of the other students ventured more considered evaluation and criticism. Following each ventured evaluation there would be an informal group evaluation as to the accuracy of the statement and sometimes argument. In general, students who had been critical of themselves did not have their self-criticism substantiated by other members of the group. Some typical comments made include:

> "My boyfriend says I'm fat; I'm on a diet. I'm supposed to be 9 stone. In 2 months time I'll be perfect." *[dance respondent number 137]*

> "I haven't got a good figure at all; don't care, I'm not bothered." *[dance respondent number 153]*

> "All people exaggerate, especially the people who don't need to lose weight." *[sport respondent number 147]*

> "My dad calls me pudgy — I think it's a joke but it upsets me." *[sports respondent number 004 (anorexia victim)]*

> "I'm not fat; not thin. But I'm not perfect." *['both' respondent number 024]*

These responses are perhaps fairly predictable given images portrayed especially in the media and perceived expectations from boys of ideal female size and shape and the students recognised the pressure on themselves to conform to the feminine stereotype which they described as not skinny or fat; toned up muscles but not too bulging; 34-24-34 'model' like; decent sized boobs — but not too big to be uncomfortable; e.g. Jane Fonda; not too tall or short; slim ankles, behind and waist; sporty. They did not envy the 'page 3' sexy, busty, curvaceous body image, but had a very clear impression of what they wanted to look like. This was very important to most students, whether they were sportsplayers, dancers or both.

The students had very definite views about muscles on women; that they were desirable and attractive up to the point where a woman looked toned rather than flabby, but developed muscles were 'well out of order' [sic]. Fatima Whitbread was used spontaneously by several students as an example of 'over the top': e.g.:

> "If you're toned and you have got muscles that's alright. But body building ... no ... that's disgusting. I saw it in a magazine. Madonna is acceptable but Fatima Whitbread is a bit gross. She doesn't look feminine at all ... I couldn't see her in a dress!" *['both' group E)]*

Clearly these students' definition of physical femininity was fairly traditionally stereotyped and yet they had given me many examples in the interview of evidence of expectations of gender equality and criticism of incidents of sexism.

This again demonstrates an unconsciousness of feminist values despite being able to fulfil some of the feminist rhetoric.

However, one very physically able, athletic student ventured nervously:

"I want to be really muscly, but boys just think it's disgusting. Muscly legs don't look right in a short skirt." [*sports respondent number 011*]

Everyone agreed that it was not just O.K. but expected that boys should be muscular. In terms of the students' perceptions of femininity, their views on body image showed they felt tremendous pressure to conform to a narrow 'feminine' image, and recognised that pressure came from the media, boys and older members of their families, and felt trapped within the need for conformity as opposed to their own well-being.

III. Summary and conclusion of findings

Despite the differences found in childhood socialisation into dance or sports activities, different leisure interests, and the importance of different role models both at home and in the media, there was a distinct commonality between sports players and dancers with respect not only to their physical self image and femininity but also perceptions of physical femininity in others. Since this was a somewhat unexpected finding, it was even more important to analyse findings as to whether perceptions of femininity alter when sports players participate in sport and dancers participate in dance, in order to tease out subtle ambiguities in a subjective yet unbiased way.

During this phase of the analysis it was found that some sports players revealed a stereotypical view of dance as being 'girlie-girlie', and of dancers as being timid and fragile. Conversely, other sports players and dancers alike respected the right of an individual to participate in almost any active pursuit they liked without drawback to their femininity. However, in practice this was not always the case for sports players due to prejudiced attitudes of peers (especially boys), inability of teachers to cope adequately and practical difficulties which often led the sports players to compromise. There was little support felt from other girls, especially for the Year 12 students, if a girl wished to be committed to sport. In the light of the ambiguity of this negative reinforcement for girls playing sport, it is hardly surprising that many girls felt they needed to compromise their view of femininity (especially when boys were around) in order to be acceptable. The conclusion drawn is that dancers more easily fit into other peoples' perceptions of femininity than sports players.

Sport evoked subtly different emotional experiences for sports players than dance did for dancers. The emotional experiences felt by the sports players were more directly attributed to the sports experience itself, whereas the dancers were more easily transported away from reality into a carefree fantasy state. It could be argued that, to some extent, the emotions sports players felt were more akin to traditional masculinity, e.g. being logical and boisterous; and dancers akin to femininity, e.g. being creative and sensitive. However, this argument 'shoots itself in the foot' when responses from the 'both' groups are analysed. These students are able to feel both sets of emotions in separate circumstances without any ambiguity whatsoever. Indeed, these students balance their sports and dance interests without apparent conflict. What the evidence from these 'both' groups suggests is that femininity has nothing intrinsically to do with the participation of girls in sport or dance. Rather, it is the bigoted attitudes and narrow stereotyped definition of femininity ascribed to by some significant others in their lives, especially boys, which asserts influence over these students. They then compromise their 'femininity' to satisfy others, in order that they may be left in peace to play their sport 'to their heart's content', just at an age when further complication to their self identity is demonstrated to be unhelpful.

*   All the data reported in this study were collected during fieldwork (conducted in 1991) for the dissertation stage of an MA Physical Education course. For consistency in terms of my own use of the data, I have used codes for respondents and response-categories. But how such codes are more widely contextualised is not central to the development of the argument of this piece.

References

Hargreaves, J. (1990) 'Changing images of the sporting female', in *Sport and Leisure* , Vol. 31, Nos. 3, 4, 5.

Lines, G. (1991) Media Interests and Sport Among 14/15 Year Olds: a Study of Gender Differences (unpublished MA Dissertation: Brighton Polytechnic).

McRobbie, A. and M. Nava (eds) (1984) *Gender and Generation*. London: Macmillan.

Scraton, S. (1986) 'Images of femininity and the teaching of Girls' PE', in J. Evans (ed) *Physical Education, Sport and Schooling*. Basingstoke: Falmer Press.

Wimbush, E. and M. Talbot (eds) (1988) *Relative Freedoms*. Milton Keynes: Open University Press.

LEISURE IN PHYSICAL EDUCATION

Lesley Lawrence
Chelsea School Research Centre
University of Brighton

I.   Introduction

In her Workshop presentation, Margaret Talbot listed 16 issues about which physical education teachers should be knowledgable, for example, the School Sport Forum, and the Sports Council's support of school Physical Education. She then made the critical comment that today's physical education teachers were not able to deal with such issues, but were at the other end of the spectrum, having to cope with the reality of teaching. It is the world of such a 'reality' with which this paper is concerned. This paper presents findings and raises issues from research undertaken on the role of leisure in the teaching of secondary school Physical Education in England (Lawrence, 1991). Although data were also collected from PE advisers and pupils, central to the research were the inter-pretations and perceptions of practising teachers — what was *their* reality, in a time of changing and increasing demands? Whilst one of the main outcomes of the research was a clarification of PE teachers' professional leisure aims and practices, determining how these leisure aims and practices were shaped by reality was as important.

After presenting some background to the research and briefly outlining the data collection stages, two main questions will be addressed:

1.   Does leisure have a role in Physical Education — in other words, how important is a leisure role in the subject?

2.   What is the nature of the leisure role in Physical Education?

A few possibly contentious questions will then be raised when considering some issues relating to the conflicting roles of 'PE *for* leisure' and 'PE *as* leisure'. The conflict between a leisure role and the academic/educational role in Physical Education will be raised. Has PE, for example, educational value in its own right, or is it to be seen as compensation or re-creation for the academic rigours elsewhere in the school? The phrase Tony Veal uses, of leisure and education being "uneasy bedfellows" (Veal, 1987: p. 79), shows succinctly that things are not straightforward when examining leisure in an educational context. (Many of these questions and issues relating to the role of leisure in education were continually raised throughout the research and while some are covered here, for fuller coverage, see Lawrence, 1991).

II.   Background to the research

While the debates are obviously still continuing, in the late 1980s the National Curriculum proposals for Physical Education were causing critical questioning and evaluation of many aspects of PE philosophy and practice in schools in England. There was concern over the survival of the subject in an age of educational accountability, leading to numerous calls to justify the subject's place in the secondary school curriculum (Tozer, 1986; Parry, 1988; Gibbon, 1989; Viant, 1989). Parry (1987: pp. 243–4) used the strong phrase "chronic problems of self-definition", and advocated "a fresh view of the concept of PE, its aims and justification". Although very little empirical evidence existed specifically on leisure aims and practices in PE, this was nevertheless one area which was being highly criticised. Particular criticism was levied at traditional leisure practice as being non-educative in what has been called the 'age of accountability'. School-based leisure programmes were also criticised and in both, the concern was with the recreational nature of programmes (e.g. by Borrett, 1982; Hendry, 1986 [*re* schools in Scotland]; Sleap, 1987; and Williams, 1987).

To rectify the shortage of data in Physical Education, the initial aim of the research was to build up a comprehensive picture of the situation as regards PE teachers' leisure aims and practices — and hopefully when doing so hypotheses would be generated for investigation in a second phase. The first phase of the research therefore, consisted of an extensive questionnaire mailed in May 1988 to secondary school PE teachers in 6 Local Authorities in England on teachers' leisure aims and related aspects: from 61 schools, 165 teachers' responses were analysed. To rectify the notable bias in previous physical education surveys (Underwood, 1983; and PEA, 1987) towards the head of department and thus the male teacher, there was a relatively even spread between assistant teachers and heads of PE departments and between male and female teachers.

The questionnaire survey proved invaluable in identifying general patterns and relationships, but did not address the contextualisation of teachers' views and teachers' responses in the light of their working situation. In addition, there was a need to examine teachers' interpretations and understandings, their reasons for what ended up as different leisure practice priorities and for what appeared to be a common leisure aim. In the case-study phase which followed, data were collected from 6 teachers in their natural setting (from interview and observation). Following this, three main elements were identified in a model of 'understanding teachers' different practice emphases': the teachers' working situation, the criticality of career and the nature of the key to the subjective meaning of leisure. While these three were primarily viewed as independent factors, a tentative connecting thread was found to be the teachers' perceptions of their work.

III. The role of leisure in physical education

The role of leisure in Physical Education can be examined on the basis of these qualitative and quantitative data bases. The findings from both phases of the research clearly confirmed the view of the existence of some form of leisure aim in the teaching of Physical Education (all teachers bar one had a leisure aim). Just over 60% of the teachers considered that their leisure aim played a part equally in curricular and extracurricular time. (For 23% of the teachers, it was mainly in curricular time, but also in extracurricular time; for 13%, it was mainly in extracurricular time, but also in curricular time.) When asked to describe their leisure aim, two aspects were striking and featured in the majority of cases: the aim was to do with participation in sport/leisure; and some reference was made to a time period. Teachers' descriptions of leisure aims were found to be similar — primarily that pupils would participate or continue to participate in sport/physical 'leisure' activity after leaving school.

The findings raised doubts, however, that this leisure aim necessarily equated with the oft-cited phrase, 'education for leisure', an assumption often made in the literature. Teachers had been asked if they thought that education for leisure was a 'commonly held' aim of PE teachers as claimed in a PE journal article (Williamson, 1987). In fact, more than one third of the teachers considered that it was not a common aim of PE teachers and almost half of the teachers expressed concern over the phrase 'education for leisure' — many found it vague and difficult to understand. One adviser who had completed a questionnaire in a preliminary phase of the research contended that "education for leisure within the context of the PE programme is an unfortunately misunderstood concept". It could be suggested that the teachers preferred other types of 'leisure aim' descriptions not necessarily through a condemnation of whatever 'education for leisure' might be, but partly because of the apparent lack of clarity over its exact meaning. Another explanation could be that there is a conflict of interest between the traditional notions of education, schooling and the subjective connotations of the word 'leisure' in particular, the association with choice/freedom. A number of the teachers were unhappy with the inclusion of the word 'education'.

Moving now to consider teachers' leisure practice, the literature points to three general areas of practice, all of which were identified by the teachers:

1. *the structure of the PE programme itself*: for example, with as wide a range of sports and physical activities as possible. This is particularly expressed in the form of some options scheme in the senior years with the choice element playing a prominent role;

2. *the facilities and opportunities to participate*: for example, community links with clubs and facilities, school extracurricular clubs. The most popular type of leisure practice identified by the teachers was, in fact, that relating to clubs outside of school. The teachers perceived their role as facilitating and encouraging pupils to join such clubs where they could participate in their chosen sports;

3. *the nature of the PE experience itself*: for example, as being enjoyable, and satisfying. This last area of practice might either be aimed at making the experience enjoyable, satisfying and motivating as a strategy to promote future activity — as a means to an end; or merely aimed at encompassing the notion of 'PE as leisure' — enjoyable and allowing a degree of freedom possibly acting as a break from the more academic subjects in the curriculum.

From the survey and case-study data, however, this basic, traditional stereotype of leisure practice, implicit in the PE literature, was not found across the board, and seems to misrepresent the reality of leisure practice in a number of ways.

First, the range and variety of practice in PE departments seem to be underestimated — there was notable variance in the way that an apparently common leisure aim was being translated into practice by teachers.

Second, although there were many common types of practice identified, the basic, traditional stereotype of practice fails to account sufficiently for individual differences in practice between teachers; different priorities and emphases were clearly identified in the case-study phase of the research. The strongest impression from this phase was of individual differences and the complexity of influences on practice. This individuality supports Ward and Hardman's suggestion in the late 1970s, following their research on male PE teachers' roles, that there is more individuality in the way teachers go about their work than is generally realised (Ward & Hardman, 1978).

Third, the traditional stereotype omits what one of the case-study teachers referred to as 'progressive' leisure practice, namely, the area of health-based Physical Education and of the health benefits of participation. This case-study teacher emphasized the 'continued doing'. He said:

> "...and then we come back to this business of leisure ... what are you going to do when you leave school ... you know — we're trying to make you aware of the benefits of exercise so that when you do leave school you will keep walking the dog; you will keep riding your bike; ... because you know that some form of exercise is beneficial to you." [CT, male, overall head of department in a school in the north of England]

The assumption underlying this form of progressive practice is that participation will continue if pupils understand the value of health, of exercise in life.

Perhaps of greatest consequence is that the literature tends to de-contextualise practice, thus failing to account for, or understand, the teachers' reality and the extent to which practice is shaped by the working situation. To give an example, the leisure practice of one of the case-study teachers (LF, a head of girls' department in a large comprehensive in the midlands) was greatly influenced by the nature of the pupil population — by the increasing number of Asian girls she was teaching and the knock-on effects of this; she was also having to contend with curriculum cuts in PE; lack of time in the day (travelling between sites in particular); negative parental attitudes; conflict with the head of the boys' PE department (which in itself would have made an interesting study); her own career aspirations; and her current state of pregnancy. Another case-study teacher (JH, male, assistant teacher in a school in the midlands) found that he had to adapt his ideal practice due to the reality of negative pupil attitudes; being unable to teach mixed PE; and his dissatisfaction with the education system in general.

While all the case-study teachers were working within the confines of a school setting and towards similar leisure aims, it was the individuality of settings which differentiated cases where leisure practice was concerned.

Table 1 summarises how the six case-study teachers in the study varied in terms of what they emphasised in practice and what some of the main constraints on their practice were.

It was surprising to find that individuality in leisure practice emerged so strongly given the nature of today's educational climate. Many of the teachers seemed to be left to their own devices within the constraints of the situation, and were involved in a process of "situational adjustment" (Becker, 1971: p. 129). As Locke (1986), in profiling the 'struggles' of seven PE teachers, contends:

> ...each teacher works in a different context, doing different things, struggling with different problems, and producing different consequences for their pupils and themselves. (p. 33)

There was a noted absence of guidance on leisure aims and practices, for example, from the LEA. It was interesting to note, however, that more than half of all the teachers in the study would welcome such guidance; the younger, less experienced teachers would most welcome it. Another consequence of this lack of guidance is that it works to promote individuality of practice.

More generally, subject status — the reality of PE as marginal and a low status subject in the school (see Whitehead and Hendry, 1976; Sparkes, 1988; Templin, 1988) — and resources were clearly identified as the two major influences constraining all the case-study teachers' practice. Lack of time emerged as particularly constraining, both in terms of the demands placed on the teachers in the day-to-day business of teaching, but perhaps more critically where leisure practice is concerned, in the erosion of time and inadequate curriculum allocation to the subject. One disturbing finding was that several of the teachers felt they lacked time to discuss and address properly the leisure aspect of their teaching, indeed many aspects of their teaching. Significantly, some teachers, due to the reality factor, felt that they were also unable to give their leisure aim its due importance.

This brings us now to consider the importance of a leisure aim. Perhaps one of the most revealing findings, aside from the variety of practice, was the high level of importance given by teachers to their leisure aim. This was a higher level of importance than might have been expected given findings from the Physical Education Association in 1987 (PEA, 1987). A decrease in importance of the

Table 1: Leisure Practice Emphases / Constraints

TEACHER IDENTITY /STATUS /GENDER	CAREER AGE-PHASE *	PRACTICE EMPHASES	KEY REASON(S) FOR EMPHASES ADOPTED (relating to working situation /career)	CONSTRAINTS ON PRACTICE
CT (Overall head) Male	30-40	ACTIVITY/ HEALTH-BASED	Dissatisfaction with the quality of the PE product (own and pupils); career move thwarted	Other PE staff/ subject staff resisting change and expansion
NY (Assistant) Female	28-33	ENJOYMENT-BASED OPTIONS SYSTEM	In Department aims - settling into school; applying for HOD post at other local school	Reduced programme - staffing, time and charging
CU (Overall head) Male	40-50/55	OFF-SITE OPTIONS/ EXTRA-CURRICULAR	Teaching older pupils; girls not 'getting much' from PE programme	Finance; lack of professionalism of others; the changing nature of school PE
LF (Girls head) Female	30-40	ATTITUDES/ EXTRA-CURRICULAR HABIT FORMING	Consequences of changing pupil population to 80% South Asian	Lack of time; parent attiudes; pregnancy (own); conflict with Head of Boys dept.
RD (Joint head) Female	40-50/55	LOCAL FACILITY BASED	Outdoor facilities loss; local Sports Centre; reduction in extra-curricular role; pupils' lack of confidence	Loss of PE time to achieve basics
JH (Assistant) Male	21-28	ADAPTED KNOW-LEDGE-BASED (SOCIAL)	Professional train-ing/experi-ence in W. Germany; 'poor' pupil attitudes to learning	Negative pupil attitudes; lack of mixed PE; Education Sys-tem in general

(Source: Lawrence, 1991)

* Career-age phase of teachers (see Sikes *et al.*, 1985) is used here as an alternative to age of teachers — it was found to be more influential in understanding teachers' leisure practice.

leisure aim had been inferred when the PEA compared their own survey findings from a 'ranking of aims in PE' question with findings from a supposedly identical question in an earlier survey (Kane, 1974). Yet, significantly, for many of the teachers in a study which investigated this issue in much greater depth (Lawrence, 1991), the leisure aim had increased in importance since starting to teach the subject (for 73% of teachers). Many teachers regarded leisure's place in society as changing — for example, becoming more important, receiving a higher profile in society — and their leisure aim in their teaching had subsequently increased in importance. The leisure aim was thus found to be important, and for some teachers it was the most important aspect of their teaching. It should be pointed out here that the level of importance was found to be a function of pupil age: the role leisure plays is stronger with the older pupils.

The reality factor kept emerging however to suggest that the importance rating could be even higher. For example, as a male, assistant teacher revealed:

> "It becomes difficult to make this aim a priority when dealing with such large numbers, shortage of equipment, space etc. It is important, but not as much as I would like."

An overall head of department said:

> "I feel I would like to make it [the leisure aim] much more important, but longer term considerations are overtaken by 'day to day' routines and tasks."

Certainly then, where the teachers in the study were concerned, leisure has a role in the school PE curriculum and an important one at that. The leisure aim would seem to be more than a mere by-product of other more important aims in PE e.g. physical skill and physical fitness or non-essential as some would argue (e.g. Wright, 1981; Tozer, 1986). Yet, the importance of a leisure aim from the practising teachers' perspective is certainly not reflected in the PE literature. With a few exceptions, and even then these tend to be the community-related initiatives involving partnerships with outside bodies and often initiated by the partner, the role of leisure in Physical Education does not seem to be a priority and is underestimated in the literature. As noted (Lawrence, 1991), it seems that just as some of the teachers in the study were revealing other priorities (many of a pragmatic nature such as coping with the reality of teaching and changing/ increasing demands), the profession's literature is preoccupied with other, less traditional aspects of the PE teacher's work: innovations, assessment, the development of examinations, and latterly, the National Curriculum (with relatively little evidence of any depth consideration of a leisure role).

It is possible of course, that the leisure aim is seen as important, but worryingly, is taken-for-granted in the profession — the implication being that this traditional area of the PE curriculum will 'take care of itself'. In the discussions in the literature relating to PE and the National Curriculum, there seems to be a policy of attaching the label 'education for leisure' to a particular section of the curriculum — the latter part of pupils' school careers (e.g. McConachie Smith, 1990) — and leaving it at that. Yet the findings and implications from this research point to the inadequacies of labelling the latter stages of a pupil's PE career as 'education for leisure' or preparation for leisure, with the assumption that it will take care of itself.

The findings support the view that PE's role in leisure needs to be structured rather than assumed (Coventry LEA, 1984: 1.08).

IV. Conflicts

There are a number of conflicts being faced by PE teachers relating to the role of leisure in the subject. The evidence from the research confirmed the literature evidence which suggested that teachers are faced with a dual role in their teaching: PE *for* leisure and PE *as* leisure. In other words, on the one hand teachers are aiming to prepare or educate pupils for a leisure time period out of the school context when the pupils will hopefully partake in some form of sport/ physical activity — the leisure aim. At the same time they are promoting the subject, particularly in the upper years, as a 'leisure' experience incorporating some of the subjective qualities associated with leisure e.g. enjoyment, relaxation, freer context. Both act to justify the PE curriculum. These two inter-related leisure roles however, seem to lead to a conflict where teachers' leisure practice is concerned, to a greater degree than is gauged from the literature.

Conflicts on another level were also identified: between the teachers' leisure role and, for example, the increasing pressures many teachers were under to assess, to get pupils involved in examinations etc. The case of CU, in his mid-forties and in overall charge of a department in a mixed-sex school in Greater London, illustrates such conflict. Giving an immediate insight into his feelings about his job is a revealing aim: this was "to get out of teaching at the moment. I don't feel that I am now being asked to do the job that I trained for". CU had many dissatisfactions and his main aim at the time was survival. He was particularly dissatisfied with the people who "say all the things that should be done", but have no idea of the reality (largely the school's senior management and the LEA PE Inspector).

Perhaps CU's overriding dissatisfaction, though, was the changing nature of PE. One resentment keenly felt, and which related directly to his leisure role, was the pressure to make the 'recreative', unpressured (for the pupils) options scheme assessable, with perhaps an award at the end of it. When setting up the scheme this was never his attention. One Deputy Head in particular, he said, was "always asking you to justify what the pupils do and assess it". CU has a 4th and 5th year options scheme, largely off-site, which has been running for just a few years, and is timetabled for the whole afternoon. Although in the 4th year options there was skills teaching and often outside help brought in (for example, a squash coach), his philosophy for the 5th year pupils was "let them play and enjoy it". The only aspects of his job he seemed to derive satisfaction from were this options programme, the extensive extracurricular club programme, and the positive relationship he believed he had with the pupils.

PE in general, and the options scheme, are seen as largely recreational in an exam conscious school; "the kids need some sort of break", a change from academic demands. Just as CU's own leisure activities allowed him to recuperate from the stress of teaching, he seemed to be appreciating a similar role for PE where it allowed pupils to recuperate from the academic nature of the school curriculum. He believed that:

> "There are times within the school day it's becoming so intense for the kids, and this philosophy of everything being geared to exams ... The kids need some sort of time to let themselves go a bit and come and do something they enjoy doing rather than, at that particular time, come in and have more crammed into them to do exams".

CU believed that:

> "With a lot of the kids, we are offering something that they enjoy doing... We may be the only department to them that does that, especially the less able kids".

His resistance to making PE academic, to introducing exams, to assessing options, was understandable in the sense that it would conflict with 'PE *as* leisure' which was so important to him. To CU, introducing assessment in a programme where the underlying rationale is PE *as* leisure strikes a wrong chord.

At the same time, his main aim as a teacher of PE was that at the end of their time in the school there would be something pupils had done in PE that they would continue to do. The conflict between role of 'educator', and feelings over what 'leisure' was, was evident, for example, when he was considering the role of physical fitness in the leisure aim. He felt that it was something that would be encouraged by PE teachers, but that he was quite happy for "people going to play snooker rather than squash". It was their decision.

> "I don't think it's for me to say that they should do this or they should do that. I want them to do something and to do something positive and that is more important to me than rigorous exercise ... at the end of the day it's freedom of choice ... but on the other hand we as PE teachers have got to encourage the health aspects so they know what is best for them, and then it is their choice".

In a sense, the teachers' dilemma is summed up in the phrase 'productive relaxation'. This was a phrase used by one female assistant teacher in the survey phase of the research. Her leisure aim, which was geared to the present and the future, had increased in importance due to the increased workloads pupils were getting. While the viability of this notion of productive relaxation is a matter of some debate, the teacher believed that "a form of productive relaxation was necessary — now GCSE exams really push pupils — some cannot cope with the work load".

'What balance should there be between education and leisure in the upper school PE programme?' becomes a key question. As a subject in the school curriculum, has PE educational value in its own right, or is it to be seen as compensation or re-creation for the academic rigours elsewhere in the school? Can, and should, PE cater for both? It could be argued that 'PE *as* leisure' has no place within the educational philosophy and remit of contemporary schooling. While there are merits in providing a solely recreational options scheme which would offer some pupils relative freedom, enjoyment, a break from the academic diet in the rest of the curriculum, many would argue that today's reality dictates that non-serious and/or non-educational PE as leisure may not be justifiable.

Perhaps both the critics and PE teachers are trying to satisfy 'educational' and 'leisure' criteria at the same time? Where critics are concerned, teachers are failing, particularly with regards to the former and there is concern over the image of the subject, of particular concern when this relatively low-status subject is in competition for curriculum time. The consequences of a non-educational approach have been broached by many (e.g. Jagger, 1982; Kirk, 1989). Robinson (1990: p. 25), for one, believes that the subject has to examine its "educational validity if it is to avoid the risk of being seen as nothing more than a recreative break from serious education". Yet, as George and Kirk (1988) argue, the 'ideology of recreationalism' actively works against the use of PE for educational ends. From their work with teachers in Australian schools, they believe the 'ideology of recreationalism', "firmly rooted in many teachers' own experiences of physical activity", leads to a "trivialization of the educational potential of Physical Education" (George & Kirk, 1988: p. 153).

> A 'wide range of activities' and 'freedom of choice' for students become the leading ideas in programme planning, and the notion that physical activity can be a medium for educational experience loses out to the idea that Physical Education is a hedonistic, playful break from the more rigorous demands of 'real subjects'. (George & Kirk, 1988: p. 149)

The teacher becomes the provider of opportunities rather than educator, and the administrator rather than teacher.

While PE as leisure is prone to criticism for non-educational rationales, doubts must also be raised over its suitability and likely success rate within the school context from the pupils' point of view. A common assumption is that participation in a so-called 'leisure' activity within a PE options programme is indicative that leisure is being experienced. Yet, on the strength of the pupil data from the research, this notion is invalid for many pupils on 'meaning of leisure' grounds. The choice/freedom element is the subjective element in leisure which seems most at odds with the compulsion of school. It can be argued that although pupils may be participating in 'leisure' activities within, for example, a PE options programme, this is still within the compulsory structures of the school — the experience, for many, is not *leisure.*

Also, how appropriate is the school context, a 'learning environment', if part of the aim of the options programme is 'Physical Education as leisure'? There is conflict between learning something in depth or 'working' at something of educational value, and the "hedonistic, instant gratification ideals associated by many with leisure" (Veal, 1987: p. 81). Martin and Mason's argument raises another area of debate: they argue that if leisure is to remain a time of free choice, "people cannot be taught what to do with this part of their lives" (Martin & Mason, 1987: p. 259).

Perhaps there is potential for exploring the merits of another leisure role in PE, namely, PE *about* leisure — leisure awareness basically or what could be called 'educ-awareness of leisure'. The evidence from the research suggested that, with only a few exceptions, teachers' approaches are not about leisure. Pupils are not consciously made aware of the significance of leisure in life; the meaning of leisure; the quality of the experience that goes with participation; or the constraints on present and future leisure. There is little critical awareness of leisure of the type advocated by Kirk (1989) — of the structure and operation of leisure, and of the leisure industry.

V. Conclusion

This paper has examined the nature of and importance of a leisure role in Physical Education, and raised a number of issues. Importantly, it has done so by drawing largely from data collected from practising teachers. It is critical to examine leisure roles and leisure practice within the context of the teachers' present reality. This avoids the accusation of being "out of touch with the everyday reality of a situation" (Threadgold, 1985: p. 214), but far more importantly, prioritises an often neglected voice in debates on schooling. In a period of changing and increasing demands on teachers, constraints and structures within the teachers' world must be taken into account. Any discussion on the role leisure ought to have in Physical Education therefore has to be tempered with pragmatics and with what is appropriate and possible in practice. The teachers' reality should be a critical consideration.

From the quantity of debates and issues that can be raised from a supposedly straightforward topic as 'leisure in education' — some of which have only been touched upon in this paper — Veal's belief that leisure and education are "uneasy bedfellows" (Veal, 1987: p. 79) can easily be supported in the Physical Education context. There are also many complexities in an area which is often taken-for-granted, over-simplified and/or given little priority in Physical Education discussions and policy. Yet, from the findings and issues raised and presented in part in this paper, it is clear that discussion on the leisure role in Physical Education, and in the school context in general, should be prioritised.

References

Becker, H.S. (1971) 'Personal change in adult life', in B. R. Cosin, I. R. Dale, G. M. Esland and V. F. Swifts (eds) *School and Society — A Sociological Reader.* London: Routledge and Kegan Paul in association with Open University Press, pp. 129–135.

Borrett, N.W.G. (1982) Leisure and Education — Towards a Leisure Education Programme in Schools with special reference to Sport and Physical Education. Unpublished MSc dissertation, South Bank Polytechnic, London.

Coventry LEA (1984) *Physical Education for Life — a Framework for Developing the Physical Education Curriculum.* Coventry: Elmbank Teachers' Centre.

George, L. and Kirk, D. (1988) 'The limits of change in Physical Education: ideologies, teachers and the experience of physical activity', in J. Evans (ed) *Teacher, Teaching and Control in Physical Education.* Lewes: The Falmer Press, pp. 145–155.

Gibbon, A. (1989) 'PE and the National Curriculum', *The British Journal of Physical Education*, Vol. 20, No. 1: p. 3.

Hendry, L.B. (1986) 'Changing schools in a changing society: the role of Physical Education', in J. Evans (ed) *Physical Education, Sport and Schooling: Studies in the Sociology of Physical Education.* Lewes: The Falmer Press, pp. 41–69.

Jagger, J. (1983) Foreword, in *The Physical Education Curriculum in the Secondary School: Planning and Implementation* (G.L. Underwood). Lewes: The Falmer Press.

Kane, J.E. (1974) *Physical Education in Secondary Schools.* London: MacMillan Education.

Kirk, D. (1989) *Physical Education and Curriculum Study — A critical introduction.* London: Croom Helm.

Lawrence, L. (1991) *Understanding teachers' leisure aims and practices in secondary school physical education.* Unpublished Ph.D thesis, Brighton Polytechnic.

Locke, L. (1986) 'What can we do? (Profiles of Struggles)', *Journal of Physical Education, Recreation and Dance*, Vol. 57, No. 4: pp. 60–63.

McConachie Smith J. (1990) 'A National Curriculum in Physical Education: processes and progression', *The British Journal of Physical Education*, Vol. 21, No. 1: pp. 226–230.

Martin B. and Mason, S. (1987) 'Making the most of your life: the goal of education for leisure', *European Journal of Education*, Vol. 22, No. 3: pp. 255–263.

Parry, J. (1987) 'Physical Education under threat', *The British Journal of Physical Education*, Vol. 18, No. 6: pp. 243–244.

Parry, J. (1988) 'Physical Education, justification and the National Curriculum', *Physical Education Review*, Vol. 11, No. 2: pp. 106–118.

PEA (1987) *Physical Education in Schools*. Report of a Commission of Enquiry, Physical Education Association, London.

Robinson S. (1990) 'There has to be more to it than that!', *The Bulletin of Physical Education*, Vol. 26, No. 2: pp. 23–26.

Sikes, P. J., Measer, L. and Woods, P. (1985) *Teacher Careers — Crises and Continuities*. London: The Falmer Press.

Sleap, M. (1987) 'Education for leisure: a suggested approach for schools', *Leisure Studies* Vol. 6, No. 2: pp. 167–179.

Sparkes, A.C. (1988) 'The micropolitics of innovation in the Physical Education curriculum' in J. Evans (ed) *Teachers, Teaching and Control in Physical Education*. Lewes: The Falmer Press, pp. 157–177.

Talbot, M. (1992) 'Physical Education and the National Curriculum', presentation to the BSA/LSA Workshop, 6/7 June; this volume pp. 34–64 contains a reworked version.

Templin, T.J. with Bruce, K. and Hart, L. (1988) 'Settling down: an examination of two women physical education teachers', in J. Evans (ed) *Teachers, Teaching and Control in Physical Education*. Lewes: The Falmer Press, pp. 57–81.

Tozer, M. (1986) 'To boldly go where no subject has gone before', *Trends and Developments in Physical Education, Proceedings of the VIIIth Commonwealth Conference on Sport, Physical Education, Dance, Recreation and Health*. London: E.& F.N. Spon, pp. 178–184.

Threadgold, M.W. (1985) 'Bridging the gap between teachers and researchers', in R. G. Burgess (ed) *Issues in Education Research: Qualitative Methods*. London: The Falmer Press, pp. 251–270.

Underwood G.L. (1983) *The Physical Education Curriculum in the Secondary School: Planning and Implementation*. Lewes: The Falmer Press.

Veal, A.J. (1987) *Leisure and the Future*. London: Allen and Unwin.

Viant, R. (1989) 'Physical Education — a justifiable commodity in the secondary school curriculum', *Physical Education Today, Perspectives 41*, School of Education, University of Exeter, pp. 14–25.

Ward, E. and Hardman, K. (1987) 'The influence of values on the role perceptions of men physical education teachers', *Physical Education Review*, Vol. 1, No. 1: pp. 59–70.

Whitehead, N., and Hendry, L.B. (1976) *Teaching Physical Education in England — description and analysis*. London: Lepus Books.

Williams, A. (1987) 'Adolescent attitudes towards aspects of Physical Education and involvement in activity outside school', *Scottish Journal of Physical Education*, Vol. 15, No. 3: pp. 4–12.

Williamson, T. (1987) 'One view of the future', *The Bulletin of Physical Education*, Vol. 23, No. 1: pp. 45–52.

Wright, J. (1981) 'How should Physical Education prepare our school leavers to live as adults in the changing society of the 1980s?', *Physical Preparation for Life from School to Work and Leisure*, PEA Conference Proceedings, PEA, Roehampton Institute of Higher Education, Digby Stuart College, London: pp. 1–10.

THE DEVELOPMENT OF YOUNG PEOPLE'S LEISURE AND LIFESTYLES[1]

Leo B. Hendry
Department of Education
University of Aberdeen

I.   Prologue

Any appeal to members of an audience to catalogue the main features of their own lifestyle will produce a response which captures not just the main features of that particular lifestyle, but also the contradictions within it. When the participants at the 'Education, Sport and Leisure' Workshop (from which this collection stemmed) were asked to list a few key descriptors of their own lifestyles, the response was revealing. Experts on sport and leisure, and on the health-benefits of exercise, listed terms like 'hectic', 'other-directed', 'semi-active', 'frenetic' and 'work-dominated' — all this on a Sunday morning in a prominent national physical education/sport and leisure department!

II.   Adolescent transitions and lifestyles

Lifestyle is a concept or term which captures both the complexity of choices (and the constraints upon those choices) which are characteristic of our everyday life, and the sense of transition which affects these lifestyle choices at various stages in our life course.

The development of young people's lifestyles is bound up with the process of transition towards adulthood. From the physical and physiological changes that herald the teenage years, the adolescent has various psycho- social 'tasks' to achieve. There are at least six 'tasks' to be attempted across the adolescent years (see Hendry, 1983 for elaboration):

(i)   developing a self-identity in the light of physical changes;
(ii)   developing a gender identity;
(iii)   gaining a degree of independence from parents;

(iv) accepting or rejecting family values;

(v) shaping up to an occupational (or unemployed) role; and

(vi) developing and extending friendships.

These six 'tasks are encapsulated in the notion put forward by Erikson (1968) that the chief task of adolescence is identity formation. Yet there are no obvious symbolic 'rites of passage' into adulthood in Western society, so the adolescent's route toward adulthood is not marked out by clearly defined signposts that indicate progress in a desired direction. Within this transition from childhood to adulthood, and within the attempted achievement of these personal and social tasks, three broad elements are discernible: (a) psychological and social changes; (b) educational and occupational developments; and (c) changes in leisure pursuits and interests.

(a) Psychological and social changes

Because there is so much change during adolescence, and these changes require effective coping on the part of the individual, the processes involved in this period of the life span are also likely to be ones needed to respond to challenges throughout adult life. Furthermore, it could be hypothesised that adolescence differs from earlier years in the nature of challenges encountered and in the capacity of the individual to respond effectively to these challenges. If this is correct, adolescence will be the first phase of the life span requiring, and presumably stimulating, mature patterns of functioning and the development of a clear-cut personal and social identity that persists throughout life. Conversely, failure to cope effectively with the challenges of adolescence may represent deficiencies in the individual's self-concept which will have negative consequences for subsequent development. The ways in which young people understand and perceive themselves, their own agency and personality, and their various social situations have a powerful effect on their subsequent reactions to various life events.

With the complexities of modern society, young people can reach physical maturity before many of them are capable of functioning well in adult social roles. The disjunction between physical capabilities and socially approved independence and power, and the concurrent status-ambiguities can be stressful for the self-image of the adolescent. But the fact is that, despite the amount of overall change experienced, most young people are extremely resilient and appear to cope with adjustments without undue stress.

Although for some young people adolescence may be a difficult time, for the majority it is a period of relative stability. Nonetheless, there is general agreement that during the teenage years major adaption has to occur. The transition between childhood and adulthood cannot be achieved without substantial adjustments of both a psychological and social nature; and yet most young people appear to cope without undue stress. (Coleman & Hendry, 1990)

Coleman (1979) has suggested that concerns about understanding gender roles and relationships with the opposite sex decline from a peak around thirteen years; concerns about acceptance by or rejection from peers are highly important around fifteen years; while issues regarding the gaining of independence from parents climb steadily to peak beyond sixteen years and then begin to tail off. Such a theory provides some resolution between the amount of disruption and crisis implicit in adolescence and the relatively successful adaptation among most adolescents. Those who, for whatever reason, do have more than one issue to cope with at one time are most likely to have problems of adjustment.

We believe that most young people pace themselves through the adolescent transition. Most of them hold back on one issue, while they are grappling with another. Most sense what they can and cannot cope with, and will in the real sense of the term, be an active agent in their own development. (Coleman & Hendry, 1990)

(b)   Educational and occupational developments

The educational trend of the 1980s and into the 1990s to equate preparation for life with preparation for economic roles may well be a reaction against the equally simplistic cries of the 1960s for education for leisure. Both demands rest upon a false dichotomy between work and leisure, and an unreal distinction between the prerequisites for pleasure and responsibility in these two areas of life. Jonathan (1982), in discussing life-long education, argued that: 'Preparation for life cannot be seen as a choice between 'educating for leisure' or 'training for work''.

While a proportion of adolescents go on to higher education more than half of British young people leaving school do so at the minimum school leaving age of sixteen years (Raffe & Courtenay, 1988). National data sets confirm that girls and those with more academic qualifications continue in secondary education longer than others. The association between duration in (secondary) education and post-school careers however suggests that 'more' does not necessarily mean 'better' in terms of life chances. A combination of structural arrangements within the youth labour market and wider normative constraints, especially in relation to gender, serve to mitigate the potential effects of additional years in school. Thus for some young people the opportunity to take up an apprenticeship is forfeited in staying on at school an 'extra' year and on leaving school such youngsters find themselves in a weaker position in the labour market as a result.

Almost paradoxically, the British government's responses to youth unemployment have addressed an alleged mismatch between school-leavers' capabilities and occupational requirements in the service and high-technology sectors which, it is claimed, contain the best hopes for future job creation. Hence the case for Britain's Technical and Vocational Education Initiative, the Youth Training Scheme (now called Training, Enterprise and Education), and the Sixteen to Eighteen Action Plan. However, educational solutions to the disappearance of jobs for adolescents produce diminishing returns (Bates *et al.*, 1984). These attempts to tighten the bonds between schooling and job requirements and to strengthen young people's vocational orientations seem problematic. Holt has argued that the vocational skills of today may well be outdated for use in future society.

> The fact about tomorrow is that it will be different from today, and will present quite new problems. New problems can be solved only by those with the personal and moral autonomy to interpret our culture — by those who have enjoyed a liberal education. (Holt, 1983)

So employment — and unemployment — have a multi-faceted impact on the life of individuals, involving such diverse matters as self-esteem and income, lifestyle, and leisure pursuits. These may be particularly important in adolescence.

(c)   Changes in leisure pursuits and interests

Leisure activities may be chosen for their personal meaning and for social expression, and these choices are, in turn, coloured by influences such as the family peers, the educational system, the media, leisure promotion industries, and changes in the general social context such as massive unemployment. A crucial point to stress in all this is the way the interplay of factors determining leisure choices varies as the focus of social interests changes across the adolescent years. Thus changes and continuities in the adolescent's leisure preferences and behaviour can be noted. The main factors influencing leisure pursuits proposed by Hendry (1983) are suggested to be age, sex, educational attainment and social class. These are hardly surprising elements, but when linked to the shifting focus of social relationships postulated by Coleman (1979), a framework can be offered to provide insights into a changing and differential pattern of leisure in the teenage years. We would want to argue that this leisure focus generally shifts from adult-organised through casual activities to commercially organised leisure, and that these transitions may occur roughly at the ages when main relationship issues — sex, peers, parents — come into focus. The differential effects of sex and social class can influence this general leisure pattern to produce possible patterns of overlap not dissimilar to those postulated by Coleman. For instance, the earlier physical and psychological maturity of girls underpins their relatively earlier transition toward a focus on peers and casual leisure pursuits, and then toward more exclusive courting couples and commercial leisure provision. Further, Hendry has argued that these differential effects of sex and social class on general leisure patterns can be explained in relation to a dynamic interplay of factors. It is, therefore, necessary to stress the variability among adolescents in aspiration, motivations, attitudes and in the values they place on their leisure interests and pursuits within their developing lifestyles.

III. The development of lifestyles

These transitions in adolescence — in educational and occupational trajectories, in social and leisure roles — all link with the idea of the development of self in adolescence: in other words, the ways lifestyles are created and crystallised. As Coleman and Hendry (1990) stated:

> Increased knowledge of this process of active agency could provide essential information to help answer two key questions: 'What distinguishes the majority who cope with the minority who experience manifest stress during the teenage years?' and, 'What is it about adolescence which makes it different from other stages in the life cycle? In our view the answers to such questions are almost certainly to do with the nature of the transition and the way it is managed.

Wenzel (1982) has defined the lifestyle of an individual as:

> The entirety of normative orientation and behaviour patterns which are developed through the processes of socialisation.

That means that understanding lifestyle is not only gauging behaviour but also includes understanding the values and attitudes of the individual inter-related into a developing pattern of living. These characteristics are also closely linked to the individual's social and physical surroundings, thus lifestyle is related to socio-economic circumstances and the material and other resources available to individuals. As Arro *et al.* (1986) have suggested, lifestyle is the relatively stable pattern of behaviour, habits, attitudes and values which are typical for groups the individual may belong to or wants to belong to. Lifestyles are developed through a process of socialisation and encompass values and attitudes as well as actions and interactions. More importantly, though we can describe the individual as having a certain lifestyle, the concept of 'lifestyle' is embedded in orientation towards others, be they peers, family or workmates. Lifestyle is clearly related, too, to socio-economic circumstances. The ease with which an individual may choose, change or adapt his/her lifestyle will depend on social situation, wealth and status. We can assume then that lifestyle is determined or indicated by three large groups of characteristics:

(a) those related to the person
(b) those related to the immediate surroundings, and
(c) those related to general social and cultural structures.

Thus our understanding of the development of adolescent lifestyles needs to take account of a 'network' of determinants. These are common to all concepts of lifestyles and include the individual with his/her socialisation process and present personality as well as his/her immediate surroundings (family, teachers, friends, workmates, youth leaders, and colleagues). It also includes connections within the social and economic environment. In this way objective conditions and subjective perceptions are contained within one model. In particular the linkages of this network help formulate a better understanding of the development of the constituent elements of lifestyles during adolescence.

IV. The development of young people's leisure and lifestyles

The Young People's Leisure and Lifestyles seven-year research project (Hendry *et al.*, 1993) studied young people's leisure and lifestyles over an extended period. The project was designed to operate at two complementary levels. There was a survey element and this involved a sampling frame of 126 schools to represent a nationwide sample of Scottish young people. The young people involved in the project ranged in age from 10-20 years. An initial questionnaire survey was carried out in 1987 and this involved over 10,000 young people in Scotland and 3,000 from selected areas in North-east England. The questionnaire (in addition to ascertaining biographical data on young people, such as age, gender, school attended and so on), also explored the composition and socio-economic status of families, their religious affiliations, leisure activities and interests, and time spent on leisure within families. An examination of the sports participation and physical activities engaged in by young people and their parents, and of young people's attitudes and reasons for leisure involvement was also undertaken. In addition, investigation into the spending powers of young people, their friendship patterns and their orientations to both their peers, family and adults outside the family formed part of the questionnaire survey. Measures of self-esteem and self-perception were attempted, together with some examination of young people's views of male and female stereotypes. Questions on health were also included, as were some attempts to measure attitudes to school, future occupational ambitions and attitudes to work. Some indications of general health statuses and attitudes to healthy living were examined together with young people's attitudes to a range of social issues including drink, drugs, smoking and relationships with authority figures. This initial survey, to provide a broad and general picture of young people growing up in modern Scotland (and North-east England), was followed by further surveys of adolescents' socialisation and leisure in 1989 and 1991.

The second element in this study was a smaller, more intensive examination of a sub-sample of 250 young people living in eleven different socio-geographical areas of Scotland. This ecological approach was intended to examine some of the implications of social environment on young people's lifestyles and leisure patterns. The areas included in the study have included rural market towns, inner cities, new towns, middle class suburban settlements and so on. The research strategy involved in this aspect of the project has been to meet these young people on at least two occasions each year and, by a variety of interpretative and illuminative research techniques, to start to tease out some of the dynamics and the mechanisms involved in the changes demonstrated in young people's lifestyles and leisure patterns. This has involved the use of leisure diaries, leisure histories or profiles, semi-structured interviews, and the use of photographic material as a stimulus for small group discussions.

The overall purpose of the research project has been to develop an explanatory picture of young people growing up in modern society.

V.   Understanding the development of adolescents' lifestyles

In what ways does the particular approach[2] taken in the Young People's Leisure and Lifestyles project help us to gain some general understanding of young people's developing lifestyles in adolescence? First, any consideration of the developmental context of adolescent lifestyles within modern Britain must start with a consideration of the structure of society itself. Despite dramatic structural shifts in British society in recent years, there is still a profound linkage between social class background and the life chances (and so lifestyles) of young people.

The approach taken in the Young People's Leisure & Lifestyles project using factor and cluster analyses enables us to examine the developmental context of lifestyles during adolescence. In order to focus in some detail on aspects of the adolescent transition, young women aged 15-16 in 1987 are particularly considered. These young women were still at school in 1987, and so we were able to follow them from compulsory secondary education to adult society and the world of work in 1989.

The factors associated with 15-16 year old women can be regarded as the dimensions underlying our 'description' of adolescence for these young people. They are: relationships with female friends and 'the bedroom culture' (e.g. Frith, 1978); life values and priorities; involvement in sport; intended educational or employment trajectories; psychological well-being and adjustment; commercial leisure and boyfriends; family conflict and 'trouble'; and disapproval of drugs and alcohol. Essentially these are the elements which inter-relate to produce the clusters which form the basis for our identification of different adolescent lifestyles (see **Figures 1** and **2**).

If we look at our clusters it is clear that adolescent lifestyles are characterised in terms of social class differences. These differences are an amalgam of the social class of origin (i.e. parental occupation), parents' experience of education beyond school (i.e. parental education), and the type of residential neighbourhood or locality as characterised by the ACORN classification (i.e. parental residence) (Shaw, 1984). These inter-related social and ecological aspects of living conditions produce a clear 'class based' differentiation of adolescent lifestyles. As can be seen from **Figure 1**, clusters 1 and 3 can be labelled as 'working class' while clusters 4 and 5 can be labelled as 'middle class'. Cluster 2 is more varied and can be viewed as a mix of social backgrounds. Brake (1985) has argued that we are born into particular social settings possessing distinct ways of life. Thus young people influence and are influenced by the perceptions, values and behaviours of these social groups. Within this complex pattern of social relations and meanings, individual adolescents begin to form a personal identity and a lifestyle. Also Giddens (1984) has identified locality as a vital social context pertaining to interactions, habits and behaviours by which lifestyle patterns develop. Put simply there are both class based differences and eco-logical differences associated with the development of adolescent lifestyles as Bronfenbrenner (1979) has earlier proposed.

But considerations of social class alone do not account for the five clusters obtained. Differences in lifestyles also emerge within social class boundaries. For example, if we look at these young women's involvement in sport, in terms of class of origin alone, we would find *no* class based differences. Yet it is clear from **Figure 1** that variations in levels of sports participation do exist among the five clusters. These variations only become apparent once we begin to dis-tinguish between different 'working class' lifestyles and different 'middle class' lifestyles. For the two 'middle class' clusters, individuals in cluster 5 are particularly involved in sport — they spend money on sports goods, they are members of sports clubs, attend sports fixtures, and play sport competitively — whereas those in cluster 4 have little interest or involvement in sport. If we had not differentiated between those two groups we would have been in danger of concluding that middle class young women are not particularly involved in sport, and certainly no more so than working class women. In summary, there are clearly 'within social class' differences in lifestyle development, and we need to take account of these in any real understanding of the contexts of adolescent development.

Importantly, some lifestyles are common to both middle and working class young women. For example, cluster 2 seems to fit one archetypal view of adolescent young women as spending a lot of time with a close girl friend, hanging about the neighbourhood in groups, being interested in find-ing a boyfriend, being in conflict with the family, and spending money on

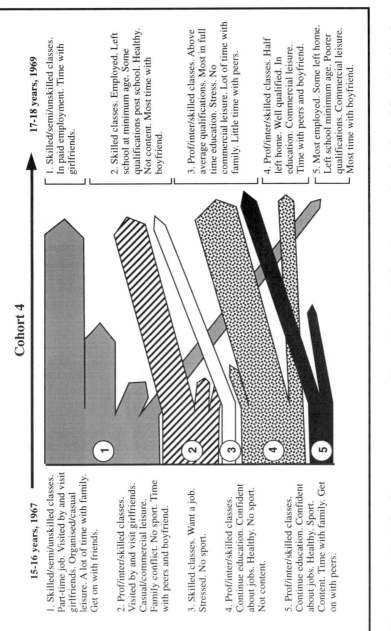

Figure 1:   Results for young women. Description of the clusters obtained and longitudinal connections between them

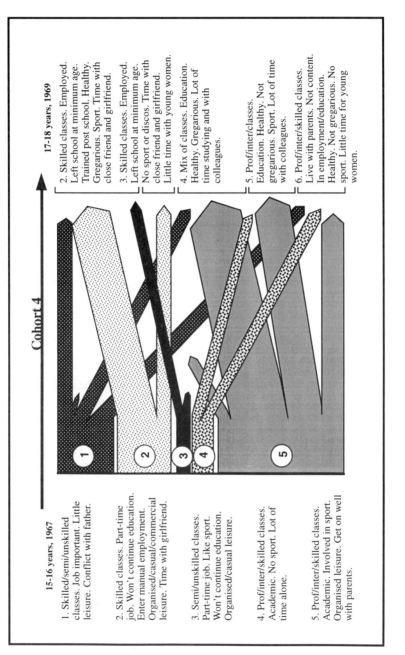

Figure 2:   **Results for young men. Description of the clusters obtained and longitudinal connections between them**

entertainments and fashion. It is interesting to note that this lifestyle pattern cuts across class boundaries in its adherence to 'youth culture' values (e.g. Brake, 1985).

When we look at the longitudinal transitions made by young women between the period when they are still at school (i.e. 15-16 years of age) and when they have left school and moved into adult society (i.e. 17-18 years of age) we begin to note identifiable lifestyles emerging. For young women aged 17-18 years in 1989 there are once again clear-cut middle class and working class clusters, with one small cluster from a mix of social backgrounds (see **Figure 1**). Additionally, from Figure 1 it can be seen that the development of these clusters over time represents an exchange between clusters within social class boundaries, and in terms of fragmentation across class boundaries the exchange is fairly minimal. Between 1987 and 1989 the class basis of these clusterings of young people is relatively stable over time. Thus the migration of individuals from one type of lifestyle to another is predominantly within social class boundaries. For example, young women from clusters 4 and 5 in 1987 move into clusters 3 and 4 in 1989. Hence these groupings of young women are differentiated by their own occupational status and educational attainments as much as by their social class origins. We can conclude that the social context has a powerful impact on their lifestyle development.

Young people in higher education, working youth and those young people on government training schemes or the non-employed do have different lifestyle patterns. Different kinds of experiences help to mould developing lifestyles — there can be pressures in aspiring towards higher education, or in being unemployed, or on a relatively uninspiring youth training scheme, or living in poor housing conditions, or getting involved in drugs misuse. Yet it is necessary to point out that, in general terms, academic and working youth do appear to have 'healthier' lifestyles than those on training schemes, the unemployed or those who are non-employed. Unemployment creates a 'limbo' for some young people in mid-adolescence which restricts their transition towards adulthood in terms of their social and leisure involvements.

When we look at young men in the 15-16 year old cohort in 1987, and again in 1989, we find some similarities with young women's lifestyles — but equally differences emerge (see **Figures 1** and **2**). Somewhat similar underlying factors to those for young women differentiate groupings of young men, and this is equally true of the clusterings for 15-16 year old males. But we see a greater differentiation of lifestyle patterns at 17-18 years of age, and gender differences do emerge. For instance, young women in middle class groupings are more likely to report ill-health and psychological stress, whereas young men of similar social class background and academic standing appear to be less outgoing and gregarious in overtly social ways.

Health-related behaviours such as smoking, drug usage and drinking, together with involvement in sport and physical activities do act as important differentiators in the variations seen within both male and female adolescents' lifestyle development. These in their turn are linked to perceived mental and physical health statuses and this may suggest the development of adolescent lifestyles which have certain important implications for later life.

VI. Conclusions: sport, health and lifestyles

Much of the existing evidence on the relationship between health and active lifestyles is confined to older population samples. In youthful populations good health is the norm, physical ailments are usually short-lived and unlikely to be seen by the individual concerned as the 'beginning of the end'. Even the effects of heavy smoking and drinking do not clearly emerge until early adulthood. Thus young people in the Young People's Leisure and Lifestyles study (Hendry *et al.*, 1993) appeared to perceive themselves as generally fit and healthy. Whilst there were gender differences in perception of physical health statuses — with young women rating themselves less healthy than young men — there were no social class differences based on parents' occupational classifications. Nevertheless, by mid-to-late adolescence the occupational status of young people themselves was associated with significant variations in self-ascribed health status, with those going on to further and higher education (including those staying on at school) and in employment having healthier profiles than those on training schemes, the unemployed or those in non-employed status (for example, housewives).

With regard to self-reported mental wellbeing, similar trends emerged to those associated with physical health and fitness. In addition, young people with organised active and/or sociable leisure interests which ensured peer group interaction and those with positive attitudes towards leisure had better mental health scores. Conversely those with little available leisure time (such as young women who were non-employed and caught up with childcare and housework) and those adolescents who saw themselves having too much leisure time or being bored in their leisure had poorer mental health scores. Various associated social and psychological factors, providing descriptive patterns of healthy and unhealthy lifestyles in adolescence are apparent. These trends develop across adolescence and distinctive lifestyles emerge.

It was clear from Hendry *et al.*'s (1993) findings that young people had reasonably positive views of their physical self and that whilst there were some variations and age trends regarding their views on health matters they were aware of the importance of self-agency in developing a healthy lifestyle. Thus they appeared to operate an internal locus of control. These findings are matched by the work of Thomson *et al.* (1988). In their study of health-related behaviour of school children they found that over 70 per cent of their sample believed that good health was mainly achieved by one's own efforts, was self determined and that 81 per cent considered that participating in sport was an important way to improve health.

Adolescents are particularly associated with risk-taking behaviours. Those of us who work with a range of young people may wonder whether this is a gross calumny resting on a well-established caricature of youth. Some young people, in some areas of their lives at least, seem very little inclined to take risks. Some of the foundation for the caricature may rest in the fact that despite their physical ability to start acting as free agents and the pressure from society to start operating independently as they move into adulthood, adolescents have as little ability as our younger children to foresee consequences, and insufficient opportunities to have learned from experience. This is not to deny, however, that for many young people in their teenage years the desire to seek out thrills will be as real as it was in childhood. As a young child the individual may legitimately seek out physical thrills in the adventure playground or on a funfair ride. Young children enjoy chance-taking in countless playground and indoor games and almost deliberately torment themselves by confronting or creating creatures or situations which horrify and yet thrill them. Once we start to make the journey into adulthood there are fewer and fewer legitimate venues for such thrill-seeking and the ones left open to us as adults often bear more serious consequences. Those who see in the current fad among young people for stealing cars and 'joyriding' only a protest of the under-privileged against those who 'have', deny the very real thrill that such delinquent activities can inspire.

Over the past decade or so, Csikszentmihalyi and his colleagues at the University of Chicago have developed a model of optimal experience. It has also been called the flow model, 'flow' being the word used by interview subjects themselves to describe the experience of intense involvement in some activity — whether it be chess, rock climbing, dancing or performing heart surgery — where there is total concentration, little or no self-consciousness and a sense of self-transcendence resulting from a merging of consciousness with action (Csikszentmihalyi, 1975). The activities which afford such experience must be sufficiently challenging to engage a full measure of the individual's skill, but not so demanding as to be anxiety-provoking. Activities which provide clear feedback, such as those just mentioned, are most likely to be flow-producing. But the matching of challenges and skills is critical. If challenges are greater than skills, anxiety results, while a lack of challenge in relation to available skills is likely to be experienced as boredom. What is certain is that 'flow' in leisure provides a highly vivid climactic set of experiences.

What the 'flow' model does seem to suggest is that certain qualities intrinsic to a variety of leisure pursuits are conducive to mental well-being. Sport, for example, offers advantages in terms of structural conditions conducive to optimal experience, but it appears to fall short with respect to such things as self-expression and individuation (Kleiber & Rickards, 1985). Comparing it with other leisure activities, sport does not offer the intrigue and free interchange of certain casual peer involvements nor the sense of a personal tutorial to be found in one-to-one hobbies (for example, working on cars). Sport in general can be a very positive experience for certain adolescents, but as Csikszentmihalyi and Larson (1984) have pointed out, so too can socialising, eating and travelling in a car. So too, we could add, can stealing and driving away someone else's car!

Thus, various leisure activities can (potentially) provide therapeutic effects and produce sound mental health. Yet little is known of the properties, contexts and motivations which generate emotional stability and positive effects for young people in present-day society. Young people who organise themselves for the purpose of playing games are well-regarded for their potential to create developmentally important experiences in the process (Devereux, 1976). But games are certainly not the only medium around which children and adolescents will organise. The possibility that illegal or deviant activities (for example, drug use) may be among the more attractive alternatives for youth should only be regarded as a challenge to the purpose of identifying and developing the wealth of abilities and interests which adolescents possess.

The psychosocial transitions across adolescence alluded to earlier seem to interact to distinguish particular lifestyles which emerge across the adolescent years. These changing patterns of lifestyle development do not necessarily relate directly to Coleman & Hendry's (1990) focal theories, though it is possible to note a combination of life events, relational issues, values, attitudes and leisure interests which interact as focal theory suggests. This allows us to consider not only social class and gender differences, but also important lifestyle variations within social class boundaries as young people make the transition towards adulthood. Such constellations of factors may be particularly relevant within leisure, and it is possible to perceive lifestyle developments which are differentiated by adolescents' involvement in organised, casual or commercial leisure; by participation in smoking, drinking and drug taking; by those young people who are particularly involved with a network of friends or with a special boy or girl friend, or those who are somewhat isolated and alone; and by those who are concerned about relationships with peers or parents; and by interest and involvement in sports. It is therefore possible using analyses such as those employed by Hendry *et al* to gain clearer insights into the various aspects of attitudes, meanings and behaviours which go to make up more conventional adolescent lifestyles within social class boundaries, and to acknowledge the variations within social classes which produce more 'youth culture' oriented leisure patterns. In this way we may begin to gain a better understanding of the role sports and leisure play in the lifestyles development of adolescents.

As Ingham (1987) has suggested, leisure may be significant in creating opportunities for identity development, social meaning, levels of competence and intrinsic satisfactions in adolescence. This is possible because alternative forms of self-presentation and style can be tried out without dire consequences should they fail to impress. At the same time these individualistic aspects of behaviour are carried out within institutionally defined roles, with relatively predictable behaviours and rules. Adolescents need to learn these skills in planning, self-orientation and organisation in the social and leisure domains as well as in cognitive and work-related spheres in order to develop a clear-cut personal and social identity.

Loss of producer roles, and the inability of education and training to guarantee life-time vocations, make young people more dependent on ascribed statuses, sometimes derived from gender and ethnicity, in establishing adult identities and independence. Thus current trends may also make young people independent of leisure activities and environments to sustain these identities, and to establish and maintain relationships that allow other aspects of the transition to adulthood to proceed despite the impossibility of stepping directly from full-time education to stable employment. Leisure is likely to grow in importance as a source of stability in adults' and young people's lives when most other aspects of society change rapidly, and are seen as being beyond individuals' control. Leisure is likely to become one sphere where people are assured of 'returns on their investments'. Access to conventional leisure of various kinds — sporting, musical, political — can assist young people who wish to preserve conventional life-styles and trajectories. Equally, adolescents who are pioneering less familiar ways of living benefit from leisure environments in which to interact and display their preferred personal and social identities. Leisure can provide opportunities for self-development and the maintenance of self-esteem. It can establish social status and identity and can also provide an opportunity for sociability, relaxation, excitement, independence of action and activity within the developing lifestyles of adolescents making the transition towards adulthood.

VII. Epilogue

Several questions emerged regarding leisure in the discussion of the paper at the workshop. First, how should recognition be given to the fact that youth is not an homogeneous category? Second, how can partnerships be evolved between schools and other agencies in the community, in other words, what is the basis of such collaborations? Third, how do young people get into any particular flow of activity?

At a time in which youth work in some local authorities is the subject of intense debate, and the expanding or at least changing role of the PE teacher is marked and widely recognised if not fully acknowledged, it is essential to remind ourselves of the influence of framing structures and contexts in the socialisation of young people as their particular lifestyles develop. As physical education, sport and leisure professionals debate the pressures and influences of the day, the views, attitudes and life world experiences of young people should not be forgotten. Continuing research on adolescent transitions to adulthood should inform professionals in the field. Nothing is more certain to fail than a professional or policy concern which is insensitive to the realities of the lives of its adolescent clients.

Notes

[1]   This paper which is based on an address given by Professor Hendry at the Olympic Scientific Congress (1992) is presented on behalf of Leo B. Hendry, Janet Shucksmith, John Love and Tony Glendinning, Young People's Leisure and Lifestyles Project, Department of Education, University of Aberdeen. The project is supported by a grant from the Health Promotion Research Trust, Cambridge. The views expressed in this paper are those of the research team but are not necessarily those of HPRT.

[2]   Here we focus on the first two sweeps of the large scale longitudinal study and attention is restricted to one cohort of roughly 350 adolescents. The young people from this cohort were aged 15-16 years in 1987 and 17-18 years in 1989. During the first sweep in 1987 they were contacted at school and the survey questionnaires were completed under the guidance of a field-worker: in 1989 they were re-contacted via a postal questionnaire and of these 50 per cent responded to the postal questionnaire two years later. Cluster analyses were performed to provide a descriptive overview of a large and complex dataset and to generate typologies which would identify differing developing lifestyles and leisure styles of young people. Factor analyses were conducted in parallel with the cluster analysis to identify the major factors underlying the data. These dimensions were used to interpret the results from the clustering process.

References

Arro, L. E., Wold, B., Kannas, L. and Rimpela, M. (1986) 'Health behaviour in school-children. A WHO cross-national survey', *Health Promotion* Vol. 1, No. 1: pp. 17–33.

Bates, I., Clarke, J., Cohen, P., Finn, D., Moore, R. and Willis, P. (1984) *Schooling for the Dole*. London: Macmillan.

Brake, M. (1985) *Comparative Youth Sub-cultures*. London: Routledge & Kegan Paul.

Bronfenbrenner, U. (1979) *The Ecology of Human Development*. Cambridge: Harvard University Press.

Coleman, J. C. (1979) *The School Years*. London: Routledge & Kegan Paul.

Coleman, J. C. and Hendry, L. B. (1990) *The Nature of Adolescence*, 2nd edition. London & New York: Routledge.

Csikszentmihalyi, M. (1975) *Beyond Boredom and Anxiety*. San Francisco: Jossey-Bass.

Csikszentmihalyi, M. and Larson, R. (1984) *Being Adolescent: Conflict and Growth in the Teenage Years.* New York: Basic Books.

Devereux, E. C. (1976) 'Backyard versus little league baseball: the impoverishment of children's play', in D. Landers (ed) *Social Problems in Athletics.* Illinois: University of Illinois Press.

Erikson, D. (1968) *Identity: Youth and crisis.* New York: Norton.

Frith, S. (1978) *The Sociology of Rock.* London: Constable.

Giddens, A. (1984) *The Constitution of Society.* Oxford: Polity.

Hendry, L. B. (1983) *Growing Up and Going Out.* Aberdeen: Aberdeen University Press.

Hendry L. B., Shucksmith, J., Love, J. G. and Glendinning, A. (1993) *Young People's Leisure and Lifestyles.* London: Routledge.

Holt, M. (1983) 'Vocationalism: the new threat to universal education', *Forum* Vol. 25, No. 3: pp. 84–86.

Ingham, R. (1987) 'Psychological contributions to the study of leisure', *Leisure Studies* Vol. 6, No. 1: pp. 1–14.

Jonathan, R. (1982) 'Lifelong learning: slogan, educational aim or manpower service?', *Scottish Educational Review* Vol. 14, No. 2: pp. 80–92.

Kleiber, D. A. & Rickards, W. H. (1985) 'Leisure and recreation in adolescence: limitation and potential', in M. G. Wade (ed) *Constraints on Leisure.* Springfield: Thomas.

Raffe, D. & Courtenay, G. (1988) '16–18 on both sides of the border', in D. Raffe (ed) *Education and the Youth Labour Market.* London: Falmer Press.

Shaw, M. (1984) *Sport and leisure participation and lifestyles in different residential neighbourhoods: an exploration of the ACORN classification.* London: Sports Council.

Thomson, W., McQueen, D. and Currie, C. (1988) *Health-related behaviour of schoolchildren.* Research Unit in Health and Behavioural Change (RUHBC). University of Edinburgh.

Wenzel, R. (1982) Health promotion and lifestyles: Perspectives of the WHO Regional Office for Europe, Health Education Programme. *Paper presented to the 11th International Conference on Health Education.* Tasmania (August), pp. 15–20 .

MEDIA AND SPORTING INTERESTS OF YOUNG PEOPLE

Gill Lines
Beal High School, Ilford, Essex

I.   Introduction

This paper is based upon research undertaken during 1991 to investigate the association between the cultural images and values consumed via the media, and adolescents' involvement in sport/PE. It developed around a consideration of the following issues:

1. Despite the growth of all areas of media there is little known about the commercial pressures exerted on young people and the extent to which media consumerism holds adolescents in its grasp.

2. It is suggested that through viewing and watching popular genres of the media the adolescent is exposed to various images and ideals concerning his/her role in society. Similarly, the ways in which the sporting image is depicted might explain how young people come to see themselves in the world of sport.
    The media selects and constructs information for the audience to consume. It portrays people behaving in certain ways and attaches status to some events, people and groups by giving them greater priority in terms of presentation, time and emphasis. It is relevant to consider how men and women are depicted in their sex roles and in their sporting roles.

3. Previous research (e.g. Scraton, 1986; Talbot, 1980) indicates gender differences in sporting behaviour that appear to accentuate at adolescence. The influence of the home and school seems to only partially explain these distinctions. Common sense and everyday observation tell us that sporting images presented by TV, magazines and newspapers can have an impact on

adolescent values. For example, the effect of Olga Korbut on girls' gymnastics after the 1972 Olympics; the increase on local park tennis during Wimbledon fortnight; and the adoption of Gazza as the nation's hero during and after the 1990 World Cup. All of these indicate that the media do have an impact. However, the problem lies in interpreting how significant it really is and in isolating its effect from other social experiences, both past and present.

In addition, research evidence (Hargreaves, 1982; McRobbie, 1984; Boutilier & San Giovanni, 1983) suggests that media imagery and ideology reinforces sex stereotyping (the notion of femininity appearing to be in direct conflict with the patriarchal hegemony of the media sporting image). The study reported in this paper developed from a belief that the gender differentiation inherent in the sporting image of media products might in some ways explain differing sporting attitudes, behaviour and participation amongst adolescent boys and girls.

A consideration of these issues made it apparent that the media as a socialising agency could be very influential. Yet despite substantial literature on children and TV, there is little research available to validate common sense assumptions about the role of the media in either adolescent lifestyles or the sports socialisation process.

In an attempt to illuminate these issues, the research (Lines, 1991) was designed to ascertain adolescent media interests and to begin to consider the imagery prevalent within them. The main focus was on highlighting significant gender differences in relation to the stereotypical sex roles and the sporting image.

The research methodology for this investigation used questionnaires completed by a sample group of 240 14/15 year olds from four different schools in the South-East region in the first half of 1991. This was followed by interviews and personal diaries with 7 case studies from the sample group. The questionnaire was designed to:

1. produce an overall view of media consumerism by young people:

    i.   discovering media interests in relation to newspapers, magazines and TV programmes watched;

    ii.   determining accessibility and availability of media in adolescent lifestyles;

    iii. determining what images adolescents identity with;

    iv.   determining which stars adolescents identify with and why.

2. determine the influence of the media sporting image on adolescents:

    i.   identifying popular sports programmes;

    ii.   cataloguing popular sports stars;

    iii. determining to what extent the sporting image influences young people.

The study produced evidence to support the following propositions:

- media consumerism is an important part of adolescent lifestyles;

- significant gender differences are apparent in media consumption;

- media imagery apparent in adolescent media interests reinforces a sex stereotyping of women and a notion of femininity amongst adolescent girls that conflicts with the image of sport;

- the media imagery of sport affirms a patriarchal hegemony that confers status on male sporting ability and achievement whilst ignoring or trivialising women's sport;

- boys and girls do gain different concepts from and have different interests in the sporting media;

- media as a sports socialising agency is different for boys and girls.

II. Media consumption

The findings offer a detailed descriptive account of the role of the media in adolescent lifestyles. It is strongly argued that media impact is significant and that its power cannot be ignored.

The findings show that media products are accessible to, and consumed by, all adolescents in the sample. The availability of TV, video, satellite, cable, newspapers and magazines was substantial. There were no cases of any adolescent who was not exposed to several of these media products. The depth of knowledge about media programmes, stars, and press revealed in the questionnaires, diaries and interviews further supported its significance to adolescents. It was clear that media consumerism is not just a meaningful experience to most young people: it is also central rather than peripheral to their lives. 80% read a daily newspaper; 75% liked or thought it was OK. 92% regularly read a magazine. Many girls purchased two or more a week and 95% of girls liked or loved reading magazines. This was not so significant amongst boys. 68 different magazines were listed by the respondents. Virtually all of the sample had TV:

70% had their own personal TV. 88% of the group watched TV 2–6 hours daily. This suggests that for some young people TV viewing takes up a considerable proportion of their lives, exceeding time spent in school in some cases. TV was clearly an important part of adolescent lifestyle: 75% really loved or liked it.

Although going out with friends was identified as the most popular interest, a significant point is that for many young girls, media interests such as reading magazines and watching TV were more important to them than playing sport. For boys, sports participation seemed to be more significant than media interests. Nevertheless media involvement amongst all young people is important.

In addition, clear patterns or trends seem to be emerging. Although a vast number of magazines, programmes and TV stars were mentioned, there seemed to be evident favourites which were similar across the four schools: *The Sun*, read by 30%; *The News of the World*, 28%. *Just 17* magazine was read by 78% of girls; *Viz* was read by 22% of boys. Despite 119 different TV programmes being listed in the top 3 choices, closer analysis shows that only a few were very popular: 'Home and Away', 'Only Fools and Horses', and 'Neighbours'. TV star selection was male-dominated: favourites were David Jason, Rowan Atkinson and Ric Mayall.

These findings do provide evidence for what common sense has already suggested about adolescent favourites. However, it must be acknowledged that this research reports the here-and-now phenomena (or the then-and-there situation). For it is difficult to determine how long media impact lasts and, especially with sports viewing, seasonal distinctions are clear. Will Gazza be as popular just after the 1994 World Cup as he was in 1990/91?

A further point to arise from the findings was that regardless of concern for negative aspects of media viewing, such as aggression and violence, comments from many adolescents suggested that they saw TV as a means of relaxing. The majority of young people selected programmes and heroes who made them laugh and who provided fun and entertainment. Violence and aggression did not feature.

The content analysis of the most popular media products confirmed suggestions previously made apparent. Sex stereotyping of men and women still continues and male dominance of the sporting image prevails. The predominance of male TV heroes and sports stars amongst adolescent choices signifies the importance of men in the media world. In the *Sun* during the two-week analysis the most frequently shown female roles were topless models and film stars;

whereas for men occupational roles were far more diverse. Politicians and sportsmen were most frequently mentioned.

The prominence of sportsmen both in the news and on sports pages indicates that aspects of their private lives are as important as their sporting achievements, but most significantly of all that sportsmen are objects of interest (and perhaps inspiration) way beyond the confines of the sports pages.

Sport coverage was seen to be an important aspect of news. Space devoted to male and female sport showed a total dominance of male sport. The adolescents interviewed initially seemed satisfied with the sport featured — boys did not think that anything was missing, yet the girls seemed more confused. Several realised that they would like to read more about netball, badminton and volleyball. They did not specifically notice that it was women's sport that was missing. Only on reflection did some feel that men dominated the sports pages. One suggested that this was only to be expected as women's cricket and football was not as good anyway.

The popularity of *Just 17* magazine intimates that imagery prevalent with it might be influential in determining adolescent girls' interests and attitudes. Content analysis highlighted the focus on looking and feeling good, with the ultimate aim of getting the man. Sport did not feature in the magazines during this time. Girls were never shown in active poses — in fact the most physically active image shown was just strolling along the promenade in the latest fashions. A "discover your inner self" quiz confirmed the perceived conflict between being sporty and being feminine. The last of four categories of types of girl identified by the quiz was classed as "Footy Mad Fiona", a girl more sport crazy than boy crazy, who did not like dressing up, was sporty and active but maybe trying to imitate boys just a little too much. Girls reading this advice might see that the female sporting image is inappropriate and damaging to one's chances of catching the man!

The popularity and impact of 'Home and Away' seems to lie not with its excitement or novelty value but rather with its intensity and regularity of scheduling and the general acceptance of it as a part of everyday life. Similar aspects of the sporting image are revealed from the content analysis. Sport is shown as a central interest of the young men — surfing, jogging, fitness training. Girls were rarely, if ever, shown in active roles.

This attempt to analyse the content of adolescents' media interests is, however, still to some extent the researcher's interpretation of the image. A further development of this work would be to view and read with the adolescents to see how they interpret the same images.

One of the most distinctive features of the findings was that despite the impact of feminism and raised consciousness concerning equality and equal opportunity, sex stereotyping was clearly evident. For as anticipated, there were obvious gender differences in the consumption of media products.

Girls and boys saw themselves as distinct consumer groups — the former continuing to follow typical sex roles, purchasing magazines which focus on femininity and self-improvement, selecting role models on the criteria of desirability to men. This acts to perpetuate the media image of women. Boys, on the other hand, selected magazines revolving around sports, computers and motor cars. Girls were more interested in soap operas; boys most frequently watched sports programmes.

75% of the sample group made no selection of female TV stars in their selection of favourite performer. This seems to suggest a lack of female role models. Adolescent girls seem to select male TV heroes as their dream man. Boys at this age still identify with male heroes and not female goddesses.

III. The sporting media and socialisation into sport

Having established that media products are an important part of adolescent lifestyles and that images perceived may be influential, the next task is to consider the association of the sporting media with the socialisation process.

The major concern at this stage is with the extent and popularity of media consumerism — might it be seriously limiting an active lifestyle?

If adolescents are watching 2–6 hours of TV per night, this suggests little time left for physical activities. A development of this research could be to discover how much of adolescent time is actively spent pursuing the sports they expressed an interest in and what ways sport is significant in their lives. The media diaries considered time spent in physical activities, but this was not significant enough to provide evidence to support the idea that those who watch more TV play less sport. It was clear from the findings, though, that many girls claim to gain more enjoyment from media interests such as pop music, television and reading magazines than they do playing sport. This was not so in the case of many boys.

Conclusions can be drawn about other aspects of sports socialisation and the armchair viewer. For it is obvious from the findings that TV sports viewing and reading of the sports pages does provide both information and knowledge about a variety of sports, does offer role models for some to adopt , and can motivate some to participate. However, its impact and extent are still difficult to determine.

What is clear, however, is that the role of the media as a sports socialising agency is different for boys and girls.

Media viewing and reading

Boys and girls expressed similar enjoyment in sports participation. However, the evidence suggests that access to and interest in media viewing and reading highlights distinct gender differences.

1 in 3 girls, in comparison to 1 in 10 boys, never read the sports pages of their newspaper. This could be explained by: (i) boys are more interested in sport than girls anyway; (ii) there is more about male sport than female in the papers; (iii) the sport girls enjoy most is not featured; (iv) girls see the sport pages as essentially for boys.

Many more boys than girls buy sports magazines — 14 different sports magazines were mentioned in boys' purchases. The girls' magazines rarely, if ever, feature sport and the only girls' sport magazine mentioned was *Horse and Pony*. Boys identified sport as their favourite magazine section. Girls identified fashion, pop music and the problem pages as theirs. Only one girl mentioned sport. This is not surprising as sport does not feature in girls' magazines, and there are few magazines available focusing on women's sports.

Sports video purchases were also gender specific. Boys purchased sports specific/sports movie videos. Girls were into dance/fitness videos. This can be explained by the lack of female sports videos in the shops, and the fact that exercise/fitness videos tend to be geared towards women and the development of body shape/diet.

In addition, although many girls do watch sport on TV, 34% more boys than girls felt that it was very important to them. Boys' feelings were similar in terms of playing and watching sport. 24% more girls preferred to play than watch sport on the TV. This could be explained by the fact that the sports girls identified as popular, such as netball, badminton and rounders, are rarely televised.

Boys, in contrast, have constant reinforcement of the importance of male sport. All of their favourite sports receive coverage and they have the opportunity to watch these at the highest level.

The findings showed that most young people watched media sport because they had an interest in sport. Excitement and the atmosphere it created were also frequently mentioned. Several did mention 'helping me to improve', 'appreciation of skills', and 'helping me to find out about different sports'. However, this highlighted a significant feature in that many adolescents were not really aware of the role of TV as a performance enhancer or a provider of knowledge. Significantly, twice as many girls as boys saw no reason for watching sport on TV.

When asked if TV encouraged them to take part in any particular sport, respondents gave a mixed response. 25% felt that it had: twice as many boys as girls. However, the number of negative responses suggests that many young people are also unaware of the influences of the media on their sporting participation and that the media as a motivational agency has yet to be fully analysed.

The motivational effects of watching TV are, it seems, different for boys and girls. Boys clearly felt encouraged to participate after watching sport, whereas girls did not express similar feelings.

An attempt was also made to discover compatibility between sports played and those watched most often. Of the sports programmes featured regularly during the time of research, 'The Match', US football and 'Sports-night' were the most popular of all the programmes listed. Except for 'Ski Sunday' and US football the number of male viewers exceeded female. 'Ski Sunday' was the only programme that showed females in action. 25% identified football as their favourite sport to watch, US football 20%, and basketball was third most popular. It seems that US football's popularity must be as a direct result of television coverage as few adolescents have had previous exposure through school PE or through parental interest or live spectating. These televised choices were similar across the four schools.

These results did show some compatibility with sports adolescents enjoy playing. Football and basketball again featured prominently. The most distinctive differences were in hockey and badminton amongst both sexes and in netball for girls. These sports feature more frequently in school PE programmes than they do in TV scheduling. The popularity of US football and skiing in the viewing interests, as expected, did not extend into playing interests. This again suggests that their popularity is as a direct result of exposure time and not previous playing experience.

The most significant point to emerge here is that playing sport appears to be more important to the adolescents than watching televised sport. This is especially so in the case of girls.

Clearly girls' sport is not featured in them, but the late night sports slot and Saturday afternoon viewing when many young people work or go shopping suggest that sports scheduling is not convenient for many young people. Maybe if a sports programme was featured around the scheduling of 'Home and Away' there would be an increase in viewing.

Sports stars as role models

Sports stars are often assumed to be significant role models for young people. The impact of televised male sporting hours, the depth of sports press coverage of male sports, and the acceptance of male sports stars as important media heroes is clearly shown in the adolescents' selection of favourite sports stars: 143 different sports stars were listed in their top 3 choices. Of these only 10 were women — 3 tennis players, 4 athletes, 1 ice skater, 1 show jumper and 1 yachtswoman. German tennis player Steffi Graf was the most popular woman. This clearly indicated a lack of identified female role models. As netball, basketball and badminton are these girls' favourite sports, it is not surprising that they do not know any top class women in these sports, for they do not receive televised exposure time. In addition, it may be that, on the basis of the media's portrayal of females in action, they are not perceived to be worthy images to adopt.

Girls' learning opportunities could be enhanced if they had female role models — they would see what their sex is capable of achieving. Perhaps by only watching men in action they believe that high level sport is both inappropriate for and unattainable by them.

What was also clear from the results was that boys were able to offer a far wider range and variety of sports hero, far beyond those receiving media coverage. Within their first choice, boys listed 47 different stars, girls only 28.

The favourite sports stars named — Gary Lineker, Gazza and John Barnes — highlights the popularity of footballers, especially during the football season. These 3 stars were at the time still reflecting in the post-World Cup hype. In addition, Gascoigne was the nation's hero and 'Gazzamania' was in its full glory. He featured in the favourite adolescent paper on 7/8 of the days of analysis. This included 8 photos, and on one day he was on 3 separate pages including the front page. He also received a full page spread in *Just 17* during this same period of time. This could explain why Gazza and Lineker were more popular amongst girls than boys. Their media exposure extended beyond the sports pages and sports programmes.

Young people's selection of their hero revealed the importance to them of skill acquisition in sport. The most popular reason for identification with a hero was because they were skilful, 'brill', or simply the best. A significant number of girls, unlike boys, selected their hero because of his attractiveness, his nice legs, or his good body. Girls liked Frank Bruno because he is "all muscles and money", as one respondent put it.

Only 12% of girls wanted to be their favourite sports star. Nearly 4 times as many boys identified Gazza, Lineker and Jordan as those stars they would most like to be. Again, the most frequently given criterion was because they were the best at their chosen sport.

Not surprisingly from previous gender distinctions, 3 times as many boys as girls felt that they were influenced by their favourite sports star. However, it was again obvious that there was some uncertainty about the influences on the young people's sporting behaviour and attitudes. Of those interviewed, some mentioned copying techniques, learning etiquette, buying similar or branded sports clothing. There was a general feeling that bad habits had not been copied.

However, sports behaviour after certain televised events can be seen to have been influenced: e.g., the "you cannot be serious" approach by young tennis players echoing John McEnroe's conduct.

The subtle conditioning that may be happening therefore needs further research that was beyond the scope of this investigation. For these is clearly a need to more fully understand the long term effects of media imagery and ideology on sports behaviour.

IV.   Implications for the physical educator

The evidence provided in this paper has implications for the physical educator interested in the context in which s/he is working, and in the major influences upon young people's attitudes to and experience of sport/physical activity.

First, teachers need to be aware of the influences of the media on the adolescent value system — that girls' rejection of certain sporting values and traditions may be because of their immersion in the ideology of femininity, and the female role models they are presented with via the media may well contribute to this.

Second, an important implication is that media involvement is significant in adolescent lifestyles and that hours watching TV are likely to far exceed sporting participation. The focus on healthy lifestyles in the PE curriculum must be of importance in presenting young people with a sound knowledge and understanding of the implications of a sedentary life.

Third, the PE department should also consider the utilisation of the media as an educational tool. For it does seem that adolescents are unaware of the extent to which the media can influence sporting behaviour, knowledge and attitudes. Many watched TV for excitement and fun, but few thought about its effects on performance. The viewing of TV sports with a PE group, perhaps during a wet weather lesson, may be useful in highlighting some of these points. In addition, with evaluation as a strand in National Curriculum attainment, viewing top class performance may help to evaluate their own and others' performance more effectively.

Fourth, this also suggests that media bias in its presentation of the sporting image needs to be a topic for discussion amongst young people. Girls' PE departments do need to highlight positive aspects of media coverage to show women in action. Girls do need to be made more aware that women's sport is often trivialised or ignored and that women's sport can be viewed in its own right, not just in comparison with men. Where televised material is not available, videos from the various sporting bodies can be purchased. In this way girls will have equal opportunity to see females perform at the highest level.

In addition, press coverage relating to activities currently being taught could be used as visual aids in the changing room, and magazines relating to particular sports could be purchased from the sports associations. This would ensure that girls do have the opportunity for similar exposure to media opportunities which may enhance their sports socialisation, or at least create a more fully developed awareness of the possible routes into sport.

References

Boutilier, M. A, and San Giovanni, L. (1983) *The Sporting Woman*. Champaign (Illinois): Human Kinetics Press.

Evans, J. (ed) (1986) *PE, Sport and Schooling*. Basingstoke: Falmer Press.

Hargreaves, J. (1982) *Sport, Culture and Ideology.* London: Routledge and Kegan Paul.

Lines, G. (1991) Media Interests and Sport Among 14/15 Year Olds: A study of gender differences. Unpublished MA Thesis. Brighton Polytechnic.

McRobbie, A. and Nava, M. (eds) (1984) *Gender and Generation,* London: Macmillan.

Scraton, S. (1986) 'Images of femininity and the teaching of girls PE', in Evans, J. (ed) *PE, Sport and Schooling.* Basingstoke: Falmer Press.

Talbot, M. (1980) *Women and Sport*, Working Paper 77, University of Birmingham.

DELIVERING EDUCATION FOR LEISURE: PROVISION, ENABLEMENT AND TEACHER-STUDENT PERCEPTION

Joy Standeven
Chelsea School Research Centre
University of Brighton

I.   Introduction

Neither sport in its wider recreational and cultural sense nor physical education in its narrower curriculum sense hold any prerogative over education for leisure, but the importance of these forms of activity has long been recognised and is well-documented in the publications of the Leisure Studies Association (see, for example, Bacon, 1982; Haywood & Henry, 1985; Murphy, 1989). Speaking at the 1985 Leisure Studies Association Conference, Leo Hendry questioned the appropriateness of the schools' physical education curriculum on the basis that it concentrated on "providing short term recreational skills training" rather than equipping pupils with the attitudes and understandings that would 'enable' leisure education. Hendry's challenging statement called for investigation and provided the basis for an empirical five-year three phase comparative investigation, involving researchers in countries on both sides of the Atlantic during the latter half of the 80s.

Different social relations underlie the concepts of 'providing' and 'enabling'. As Hendry put it, the one is a paternalistic relationship characterised by a kind of professional imperialism, the other empowers the client. Hendry was by no means alone in addressing the practitioner-client relationship in schools; a number of papers delivered at the 1981 LSA Conference pursued the same theme. David Hargreaves, for example, in his paper on 'Unemployment, Leisure and Education', focused on how teaching needed to change and improve "so that the productive orientation can be fostered in pupils". Most secondary schools, he found, were "steeped in hierarchy":

... the curriculum is imposed and evaluated unilaterally by the teacher, rather than chosen, organised, judged by, or even debated with, the pupils themselves. And it is quickly defined as 'work' and soon becomes linked in pupils' minds with an unpleasant obligation which is fulfilled only under the ever-watchful and mistrustful eye of the supervising teacher. (p. 136).

In his discussion of 'education for leisure' Hargreaves dismissed the idea of a separate curriculum addressing 'leisure studies' or 'leisure skills' since "Much of the present curriculum has relevance for leisure..." (1982: p. 133). But two kinds of reconstruction, he considered, were needed: first, in terms of social reconstruction, there was a need to "change our understanding of the relations between education, work and leisure" (1982: p. 135); and second, educational reconstruction needed to focus upon changing pedagogies, and specifically upon changing the practitioner-client relation. Lacking the opportunity to take responsibility for their own learning, according to Hargreaves, will result in young people having a 'receptive' orientation of passive and alienated consumerism; or, to use the terms Hendry was working with, they will be 'provided' rather than 'enabled'.

The kind of political action necessary to achieve the radical restructuring which Hargreaves believed was needed would involve "decentralisation of government and decision making to levels of society where local communities would gain effective control over the organisation of their own affairs" (Bacon, 1982: p. 17). Power devolved in this way can transform the 'receptive orientation' into a 'productive orientation' where "men and women are active participants exercising genuine power and influence" (Hargreaves, 1982: p. 135). The kind of community education Hargreaves advocated was about more than shared premises by schools, colleges, libraries and leisure centres, and more than "some advance in the democratisation of teacher-pupil and teacher-parent relationships" (Hargreaves, 1982: p. 135), though both of these were seen as desirable. Community education was also about more than dissolved boundaries between the different communities, it had to have "a distinctive style" which "prepares young people for new community structures" (Hargreaves, 1982: p. 135). Schools in this kind of society "would need to give young people a rich and active experience of participation in multiple communities" (p .135), and "the root of such an education would be the development of the productive orientation" (p. 135). But what was "platitudinous" to members of the LSA was recognised as likely to be thought "dangerously radical" to others "and especially to politicians" (Hargreaves, 1982: p. 132). In this context, Hargreaves quotes at length Leigh (1971), emphasising Leigh's view that "the primary skills in which schools must train young people are social organisation ones" (Hargreaves, p. 137). But Hargreaves urges that Leigh's ideas "have had very little influence ... on educational practice" (p. 138) and unless or until the relationship between education and society is reconceptualised he doubts "they ever will" (p. 138).

II. Changing roles

Appraisal of government and professional publications indicates that the focus of the 80s was predominantly concerned with the 'provider' relation. The 1980-81 Annual Report from the Sports Council addressed participation, facility provision and excellence and it stated:

> Since 1978 the Sports Council has concentrated on the provision of local facilities which it regards as the *greatest single need for sport in this country*.. (Annual Report 1980–81, Sports Council, p. 9) [emphasis added]

The Council recorded that it had put a capital investment of £7.6 million into sports facilities and the same Report goes on to say:

> Never before has the Council allocated so much of its resources to this side of its work (Annual Report 1980-81, Sports Council, p. 10).

The 1981-82 Annual Report referred to the 1971 publicly announced targets for the provision of golf courses, sports centres and swimming pools with a target date for provision by 1981 and reported that:

> The present Chairman has expressed his satisfaction that the momentum for providing facilities has been maintained and even increased... (Annual Report 1981-82, Sports Council, p. 11).

A year later the Council set new targets for facility provision in the period 1983-88 which included 800 indoor dry facilities, 200 refurbished swimming pools and 50 new ones, and additional provision of outdoor sports facilities and access to water and the countryside for sport. However, it was acknowledged that facility provision would not automatically achieve the social welfare objectives espoused by the public sector. In *Sport in the Community: Into the 90s* (the 1988 update of its Strategy *Sport in the Community ...The next Ten Years*) the Council reported that the target for providing swimming pools had been met, that for other indoor sports had not, and an additional £9 million was claimed from the government "to support the provision of facilities...." (Sports Council, 1988: p. 3).

In one of its most recent publications (*Provision for Swimming*, 1992), the Sports Council is described as moving to a 'sports planning' approach in contrast to its former 'facilities planning' model since it recognised :

> In the last decade ... there has been growing realisation that the provision of public facilities does not automatically achieve social welfare objectives.... More recently there has been increasing awareness that [a] "target group" approach is significantly better than simply providing facilities.... (Sports Council, 1992: p. 8)

This document acknowledges that "in the past" pool provision has been overemphasised "rather than effective management and use" (Sports Council, 1992: p. 51).

An appraisal of the 1981 Volume 1 editions of the newly published journal *Leisure Management*, as an example of leisure industry literature, confirms the industry's focus at that time on facility provision and equipment. A glance at the 1992 Index to Volume 12 shows that a broadened concept of leisure management has been embraced with a focus on issues more than upon facilities *per se*.

This key professional journal described the significance of the 1988 Local Government Act, and the subsequent order which introduced compulsory competitive tendering (CCT) into local authority leisure services, as "one of the most significant days in the history of the industry" (*Leisure Management, 1988:* p. 3). In effect, CCT shifted the base of local authority leisure services from a concentration solely on facility provision and management to a concern with sport and recreation initiatives and development. CCT legislation has increased the importance of market forces and, ostensibly anyway, will increase consumer choice. In keeping with the whole concept of the Citizen's Charter and entitlements of the individual, council leisure services are seen to have an 'enabling' role, one which empowers the customer.

In a different though arguably parallel case, the National Curriculum's PE process model has been seen as 'taking the road towards independence' (Casbon, 1992: p. 6). Casbon states:

> It is my belief that our role is to enable children to become actively independent. That is to say that they should become thinking, reflective learners who can make a positive contribution to the society in which they live.... The framework of the programmes of study form a sound starting point for the creation of the independent child. (Casbon, 1992: p. 6-7)

In broader terms, the teacher's role can be construed as that of facilitator or 'enabler' — the learner is to be given greater responsibility in a shift towards increased learner-centred control.

Thus in education on the one hand, and in leisure services on the other, the 80s can be characterised as the decade of 'providing'. In the changing social relations of the 90s new emphases are being placed upon the 'enabling' role of the service and the empowering of the client. Given this context, it is unsurprising that the international research project conducted in the latter half of the 80s found Hendry's claim substantiated — from the pupil's point of view their physical education curricular experiences did not, in the main, influence their leisure. The result of their experiences found them 'provided' rather than 'enabled'. In the next section the basis and outcome of the project are summarised.

III. The international project

In the first phase of the international project a localised pilot study assessed whether school physical education and recreation programmes matched stated or implicit leisure education objectives with appropriate programmes and practices in two high schools in England and Canada (Standeven & Thompson, 1986). The sample included pupils in their final two years of schooling (n=405, 15–18 year olds), and their physical education teachers (n=10).

Three English and four Canadian teachers thought leisure education should be mandatory, and all but two of the teachers (English) felt the curriculum they taught embraced leisure education. However, less than half the pupils surveyed (46% of the Canadian students and 39% of the English students) believed that their school's physical education programme had influenced what they did in their spare time. This preliminary finding suggested that despite the teachers' belief that leisure education could have a profound effect on adjustment to one's entire life, and despite their acknowledgement that one function of their curriculum was to provide leisure skills and develop positive attitudes to leisure, the curriculum they taught had had little influence on how their pupils used their leisure time.

In phase two, the study was extended to a four-country investigation and used regional (instead of local) samples of 15 to 17 year olds (n=1,658) in Canada, England, the Republic of Ireland and the United States and included 99 teachers. One important aspect of this phase of the comparative study focused upon the perceived relationship between the schools' physical education programmes and leisure education.

In four out of the five indices used to gauge pupils' and teachers' perceptions of their physical education programme's contribution to education for leisure, the pupils' response suggested their programme had not, in their view, influenced their interest in leisure activities, and even fewer found that it had helped them to get started in leisure activities. Nor had physical education helped them to 'know more about leisure', it had not helped them to develop 'feelings about leisure' and only a marginally more positive view was expressed in terms of whether it had 'helped them to become aware of future leisure potentials'. However, pupils thought that leisure education should be one of the major curriculum objectives for physical education in their schools. The teachers surveyed were under the impression that their programmes were more influential than they turned out to be. The largest discrepancy between pupils views and those of their teachers concerned the effectiveness of the physical education curriculum in getting young people started in leisure activities. Teachers across all four countries appeared to hold an inflated assessment of the success of their programmes in this respect. Nevertheless, despite their misperception, teachers agreed that leisure education was inadequately provided for in schools.

The third phase of the project used nationally representative samples of secondary school students aged 15 to 17 in Canada, England and the Republic of Ireland (n=4,172). Amongst the topics surveyed were the students' perceptions of the type and extent of leisure education content in their physical education programme. The kinds of statements students were asked to respond to included:

The school physical education programme has taught/is teaching me:

- where to go to get information about the kinds of sports clubs that are open to me if I want to join;
- how to go about learning new physical activity skills so that I shall be able to feel confident starting something I haven't done before;

- how to identify and understand what I'm good at and not good at regarding physical activities for personal benefit and enjoyment.

The responses showed that students in all three countries were either uncertain or did not believe that leisure education was included within their physical education programmes.

Statements were used in the survey to assess in a general way an individual's feelings as to whether or not their school physical education programme had made them aware of the benefits of leisure activities. For example:

- I think taking part in physical education will help me to have interesting leisure activities when I leave school;
- The school physical education programme has helped me to get interested in leisure activities;
- The school physical education programme has provided instruction to help me define and know more about leisure in general and the possible benefits to me of taking part in physical sport activities.

The results of this large and comprehensive survey indicated that across the three national samples, students were not at all certain that their physical education programmes were teaching them the basic elements of leisure education or contributing to their knowledge of leisure. If schools are serious about their intentions to deliver leisure education, and if we can trust the response of 4,200 students in three different countries, it is clear that significant changes are needed in the delivery of physical education programmes if objectives of leisure education are to be achieved.

The English student population felt their schools taught more about leisure than did pupils in the other countries. Unsurprisingly, given the continued association of sport with masculinity, males in all countries scored their experiences significantly higher than did their female counterparts, indicating an assessment that was slightly more positive in terms of the perceived extent of leisure education in their physical education programmes.

From local to regional to national samples, the message from all three phases of the study (n=6,235 students) was clear — physical education programmes as they have been conceived and taught have had very little influence, in the students' estimation, on their leisure attitudes and behaviours, specifically on their participation in physically active forms of leisure. The leisure knowledge, attitudes and skills students have developed have been irrespective of, rather than due to, their experience of physical education. Being educated for leisure in the sense of being 'enabled' has not been a perceived outcome of physical education for this sample of the school population internationally.

That the results of all three phases of the survey should show such a large measure of agreement between samples drawn from different cultures suggests that the issue is more of a curricular one than a cultural one. Yet, it could be argued that it is the survey research method itself that is masking interesting cultural differences, for whilst survey method is appropriate for dealing with large-scale cases and documenting cross-national generalities, it is inappropriate for understanding the differences in meaning of a leisure experience and too blunt an instrument to expose the subtle nuances in respondents' terminology that are culturally specific. Survey method, for example, cannot fully illuminate cross-national differences in meaning of the leisure experience, nor does it help us to understand what sense young people are really making of the experiences they are offered. For this reason a more qualitative approach was proposed for part of the third phase of the study.

It was of interest to the research team to better understand young people's experience of physical education, the meanings they attached to that experience and the contexts in which those meanings were forged, in order to begin to unravel the contextual factors that might enable or constrain education for leisure.

To explore these questions the researchers first observed a series of physical education lessons in a school setting from which survey data had previously been obtained. Second, a small number of students from the class observed kept a seven-day time diary which formed the basis of an in-depth interview. The tape-recorded interview was designed to focus upon questions to do with the respondent's sports-type leisure participation during the week prior to the interview, and more generally, and the way in which their choices had, or had not, been influenced by their school experience of physical education. A third stage of this qualitative approach was curtailed due to lack of time, but was intended to return to the field and involve participant observation of the time-diarist's 'at leisure'.

Analysis of the data obtained from the first observation and the follow-up interview pointed to four contextual conditions that seemed to enable or constrain the possibilities of effective leisure education taking place in the school physical education setting: choice; relevance; understanding rationales; and institutional conditions to do with social relations.

Creating the opportunity for student choice was important as a potentially enabling condition, though choice per se was insufficient. Students themselves needed to influence setting the agenda of activities from which choice was made. Here, then, there are clear indications of a need for a shift in social relations between teacher and learner. Hargreaves (1982) pointed to the need for the curriculum to become a matter for teacher-pupil negotiation ten years ago; yet this cross-national study, even at the end of the decade, found no evidence that pupils had any say in what they were taught, or how.

The agenda for choice had to have currency — to be seen as fashionable, desirable — if it was to have relevance for the students in terms of educating them for leisure. This condition, therefore, challenges the whole idea of teaching for the 'future' rather than teaching for the 'here and now'.

Students needed to have rationales made explicit in order to avoid the mindless pursuit of activity simply for its own sake. Negotiating the agenda in the first place had the potential to contribute positively to understanding the rationale behind the choice.

Fourth, but by no means least, institutional conditions were of key importance. Compliant relations — characteristic of the school setting — are rendered problematic as a basis for 'enabling' leisure. Furthermore, the delivery of leisure education in school (that is in the pupils' non-leisure) time necessarily implies that it will be compatible with the 'dominant legitimation structure' (Corijn, 1987). This necessarily questions the concept of leisure it embodies, and raises the issue as to whether the school, given its inherent social relations, can provide the site for delivering education for leisure? Since choice, relevance and understanding (the first three identified conditions for effective leisure education) will be inextricably linked with the institutional setting, it seems that it is upon the school's social relations that effective education for leisure pivots.

An important contribution of the qualitative phase of the project was the confirmation of the key issue as one rooted in the theory of power and social control as the pivotal condition for enabling or constraining leisure education. It is not, then, so much a curricular issue as a wider institutional and cultural one — a matter more fundamentally bound up with the cultural experience of pedagogy than with the concept of curriculum as content.

Hargreaves (1982) had recognised pedagogy as the critical limiting factor inhibiting young people's conception of education as 'leisure-orientated'. Curriculum content he saw as less significant, though in order "to foster intrinsic learning for its own sake" curriculum content would need to be regarded "as the product of negotiation and joint contribution". In the same vein, Hamilton-Smith argued that leisure education is to do with:

> ...enabling people to learn about the attainment of freedom, intrinsic satisfaction and sense of relationship to one's own culture. (Hamilton-Smith, 1982: p. 59)

The right direction for leisure education, Hamilton-Smith maintains, is one in which the educational experience is "unconstrained, freely chosen, intrinsically satisfying" and culturally congruent. In this scenario leisure education "is about the liberation of education from institutionalised constraints" and implementation involves rethinking the role of school, of ways of creating intrinsically satisfying learning environments, operating in terms of 'options and values' rather than 'recipes', and of generating "the capacity for critical reflection".

Thus whatever the opportunities or expectations of the National Curriculum at the later stages of the secondary school, this international research project and complementary findings from other studies indicate that no programme of education for leisure will attain its objectives successfully unless it is first treated as a question of cultural experience and meaning, a question of genuine responsibility being devolved to the learner within an appropriate deinstitutionalised learning environment. And even then, sports-type leisure pursuits will not appeal to all individuals. If leisure is to have individual meaning then non-participation in such activities must be a democratic right. What is essential, then, is that all schools need to enable and empower all students to make their own informed choices, understanding the implications of both participation and non-participation upon themselves and upon others.

References

Bacon, W. (ed) (1982) *Leisure and Learning in the 1980s*, LSA Publication No. 14, Eastbourne: Leisure Studies Association.

Casbon, C. (1992) 'The National Curriculum — taking the road towards independence', *The British Journal of Physical Education*, Vol. 23 No. 1, Spring, pp. 6-7.

Corijn, E. (1987) 'Leisure education and emancipation in today's context', *European Journal of Education*, Vol. 22 Nos. 3/4, pp. 265-174.

Hamilton-Smith, E. (1982) 'Leisure education — what and by whom?', *New Zealand Journal of Health, Physical Education and Recreation*, Vol. 15 No. 3, pp. 58–61.

Hargreaves, D. (1982) 'Unemployment, Leisure and Education', in W. Bacon (ed) *Leisure and Learning in the 1980s*. LSA Publication No. 14. Eastbourne: Leisure Studies Association, pp. 129–146.

Haywood, L. & I. Henry (eds) (1985) *Leisure and Youth*. LSA Publication No. 17. Eastbourne: Leisure Studies Association.

Hendry, L. (1985) 'Young people and leisure: developing meta-cognitive skills?', in L. Haywood & I. Henry (eds) *Leisure and Youth*. LSA Publication No. 17. Eastbourne: Leisure Studies Association, pp. 1.2.1–1.2.51.

Leigh, J. (1971) [quoted in Hargreaves, D. 1982, *op. cit.*] *Young people and leisure*. London: Routledge & Kegan Paul.

Leisure Management (1981/82) Volume 1.

Leisure Management (1988) Editorial, Volume 8, No. 6.

Leisure Management (1992) Volume 12.

Murphy, W. (ed) (1989) *Children, Schooling and Education for Leisure*. LSA Publication No. 36. Eastbourne: Leisure Studies Association.

Sports Council (1980-81) *Annual Report*. London: The Sports Council.

Sports Council (1981-82) *Annual Report*. London: The Sports Council.

Sports Council (1982) *Sport in the Community: The next Ten Years*. London: The Sports Council.

Sports Council (1988) *Sport in the Community: Into the 90s*. London: The Sports Council.

Sports Council (1992) *Provision for Swimming*. London: The Sports Council.

Standeven, J. & Thompson, G.B. (1986) 'Education for leisure: A comparison of current physical education and recreation approaches in selected English and Canadian high schools', in E. Broom, R. Clumpner, B. Pendleton & C. Pooley (eds) *Comparative Physical Education and Sport Volume 5*. Champaign, Ill: Human Kinetics Books, pp. 361–367.

IV.

APPENDICES

APPENDIX 1:

Membership of the National Curriculum Working Group on Physical Education [England and Wales]

Chairman: Mr. Ian Beer, Headmaster of Harrow School

Members: Professor Denys Brunsden, Professor of Geography at King's College London

Mr. John Fashanu, Footballer with Wimbledon FC

Mrs. Ann Harris, Head of Binfield Primary School, Berkshire

Miss Susan Jackson, Deputy Head of Connah's Quay High School, Clwyd

Mr. Tim Marshall, Lecturer at Birmingham University Medical School

Miss Elizabeth Murdoch, Head of Chelsea School of Human Movement, Brighton Polytechnic

Mr. Phil Norman, Director of Customer Communications, NatWest Bank

Mr. Steve Ovett, Athlete and broadcaster on athletics

Ms. Maggie Semple, Director of Arts Council Project on Arts Education

Mr. Keith Sohl, Senior Manager with IBM

Professor Margaret Talbot, Carnegie Professor and Assistant Dean, Leeds Polytechnic

Mr. Michael Thornton, Deputy Head of Greenfield Comprehensive School, Newton Aycliffe, County Durham

Assessors: Miss Jane Benham, Department of Education and Science

Miss B. J. Lewis, Her Majesty's Inspectorate

Appendix 2:

Membership of the Physical Education Working Group [Northern Ireland]

Chairman: Mr. Jim McKeever, Head of Faculty (Practical Subjects),
            St. Mary's College, Belfast

Members: Ms. Linda Barclay, Head of Programmes, Northern Ireland
            Health Promotion Unit

            Mr. Neil Barr, Vice Principal, Holy Family Primary School,
            Aileach Road, Derry

            Mr. Walter Bleakley, Senior Lecturer, University of Ulster,
            Jordanstown

            Miss Jennifer Boyd, Teacher at Bangor Central Primary School,
            Bangor

            Dr. Mike Bull, Physical Educationalist; twice Commonwealth
            Games Gold Medallist

            Mrs. Roxanne Connor, Leisure Arts Department,
            St. Genevieve's High School, Belfast

            Mrs. Moya Gibson, Head of Physical Education Department,
            Glenlola Collegiate School, Bangor

            Mr. Raymond Gilbert, Lecturer, Physical Education, Stranmillis
            College, Belfast

            Mr. William Gribben, Vice-Principal, Edenderry Primary
            School, Portadown

            Mr. Robert Irvine, Vice-Principal, Newtownbreda High School,
            Belfast

            Mr. Sean McGourty, Head of Physical Education Department,
            La Salle Boys' School, Belfast

            Mrs. Joyce Millar, Head of Secondary Department, Fleming
            Fulton Special School, Belfast

            Mr. Danny O'Connor, Sports Council for Northern Ireland
            (Officer)

            Miss Musgrave Davidson, Inspector DENI (Assessor)

Appendix 3:

Assessment of Practical Performance[1]

Guidelines

Within the context of a practical activity the teacher should focus on what each pupil knows, understands, and can do. The evidence upon which such judgement can be made will emerge as teachers engage in practical activities. Assessment should therefore be a continuous process with teachers observing and recording pupil achievement within the context of a practical activity. Assessment should be based on the statements of attainment and levels of attainment [namely performance and appraisal (AT1) and evaluation of performance (AT2)] as outlined in the Northern Ireland curriculum[2].

Both attainment targets (for Northern Ireland) can be assessed within one specific practical situation or a single practical task. For example, a pupil could be asked to plan, perform and evaluate a dance or a gymnastic sequence and suggest and implement strategies to improve performance. Equally, pupils could be given a problem to solve within the context of a game. The pupils' strategies to resolve the problem will be apparent within the dynamics of the game situation, and therefore the teacher will gain valuable evidence of pupil competency in performance and in appraisal and evaluation simultaneously. Alternately, some pupils might be asked on a reciprocal basis to focus on performing while others focus on appraising and evaluating that performance. Therefore, within practical activities, pupils should at all times be asked to perform to the best of their abilities and to reflect critically on their performance. They should be required to review critically their cooperative and competitive roles in, for example, team games.

The assessment of such practical competency is more meaningfully achieved when the activity context is relevant to the pupil. It is more appropriate and less time consuming to assess pupils' abilities within the context of the game than it is to assess achievement within the component techniques and skills of the game. Similarly, to assess achievement in gymnastics or dance the composition and presentation of a sequence of moves will provide evidence of ability in all the contributing actions. Only if pupils experience difficulty with the complexity and dynamics of the practical activity should it be necessary to isolate component parts for assessment.

The implementation of such an assessment strategy will only be possible if teachers are able to step back from the direct process of teaching and thereby shift the responsibility for personal decision making within a particular practical activity over to the pupils. How pupils respond to such responsibility will become immediately apparent and tangible evidence of progress on the AT2 visible. The rational application of the Spectrum of Teaching styles will be a direct facilitator to such evidence and teachers will have to become familiar with alternative presentational teaching styles if they are to do justice in equal measure to AT1 and AT2.

Initial considerations in the assessment of Physical Education

Physical Education has been designated non-statutory as far as assessment is concerned. This means that the subject will not be formally assessed in the manner of English, mathematics and science. However, pupil progress will be monitored and reported periodically, and especially at the end of each Key Stage. Assessment will be based on the statements of attainment and reporting will based on Levels of Attainment in relation to the two Attainment Targets. Teachers will therefore be required, under Legislation, to show how they are responding to the challenge of assessment. They will be required to clarify the mechanism for assessment in their department and show how these procedures provide appropriate evidence of pupil progress in the various programmes of Study which make up the Activity programme in their school.

Pupils' experience in and through physical education

Every pupil has the right to expect that the experience of physical education in the school curriculum should be challenging, vigorous and individually purposeful. In physical education, pupils should be involved in planning for and preparing to perform, performing, and reflecting and evaluating performances in a variety of contexts. Often in physical education these experiences occur in cooperation and/or competition with others, and so each of these phases offers a variety of learning opportunities for the pupils. It is important therefore that, when the teaching environment and pupil experience permit, pupils are provided with the opportunity to negotiate with their peers and to make personal and collective decisions about the tasks set by the teachers. This can only be achieved through the explicitly planned and rational actions of teachers. By so doing, teachers will be recognising and taking account of the unique learning abilities of each pupil and providing a safe learning environment which offers great opportunity for pupils to learn beyond the mere act of doing. Indeed, the choice of subject matter and the manner in which the subject is presented to pupils in many respects can dictate the nature of learning outcomes and ultimately the quality of experience for the pupils involved.

In order to assist teachers in making appropriate selections of both content and presentation method, the following guide is offered for consideration.

Choice and presentation of curricular material

An activity is worthwhile in terms of its potential to offer pupils both task and process learning if, in its presentation to pupils, it fulfils the following criteria:

1. The opportunity to share the planning, implementation and appraisal of the activity with others.
2. Permits informed choice in executing tasks.
3. Involves pupils in the meaningful application of rules and regulations.
4. Requires pupils to practise, review, repeat alternatives in order to improve/ peer performance.
5. Requires pupils to examine physically and intellectually ideas/concepts/ problems in selected contexts.
6. Involves pupils in recalling situations from previous lessons.
7. Asks pupils to enquire into alternatives.
8. Involves pupils in active learning.
9. Challenges each pupil in terms of personal abilities.
10. Successful completion of the activity is within the competency of all pupils.

Teacher delegation and pupil learning

Such criteria cannot be successfully pursued in lessons in which the teacher takes responsibility for all the task-related decisions. The lesson which follows the Explanation/Demonstration/Practice model encases the teacher and pupil in the respective roles of leader and follower, and thereby restricts pupil access to process learning. Indeed, if a teacher takes responsibility for all the decisions, then pupils will be denied access to personal decision-making and the consequences of those decisions for themselves and others. Pupil learning is consequently restricted to the task or end-product with little opportunity for pupils to experience taking a greater responsibility for their own learning and that of others.

The Department of Education and Science in its 1983 Statement of Entitlement reinforces the application of such criteria as well as warning against an over-authoritarian/didactic approach to teaching physical education when it states:

> The aim to extend pupils' movement vocabulary and to develop curiosity, independent thought and self esteem will not be achieved by teaching which relies excessively upon instruction and a didactic approach. Teachers should be at times listeners, at times partners, at times assessors, knowing when to question, cajole, encourage, guide and intervene.

Such a statement actively encourages teachers to provide opportunities for pupils, in a phased and gradual manner, to share the responsibility for assisting themselves and others to learn. The emphasis within such teaching approaches is upon the *production, application* and *appraisal* by pupils of alternative solutions to practical tasks and problems set by teachers. Pupils are encouraged to negotiate and share alternative approaches with others and to critically examine these in context. However, such discovery learning can be balances by the need for pupils to *reproduce* and *practise* techniques and skills which form the basis of all practical activity and can justifiably claim to be an essential element in the development by the pupil of basic movement competency.

It is essential therefore that pupils are provided with the requirement to both *produce* and to *reproduce* practical ideas in relation to stimuli provided by the teacher throughout the physical education programme. Such approaches will contribute to a balance between teacher-directed and pupil-centred activity, and can therefore begin to facilitate a gradual shift of responsibility away from the teacher and towards the pupil. This process of responsibility shift may coincide with the natural physical and emotional maturation of the pupil.

Potential outcomes for pupils

If teachers are able to implement such teaching strategies, then the anticipated problems associated with the Appraisal and Evaluation Attainment target will be somewhat ameliorated. Pupils will have experienced a balanced teaching approach in physical education and will therefore be provided with the opportunity to develop:

- a good basis of movement competency across a range of physical activities;
- personal confidence in their own movement learning capabilities;

- adaptability in applying what has been learnt in different movement contexts;
- knowledge of how to prepare the body for vigorous exercise and what happens to the body while exercising;
- health and safety relative to particular activities;
- enthusiasm for further participation and an awareness of the role of exercise and nutrition in the development of a positive leisure life-style;
- the ability to communicate ideas and feelings through expressive and rewarding movement in concern with others;
- the ability to plan and initiate purposeful personal training programmes and monitor progress;
- an awareness of the leisure industry and its career potential.

E. W. Bleakley
Senior Lecturer, Pre-Service Education
University of Ulster
Member, Physical Education Working Group (Northern Ireland)

Notes

1 A version of the following was first published in *Bulletin of Physical Education*, Vol. 27, No. 1 (Spring 1991): pp. 14–20.
2 NB there is only one attainment target in the curriculum for England/Wales.

NOTES ON THE CONTRIBUTORS

JOHN ALDERSON is Head of the Division of Leisure Management, in the School of Leisure and Food Management at Sheffield Hallam University. Over the years he has written provocatively on sport and physical education. His involvement with examinations in physical education, which dates from 1975 — as CSE Moderator and first Chief Examiner of the A-level Sports Studies, as well as one of its designers — motivates his commitment to the value of scholarship in this area.

AMANDA BRYANT is a BSc (Hons) Psychology/Sociology graduate of the University of Southampton. She joined the PE department at the University of Southampton in 1991 as a research student, sponsored by the University. Her research interests centre on the provision of Physical Education in the Primary Sector.

JOHN EVANS was a Senior Lecturer in the department of Physical Education at the University of Southampton, before becoming Professor of Physical Education at Loughborough University. He is author of *Teaching in Transition: The Challenge of Mixed Ability Grouping* (Open University Press, 1986) and editor of *Physical Education, Sport and Schooling* (1986), *Teachers, Teaching and Control in Physical Education* (1988), and *Education, Equality and Physical Education* (1993) — all published by The Falmer Press. His research interests currently centre on the impact of the ERA on the provision of sport and PE in England and Wales.

SCOTT FLEMING is a Lecturer in Physical Education and Sports Science at the Chelsea School, University of Brighton. He has presented findings on the role of sport in South Asian culture at national and international conferences, and has published them in various places. He is also co-author (with Stephen J. Bull and Jo Doust) of *Play Better Cricket*.

LEO B. HENDRY is Professor and Head of Department of Education, University of Aberdeen. He has published over 70 journal articles, the most recent being: Hendry, L. *et al.*, (1992) 'Adolescents' perceptions of significant individuals in their lives, *Journal of Adolescence*, 15(3) 255–270, He has written 16 book chapters including, most recently: 'The developmental context of adolescent lifestyles', in *Adolescence in Context*, Silbereisen, E. and Todt, E.

(eds), New York & Berlin: Springer (1993); and authored or co-authored 12 books, including *The Nature of Adolescence* , London: Routledge (1990) and *Young People's Leisure and Lifestyles*, London: Routledge (1993). He has been involved in a number of nationally-funded research projects including a 7-year longitudinal study of 10,000 Scottish adolescents (1985-1992), *Working with Young People on Drugs Misuse and HIV/AIDS* (Grampian Health board, 1991) and *The Benefits of Youth Work* (SOED, 1991).

LESLEY LAWRENCE was a teacher of Physical Education before undertaking doctoral research on leisure/physical education teachers. She is currently Research Fellow at Chelsea School, University of Brighton, working on a range of leisure projects in the areas of countryside recreation, tourism and leisure participation.

GILL LINES is currently Head of Girls Physical Education, Beal High School, Ilford, Essex. She has been teaching Physical Education in mixed comprehensives since 1977 and completed a 3-year part-time MA(PE) course at Brighton Polytechnic in 1991. Since then she has been involved in delivering INSET National Curriculum courses for fellow PE teachers within her authority.

GRAHAM McFEE is Senior Lecturer in Philosophy in the Chelsea School, University of Brighton, and Course Leader for the MA (Physical Education). He writes on philosophy (especially on dance aesthetics), on the epistemology of educational research and on leisure and the media. His publications include *Understanding Dance* (Routledge, 1992) and *The Concept of Dance Education* (Routledge, 1993).

BEVERLEY MILLER has been a Physical Education teacher and Head of Department in a large comprehensive school in Sussex for eighteen years. Her academic interest in Physical Education was formally re-awakened through her MA in Physical Education at the University of Brighton, completed in 1991. She has since written a number of articles on the subjects of femininity, feminism and female sexuality in relation to sport and dance.

ELIZABETH MURDOCH has been a member of both School Sport Group and the National Curriculum Subject Working Group in Physical Education. She is currently Chair of the British Council of Physical Education and Chair of South East Region Sports Council's Workshop Group on a policy for Sport and Young People.

DAWN PENNEY is a BA (Hons) Sports Studies graduate from Bedford College of Physical Education. Formerly a Development Officer for the National Coaching Foundation, she joined the PE department at the University of Southampton in 1990 as a research scholar, sponsored by the Sports Council.

JOY STANDEVEN is a principal lecturer in the Chelsea School of the University of Brighton. Her academic responsibilities include leading the School's BA (Hons) Leisure [Policy and Administration] route and teaching social perspectives of sport and leisure. Her research interests include education for leisure, leisure markets and cultures, sport and tourism.

MARGARET TALBOT is Carnegie Professor at Leeds Metropolitan University. She was a member of the DES Working Group whose proposals constituted the National Curriculum for Physical Eudcation. She has been an activist, researcher and writer on issues relating to sports enquiry for many years, and co-edited (with Erica Wimbush) *Relative Freedoms — Women and Leisure* (Open University Press, 1988).

ALAN TOMLINSON is a sociologist and social historian, who has worked in Chelsea School/University of Brighton since 1975. He is currently Professor and Reader in Sport and Leisure Studies, Director of the Leisure Research Unit and Manager of Chelsea Research Developments. His current research interests are sport, popular culture, leisure theory, leisure trends, and the application of cultural studies to the analysis of sport and leisure.

Index

free market *20, 21, 31, 33*
Frith, S. *168*
Fuller, P. *106*

G

Gajadhar, J. *121*
Galbraith, J. K. *94*
GCSE (General Certificate of
    Secondary Education) *49, 51,
    52, 86, 155*
gender *41, 42, 43, 46, 164, 181,
    186, 190*
George, L. & Kirk, D. *156*
Gibbon, A. *146*
Giddens, A. *26, 169*
Glanville, B. *119*
Gleeson, G. *83*
GMS (Grant Maintained Status) *21,
    75*
Griffith, D. *130*
Grinter, R. *126*
group interviews *136*
gymnastics *44, 83*

H

Hamilton-Smith, E. *202*
Hargreaves, D. *193, 195, 201*
Hargreaves, John *120*
Hargreaves, Jennifer *182*
Harris, Anne *56*
Haywood, L. & Henry, I. *193*
health *8–15, 39, 46, 51, 53,
    54, 75, 82, 83, 84, 116,
    167, 173–179, 191*
HEFC (Higher Education Funding
    Council) *104*
Hendry, L. *10, 146, 161, 165, 166,
    173, 174, 193, 194*
Hewlett, M. *80–81, 82*
hidden curriculum *128*

Hill, D. *123, 124*
Hill, M. *23*
Holt, M. *164*
Houlihan, B. *93*

I

ideology *20, 24, 30, 41, 94–95,
    182, 190*
implementation *22, 23*
individual racism *123*
Ingham, R. *33, 176*
INSET (In-Service Education and
    Training) *37, 48, 74*
institutional racism *123*
instrumentalism *88*

J

Jackson, Sue *56*
Jagger, J. *156*
Jarvie, G. *129*
Jonathan, R. *163*

K

Kane, J. *150, 152*
Kansara, B. *121*
Katz, J. *121*
Kew, S. *123*
Key Stage *5, 6, 7, 8–9, 28,
    38, 48, 49, 52, 55*
Kirk, D. *29, 156, 157*
Kleiber, D. & Rickards, W. *175*

L

labour market *164*
Lashley, H. *124*
Lawrence, E. *122*
Lawrence, L. *10, 145, 146, 152*
Leaman, O. *121, 123*
Leaman, O. & Carrington, B. *120*
Leigh, J. *195*